BEYOND MY HORIZON

An Σducational Ωdyssey & Combat Memoir

By

CLAUDE REGIS VARGO

First published by Dog Ear Publishing
4010 W. 86th Street, Ste H
Indianapolis, IN 46268
www.dogearpublishing.net

ISBN: 978-160844-565-3

This book is printed on acid-free paper.

Printed in the United States of America

This book's title,

BEYOND MY HORIZON,

is in honor of Conrad N. Hilton, benefactor of the college bearing his name.

"BEYOND <u>THE</u> HORIZON"

is the title of a speech given by Conrad N. Hilton October 28, 1969, in which he said, "I am making this gift to the university [of Houston], to see that there are young men and women prepared to reach that horizon and beyond."

In the subtitle of the book,

An Σducational Ωdyssey & Combat Memoir,

the Greek letters Σ (Sigma) and Ω (Omega) signify the total and final commitment I made to complete my education goals.

DEDICATION

To my best friend, soul mate, and bride,
GLORIA,
Who is always at my side.
To all my college professors
&
The Marine tankers
Who kept me alive.

ACKNOWLEDGMENTS

I would like to thank the following Marines, who kept me either alive or in stitches: Andy Anderson, Larry Basco, Dale Wayne Sandifer, Joe Harrigan, Sergeant Robert "Bob" Dougherty, Frank "Smitty" Smith, Sergeant Soto, Robert "Bob" Mendez, Staff Sergeant Lowery, Staff Sergeant Jim Jewell, Sonny Venturi, Rene Cerda, Leonard Coco, and especially Lieutenant Peter J. Ritch. To Jack Butcher for sharing his photos that were right on.

In memory of our two closest tankers who went with us through hell and who are now peacefully guarding heaven's gate and are always in our brothers' prayers: Robert M. "Satch" Walkley and John M. Forster. And to John Wear, president of the USMC Vietnam Tankers Association, and veteran author Robert "Bob" Peavy, vice president, who pointed me in the right direction.

To all the deans past and present who guided me educationally: James "Jim" Taylor, Alan T. Stutts, and particularly John T. Bowen for his critical evaluation. And to my Cornell professor, closest friend, and business partner, John B. "Jack" Corgel, and my best Cornell study partner, Tom Lewerenz.

To all my University Houston and Hilton College professors and staff who gratefully took me into their family: Agnes DeFranco, Alex Ignatiev, JeAnna Abbott, Stephen "Steve" Barth, Glenn Cordua y Cruz, Mary Dawson, Nancy Graves, Ron Jordan, Ron Nykiel, Kevin Simon, Kathleen Baird, Clinton Rappole, Rudolpho Casparius, and James "Jim" Wortman. And to my best academic friends and classmates—Kyle Bowman, Eric Morse, and Lydia Westbrook—for setting the bar high for me to reach.

To my friend and confidant, Janet Williams, who urged me to record my story.

To our children—Christina, Dennis, Travis, and Amanda—for giving up what I should have provided and where I should have been, and for the grandchildren they did provide: Annika; Kaylee, Kenzie, Emily, Addison, and Broden; Charlotte and Violet; and Peyton. And to my mom and dad, Frank J. and Rita M. Vargo, who gave me the seeds to carry me through life with good moral values and a great start, and my brother and special friend, Mark.

To Jon and Lindsey Wedemeyer, the most "Dangerous Writer" and editors on the planet.

And to the "team extraordinaire" at Dog Ear Publishing, especially Stephanie Seifert Stringham Matthew Murry, Amber Ortner and Adrienne Miller.

UNCOMMON HONORS

Summa Cum Laude

"A Latin phrase meaning 'with highest praise'—the highest distinction attainable as part of a university degree."

Disability Rights Advocates

United States Marine Corps

November 10, 1775 ~ Present

STANDARDS OF PERFORMANCE: 4.9 ~ 5.0

"Does superior work in all duties. Even extremely difficult or unusual assignments can be given with full confidence that they will be handled in a thoroughly competent manner."

Para 4007.7a (IRAM)

STANDARD OF CONDUCT: 4.9 ~ 5.0

"Observe[s] spirit as well as letter of orders and regulations. Demonstrated positive effect on others by example and persuasion."

Para 4007.6a (IRAM)

PRESIDENTIAL UNIT CITATION

"The degree of heroism required is the same as that which would warrant award of the Navy Cross to an individual…making the Navy Cross a combat-only award and second only to the Medal of Honor." (See Appendix A.)

Wikipedia

PURPLE HEART

"The original Purple Heart, designated as the Badge of Military Merit, was established by General George Washington on August 7, 1782. It is also the nation's oldest military award [resulting from direct] enemy-related injuries [or death] by bullet, shrapnel, or other projectile created by enemy action."

Wikipedia

To see Claude's college transcript,
USMC discharge documents, more photos, and other cool "stuff" please go to

www.GetYourDamnDegree.com

CONTENTS

PART III
SUGGESTIONS & RECOMMENDATIONS

PART IV
MY ACADEMIC GOAL LINE

APPENDICES

INTRODUCTION

"Yes, there are two paths you can go by
But in the long run
There's still time to change..."

Led Zeppelin—"Stairway to Heaven"

It really is never too late to go after your unfulfilled dreams and goals in life and to accomplish them, possibly beyond your wildest expectations. I am living proof of this.

It took me decades to finally pursue what I had always really wanted to do with my life. In my case this was to go back to college and, specifically, attend Cornell University. In fact, I struggled with this decision so ferociously that I just kept putting it off throughout my adult life. But then I was pushing fifty years old and starting to look at my life in the rearview mirror. Every day I would look back and ask myself why I had let all those years I saw there get behind me.

The sad part is, waiting all those years and making my decision was terrible agony on me and a needless waste of time and energy. In the end, it took only some spare change and one simple phone call to completely change the path my life was on and allow me to accomplish my lifelong goals. During the process, I also achieved a private, personal goal of my own that seemed so unlikely, I had never dared to share it with anyone at school and had kept it solely to myself.

When I say I struggled ferociously to decide, I meant it. I served two tours as a combat Marine Corps tank commander in Viet Nam, so I've been in many battles, and deciding to go back to college was one of the toughest I have been in. I had failed high school miserably, and junior college had been no better. I had been programmed to hate school, and yet I wanted to go to an Ivy League college, so trying to justify the sacrifices it would take to go back to school at my age, and seriously doubting whether I could pull it off at all academically, was pure hell and total mental warfare. I had never been so damn afraid to fail in my entire life, which was my real anguish in deciding and actually getting started. I was scared to death of making the wrong decision this late in life, but it would end up being some of the best short years of my life.

Putting things off and avoiding them is the complete opposite of who I really am and my normal behavior. I have always been a go-getter in every other aspect of my life. Ever since I can remember, I have been driven and have always worked harder than any other two or sometimes even three people. I have always tried to excel and be the best I could at everything I do...except school. When I was seventeen years old, I would work sometimes as many as twenty hours a day, seven days a week, at a Hilton hotel in Houston. I did everything to perfection at work, because I totally loved what I was doing and couldn't get enough. I learned from the best and tried to emulate the best. The hotel industry became my passion in life, and from that early point on, I knew I wanted to go to the best hotel college in the country at Cornell University.

As a Marine I was also just as passionate and driven to perfection. I was patriotic and ended up excelling and gaining some of the highest ratings possible in the Corps, again because I loved it completely and just had to give it my personal best. As a Marine, I would survive two of the most brutal sieges in military history and bring home a couple of medals, along with the physical and emotional baggage that came with them. That experience would both shape me and scar me for life. It made me who I am today in too many ways to even begin to unravel, and I don't ever want to try. Needless to say, the experience gave me strength, discipline, and courage, but it also gave me the crippling effects and challenges of being a combat vet. Ironically, though, it would also give me the keys that would enable me to change the road I was on, to finally achieve my real goals and fulfill my life goals.

In my case, as I suspect with most people who have unfulfilled goals, life kept getting in the way, and my spouse and children took priority. Right after my time in Viet Nam, in storybook style, I came home and married my childhood sweetheart. I was on top of the world, worked hard to save up money, and immediately went to junior college to get started on my way to Cornell. I quickly got a harsh lesson in the realities of the times and the prevailing attitude toward Viet Nam vets and reluctantly dropped out of college after a tough try. That's when life got in the way. Soon, I had a growing family and was working two and three jobs at a time to help provide for them. My wife and I both worked overtime and put our kids through college. Finally, after the kids were grown up and in college or graduated from college, I began to think about my own life again—another very familiar scenario, I am sure. I had (and still have) absolutely no regrets about putting them all first, but that's when I finally made my decision to go back and try college again.

This book is the complete and true story of how I went from a high-school and junior-college dropout, with failing transcripts to match, to graduating summa cum laude in just two years by attending two major universities and three colleges in two different states at the same time. The time span covered in the book is very long, so I have tried my best to keep the timeline straight and tell the events as they happened, in an entertaining and informative way. I have gone back and used my own military records and historical military data for the sections about Viet Nam and the military. I have used a room full of tape recordings, exams, notes, and my actual transcripts for the academic information, which is where I begin my story.

Everything I have quoted, I actually heard at some point...there are some things you hear in life that you just can't forget. As so much time has passed, I am sure some of the quotes are not verbatim, and I'm just not certain exactly who said what sometimes, so I can't attribute some of them; please forgive that.

For those readers whose goal is to go back to college, especially my brother military veterans, I have tried to outline exactly how I pulled this off and what options may be available to you. The same applies to moms, nontraditional students, and anyone else who decide to finally go back and get his or her degree at a later age in life. I describe my initial approach to college and how this quickly changed. I explain all my revised approaches to going to college as I developed them and how I implemented and used them. I try to describe how I chose my professors and classes and got registered; how I studied for class, studied for tests, took tests, got tutored, and even set up my home office. I hope this book will serve as both an inspiration to help you make your decision to take the plunge to go back to college and as a guidebook to help you with your college experience so you can finally GET YOUR DAMN DEGREE!

For others whose goals may be different, I hope my story will inspire you to take some kind of action to achieve what you really want in your life, then give it your all. No matter how impossible or difficult it may seem to accomplish something you want in life, in the end, the only thing really stopping you is yourself. Whatever it is you really want to do with your life, whether it is going back to college or anything else, the key is to first take some type of action, some first step that will get you started on your way. Then, give it everything you have and enjoy the ride.

I hope readers will come away inspired and with a renewed sense of hope, optimism, and a true belief that they can do whatever they want to with their lives. Go for your dreams today. Stop waiting until tomorrow. I wish you all the best of luck on your journey.

MAP OF I CORPS—SOUTH VIETNAM 1968

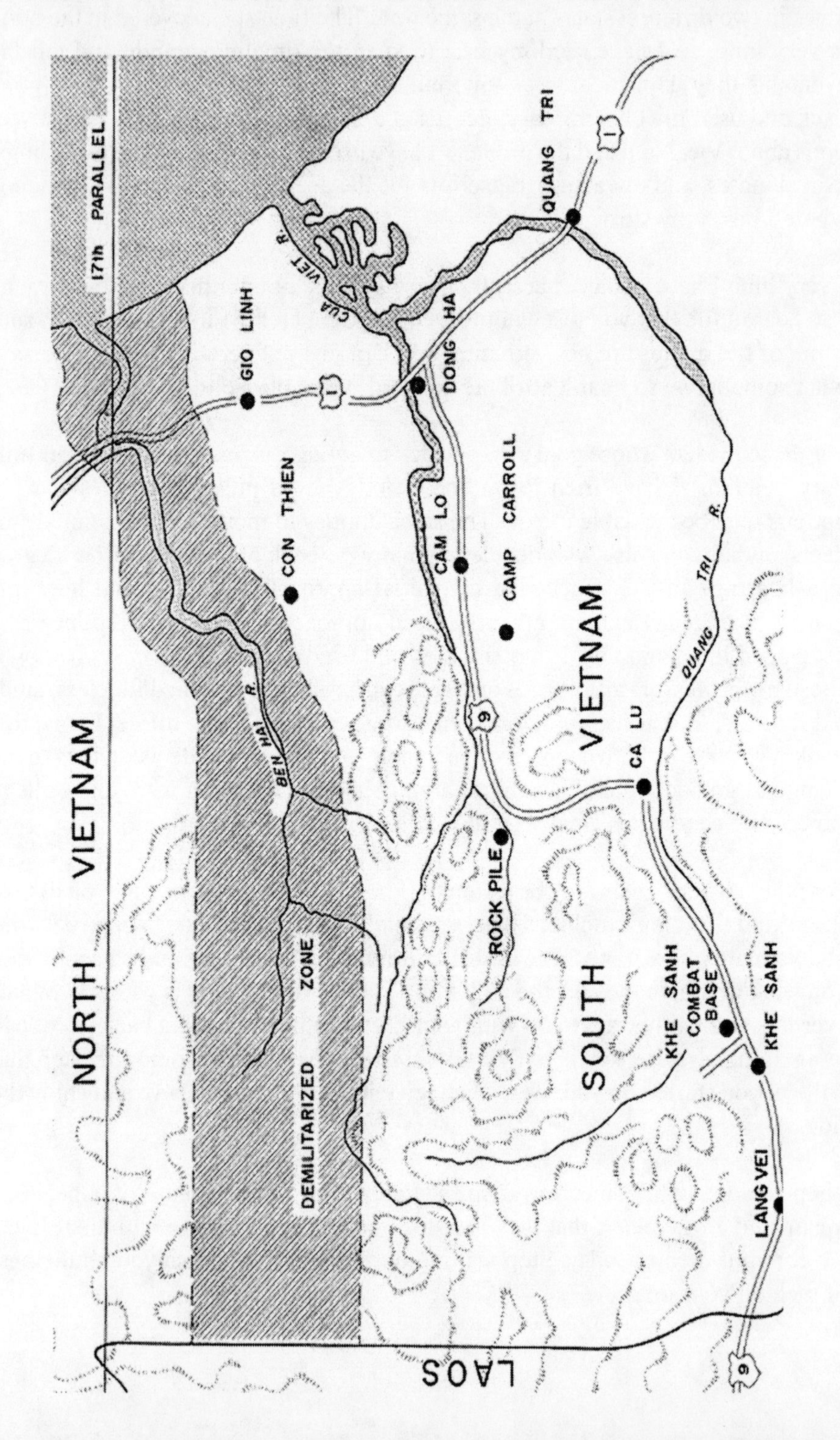

MAP OF KHE SANH and ROCK QUARRY, 1968

Note the location of the Quarry

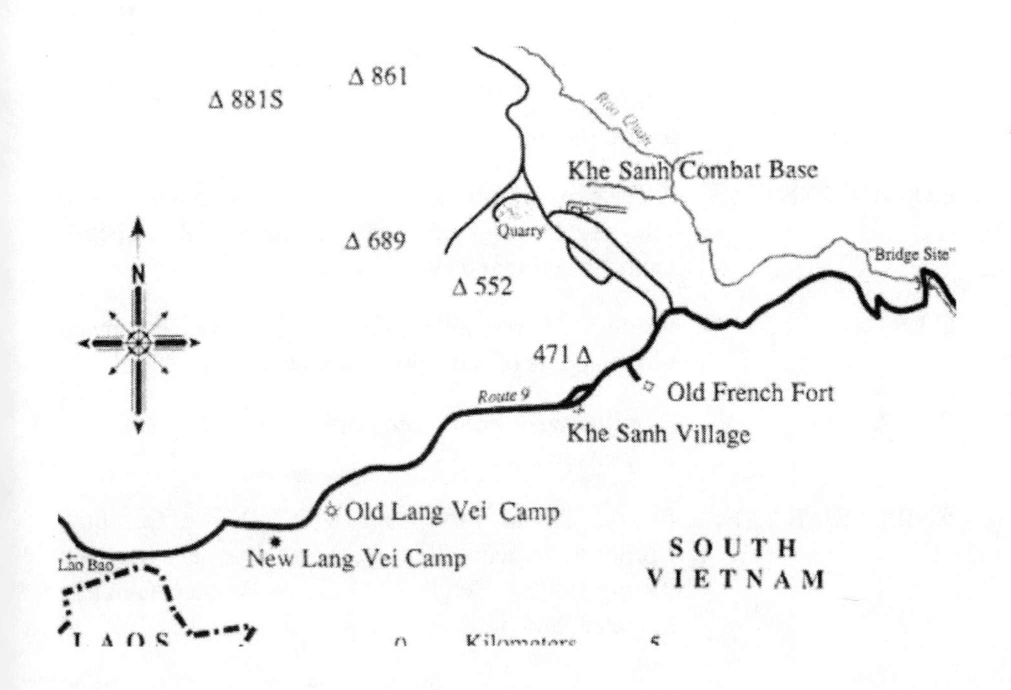

U.S. MARINE CORPS GLOSSARY—VIET NAM, 1968

A.R.V.N.*	Land-based military forces of the Army of the Republic of South Vietnam.
B.M.O.C	Big Man On Campus.
BROWN BAR*	Second lieutenant, the lowest commissioned officer military rank in many armed forces.
C-130*	A four-engine turboprop military transport aircraft capable of using unprepared runways for takeoffs and landings.
C.O.	Commanding Officer; the officer in command of a military unit.
COSMOLINE*	A class of rust preventatives that are a brown-colored wax-like mass, have a slight fluorescence, and a petroleum-like odor and taste.
C.P.*	Command Post; a military headquarters for a command group and its officers during an operation.
D.M.Z.	Demilitarized Zone; geography separating two belligerents in a war.
ENLISTED RANKS	Private, Private First Class (PFC), Lance Corporal, Corporal, Sergeant, Staff Sergeant, Gunnery Sergeant (Gunny), First Sergeant (Top) or Master Gunnery Sergeant, and Sergeant Major.
GOOK*	A derogatory term for Southeast Asians, used especially for enemy soldiers. It is apologetically repeated in this book as was used in a time of war.
K.I.A.	Killed in action.
M.I.A.	Missing in action.
OOH-RAH*	A spirited cry common to Marines commonly used to respond to a verbal greeting or as an expression of enthusiasm.

P.A.V.N.* Vietnamese People's Army, or People's Army of (north) Vietnam.

POGEY BAIT Tangible temptation, as in candy bars, beer, booze, girls and more girls.

POGUE As in office pogue, Remington raider, or rear-echelon paper-pusher. I never met one I didn't like or one who wouldn't give up his typewriter to go out in the field.

QUONSET HUT* A lightweight prefabricated structure of corrugated galvanized steel having a semicircular cross section.

R.P.G.* Rocket Propelled Grenade; any hand-held, shoulder-launched anti-tank weapon capable of firing an unguided rocket equipped with an explosive warhead.

P.T.S.D. Post Traumatic Stress Disorder.

SEMPER FI* Semper Fidelis, Latin for "Always Faithful"; well known as the motto of the Marine Corps.

SKIVVIES* Undergarments worn under other clothes. They keep outer garments from being soiled by perspiration, urine, semen, feces, and other discharges.

STEWARDESS A flight attendant or member of an airline cabin crew. At each stopover and closer to home coming back the more beautiful and lean they became.

TANK (M48A3) Specs: Weight ~ 52 tons; Length ~ 30.22'; Width ~ 11.86'; Height ~ 10.07'; Crew ~ 4 (commander, gunner, loader, driver); Armor ~ 4.89"; Armament ~ 90mm; gun; Secondary ~ .50 caliber; .30 caliber; Engine ~ 750 hp; Range ~ 287 miles; Speed ~ 30 mph.

T.C. Tank Commander, in charge of the driver, loader and gunner.

TET (OFFENSIVE)* An all out military campaign during the Vietnam War that began on January 31, 1968.

V.C.* Viet Cong; officially the National Liberation Front (NLF); a political organization and army in South Vietnam that fought the United States and South Vietnamese governments during the Vietnam War (1959–1975).

WATER BUFFALO Usually a 250+ gallon drinkable-water tank mounted on a moveable trailer.

W.I.A. Wounded in action.

WILLIE PETER* White phosphorus (WP) is a chemical element of phosphorus that is used in smoke, tracer, illumination, and incendiary munitions.

* Definitions derived in part from Wikipedia.

PART I

THE SCHOOL OF HARD KNOCKS

CHAPTER ONE
Waking up at Cornell

"There are no secrets to success.
It is the result of preparation, hard work,
and learning from failure."

Colin Powell

The huge chalkboard stretched along an entire wall inside the classroom at Cornell University. I was about to begin leading a Hotel School study group and had just finished writing my name on the board when I spaced out and just stood there with chalk in hand, staring at it. A reality check of some sort, I suppose. I felt a wave of panic and asked myself, quite urgently, "You're just a freshman, you've never taught before, and you're almost fifty years old. What the hell are you doing up here, trying to teach?" Then, as I continued to stare at my name on the board, I had what could only be called a moment...and an epiphany.

It was a completely uncomfortable moment. I really doubted myself, which for me is very unusual. I get panic attacks in which I get nervous, but those are different than this and for completely different reasons. I am not the type of person who ever really doubts my ability to do something. I tend to meet life head-on and tackle things full-speed, and I am definitely not afraid of anything or anybody. But I was just a first-semester freshman student, not a professor, and here I was standing in front of a junior/graduate class getting ready to teach for the first time in my life...and I was having serious doubts.

The class we were taking was a whirlwind real-estate finance class at the number-one, most prestigious hotel-and-restaurant college on the planet. I had felt I knew something about the subject and had thought it would be a piece of cake—turns out it was anything but. Compared to this class, all of the other real estate classes I had taken put together were just kindergarten. I had organized this study group and had let it slip earlier that I held a Real Estate Broker's License in Texas to impress everyone, but also to help build up my thin confidence. I had also told everyone about all my restaurant successes, but of course not the failures. So now I was in deep shit and there was no escaping this one.

As the reality of my current predicament began to set in, a flood of memories began running through my head. After all, they say your whole life flashes in front of you before you die. Now, of course, my current little drama wasn't quite as serious as all that. I had experienced that situation many times before in my life, and this was definitely not it. But in just those few seconds of gazing at the chalkboard, I had replayed all the major events that had transpired in my life to allow me to walk up to the board that day and write my name on it.

That actually seemed to help calm me down, and as my moment of doubt and the uneasy feelings began to pass, I refocused on my class. But all those memories had done their work quite nicely, as they had sharply and unforgivingly reminded me of just how lucky I was to even be standing there at all. They had also been somehow liberating and self-affirming, because they made me realize that if anyone deserved to be here, I did, and hell, being my age was good cover for being just a lowly freshman.

What struck me so profoundly after my moment—my epiphany—finally passed was the realization that after spending most of my life wanting and waiting to be standing exactly where I was, it was done. In an instant, all the aching to be here was over and gone. Now I could live out my dream. It had taken me more than thirty-five years and had been a very long ride, but in that simple stroke of a piece of chalk, I realized it was done. The waiting was now just part of my past. My future was right here and now in front of me. I was here, fulfilling my life-long goal of attending Cornell University.

As I looked out at the young students before me, what also struck me was how long the odds had been for me getting here at all, and I how I had overcome all of them to get here. This made any doubt that was left in my mind quickly past, and I felt an exhilarating wave of confidence as my excitement quickly grew. A smile of satisfaction crossed my face, and I nodded. I started to feel proud, strong, and confident, and I turned and began teaching my first of many study groups to come.

A lot of other fifty-year-old freshmen have made it to Ivy League colleges; you may end up being one of them. But I know for a fact that my road has most likely been a much longer and harder journey than most of theirs and, probably, yours. A lot of men my age already have their bachelors or masters degree or both or are working on their second masters or Ph.D. Others are even getting ready to retire, like my brother, who is just eighteen months older than I. But as for me, on that day, I knew that I was just getting started. I had just woken from a very long, bad dream to find myself in a whole new and different life. It gave me an adrenaline rush and a burst of energy like I'd never felt before.

Compared to the other students, I knew, I had much more life and industry experience, but I also knew that I was not as bright as a lot of them. In fact, I had never taken an SAT exam and had flunked and been booted out of my junior high. These students would probably have laughed me out of the room if they had known that in high school, my standing would have been 112 out of a class of 125. I said would have been—if I had graduated, but I never finished high school.

I wouldn't dare to tell them that two of my four children were older than they were. I was fortunate that I looked a lot younger than I really was. I still had almost all of my hair and a nice bright smile to contrast a deep, Texas-style summer tan. I also pumped weights five days a week and was fairly chiseled for my age. I was still at about 230 pounds and stood a solid 6' 5 3/4".

A beautiful young lady in the classroom raised her hand and started to ask me a question, snapping me out of my thoughts. After I answered her simple Real Estate 101 question, I looked around the room and thought about how lucky these kids were to have this incredible opportunity before them at their young age. In casual conversations with them, I could tell they were hotel brats whose families owned and managed multiple hotel brands in several states or countries. How fortunate they were that they were second- and third-generation children of hoteliers whose parents and grandparents were alumni. It had all been just given to them.

I thought for a moment about their money, their brains, and the upcoming business positions they were being groomed for with silver spoons. For now, I was living in a fifth-floor gabled room-cave, in an old house in Ithaca, New York, where I couldn't even stand up straight. As I looked at the class, I knew these silver-spoon kids were living in bought-and-paid-for off-campus condos with personal maid service that their daddies had bought for investments. I was not envious at all, seriously...I was damn jealous.

Most of them really did not have a clue how lucky they were. They talked and parroted things they heard at the dinner table, passing them on to their classmates to impress each other, but they really knew nothing about the business, nor had they ever experienced any of it in a real-world working situation. In my case, I had so much experience, it was sickening, but I had almost nothing to show for it.

I suppose that is not entirely true. My wife, Gloria, and I are still married, and we have raised four healthy, good-looking, and lovable children who have all graduated from private schools and public colleges. Had it not been for a war, several unwanted personal and business lawsuits, putting the kids through college, and more of life's distractions that were thrust upon me, along with the money I paid to various attorneys, I would have already gone to college and graduated years earlier. So now here I was, broke and undereducated, but I had made it to Cornell! I was so giddy and happy, the thought briefly crossed my mind that after I graduated, I would have to look into law school, just for insurance.

Then I closed my eyes and shook my head in what could be considered the actual beginning of a sense of remorse, as I had a quick flashback and wondered what the students in front of me would think if they knew how many enemy soldiers my tank crew and I were responsible for eliminating. I knew they would think I was some kind of pariah, a mass murderer, even. But they would never know, because I was never going to tell them. I could easily have worked my way into a survivor's guilt trip, a stupid guilt tizzy, or at least another panic attack if I had allowed myself to. But after thirty years of training, I was a professional at going from confident to insecure and into a full-blown panic attack in a New York minute.

If I had once thought I could escape from the daily panic attacks I had from the war, I was wrong; they would never go away. They always catch up to me, no matter how fast or how hard I work. The only cure I have ever found is to run everything I do in my life as fast as I can. If I slow down below 100 mph, the panic creeps back and catches up to me. I must constantly drive myself to distraction by staying busy. I always have to run my life on a fast-track to keep the demons and the panic away, and school was no exception. I realized then that this school stuff was going to be as much of a psychological war as the real one I had experienced thirty years before.

As that last random thought ran through my head, I again quickly focused back on the class, and to bring myself back into that confident state, I used one of the Anthony Robbins' non-noticeable techniques; I smiled brightly from ear to ear with my mouth full of pearly white veneers. These kids had been born into the hotel business, but I knew I had earned my rightful place at the table the hard way, and that made my smile grow wider. Unlike most of them, my passion for hotels and the hospitality business had been born with my very first job as a teenager, at one of the most beautiful hotels in the world. I knew even way back then that hotels would be my life. That was decades earlier and a million of those Anthony Robbins smiles ago.

But class was now in session, and it was time to get down to business. Claude Vargo had arrived...doing 120 mph.

CHAPTER TWO
A Thirteen-Year-Old Shamrock

I got my first taste of working in the restaurant business in 1953, at the age of five. It was at my family's restaurant, Vargo's Delicatessen, in the one and only shopping center in Bay Village, Ohio, a quaint suburb of Cleveland, and my first—and of course unpaid—job was to make potato salad and assist my dad and uncle.

A few years passed, and the two Vargo brothers decided to move their families to Houston, Texas, to seek prosperity in a full-service Texas steakhouse called the Black Angus Restaurant, which they established in 1957. At age thirteen, I asked my dad if I could actually start drawing a paycheck by working for him. Of course his answer was a prompt "no," but he graciously told me I could still work there for free as part of the family to earn my keep. Then he also oh-so-graciously told me that if I found another job, I could keep it. I guess he thought I would end up pumping gas, washing cars, or sacking groceries like the Beaver and Wally Cleaver.

But I already had an entirely different and much more robust career in mind. While growing up, I had listened to my uncle tell me endless stories about his experiences in the International Club at the Shamrock Hotel. I would listen to him over and over again, mesmerized by the fascinating stories, and hooked on the gaiety of the hotel business and nightlife. I knew then I wanted to have the same life of glamour and pizzazz.

My budding talents were not appreciated in my family's restaurant, both because of my young age of thirteen and because the Black Angus had waitresses and Mexican busboys; I just didn't fit in. So, after a few more weeks of scrubbing pots and pans without a pay envelope, I decided to go out on my own to seek fame and fortune. My dad let me, as he thought I would very quickly grow tired of working and I didn't really need to work in the first place—not like he had as a kid and young adult to support his parents during the Great Depression. Yeah right, like all the stories we had heard about how he had walked to a job five miles in the snow, uphill, both ways.

In 1961 I got my first real job, along with a real pay envelope, at the Shamrock Hilton Hotel in Houston, Texas. I was still only thirteen, but they didn't seem to have a problem hiring me, as I was tall for my age and had insisted that I was sixteen. The hotel was originally built by Glenn McCarthy, an oil wildcatter extraordinaire. But, like all the booms and busts of oil, McCarthy's Irish luck ran out, and Conrad Hilton stepped in and bought the hotel from him in 1955, just a few years after it had opened.

Houston Press Photo
Shamrock Hilton Hotel
Olympic-sized swimming pool, circa 1960.

The Shamrock Hilton Hotel was like a city in itself. It had 1100 rooms, all with the then-new luxury of air-conditioning. In addition, it had a large swimming pool, and I don't just mean large, I mean Texas-style large. This was a pool so massive, they would float a ski boat pulling a triple-decker triangle of everglade skiers behind it as part of the entertainment.

When I applied at the Shamrock, I figured I would get hired on the spot. Instead, I went through the back loading docks and waited for an appointment in the personnel department. After much to-do, and many nagging return visits, I was hired, on probation. Once hired, I just knew I would be issued a tuxedo to wait on the nouveau-riche Texas oil millionaires and the starlets fresh from Las Vegas.

Instead, my first duty was to shovel the cow manure that the Texas steers had dropped while meandering around the main ballroom among the inebriated guests. At that time, the steers and the grand champion were auctioned off at the Houston Fatstock Show and Rodeo and traditionally paraded in front of all the drunken bidders. That exercise of shoveling shit would come in handy again in my life, just much sooner than I ever imagined. Even so, from that moment, I was forever hooked on the hotel and food business.

My next duty station in the hotel was working as a bus boy in the Charcoal Terrace, overlooking that huge swimming pool. Even in winter, it looked like a warm tropical paradise, with palm trees swaying in the night breeze and their reflections shimmering in the pool's underwater lights. On holidays and weekends and during the summer, I went to work early in the day for breakfast and lunch, in addition to the dinners. In fact, I would work the early-morning breakfast, regular breakfast, brunch, lunch, afternoon teas, dinner and dance, and midnight buffet. At fifteen, I would sometimes work twenty hours a day and still have energy to burn.

The dinners and midnight dances were especially glamorous with the table-side carvings, tossed Caesar salads, and flambé dishes. I always watched and waited while the wait staff was busy, just to be around when the Chateaubriands were carved, so I could hold the dishes while the Maitre d' Hôtel carved. I loved the parades of waiters and captains that would display Baked Alaska and flaming shish kabobs made of the finest prime and choice beef skewered on two-foot-long chrome-and-brass swords. It was exhilarating to be a part of a truly professional dining room staff.

To make things even better, I was also on the Shamrock diving team. The team would compete against city and country clubs in and around the Houston area. I was not a great diver, just good. Back then I was lean as a rail, and the faction of Mexican hotel laborers nicknamed me Flaco, Spanish for skinny. At work I wore tuxedo shirts with the smallest neck size, and they were still too big. The bowties would always droop downward, and the cooks in the hotel's kitchens would call me Chicken Neck. But I could dive from the three-meter springboard and had basic rotational, tuck, pike, and free-positions skills such as dives, jumps, somersaults, and back flips. On the Olympic ten-meter platform I was adept at basic jump and dive, nothing fancy or too risky.

All of these kinetic diving maneuvers earned me a place as the center of attention during the summertime poolside Hawaiian-type luaus out by the Shamrock's cabanas, which were separate from the hotel. A diver was only needed on certain nights, and I was always available and readily volunteered to do a swan dive from the high platform...while I was on fire! I would quickly change from a bus boy's uniform to a frogman-type costume with strips of burlap soaked with flammable Sterno. Once the burlap strips were ignited and the outside lights around the cabanas dimmed, I would do a swan dive into large flaming hoops on the water's surface. It really was spectacular, and I still get a rush thinking about this early adventure in my life. Everyone who was at the poolside cabana buffet would go wild over my dives, especially the ladies...and me over them. I relished in the glory, especially during the sorority conventions, even though some of the ladies were my mother's and grandmother's ages, and even had the ruby-red gummy lipstick and the pancake makeup.

It was at the Shamrock's poolside restaurant, the Charcoal Terrace, that I waited on (and gawked at) such starlets as Debra Paget, Liza Minnelli, Nancy Sinatra, Doris Day, and Juliet Prowse and waited on celebrities such as Pat O'Brien, Gary and Wayne Newton, and Mr. Conrad N. Hilton. It was way back then, during my early time at the hotel, that I proudly announced to Mr. Hilton my dream of attending Cornell University and becoming a hotelman. I knew his son Nicky had gone there, as had the general manager of the hotel. Little did I know at the time that Mr. Hilton would become the benefactor of a college in Houston that would bear his name and that, much later in my life, I would proudly attend.

The Shamrock Hilton was not just any hotel, it was my hotel...my own personal playground. I worked all over, in as many capacities as I could worm my way into. Over time, I graduated to banquets, room service, and the Cork Club. I worked all the flower and jewel rooms: the Magnolia, Azalea, and Emerald. Even when I was off the clock, I pretended to be on and asked anyone and everyone if I could help them do something: bus tables, make beds, polish silver, run to get a pack of cigarettes or matches, anything just to be there.

In the upper suites with private bars, I would listen as the old-time waiters told stories of the wildcat oilmen a couple of decades before getting in fistfights when they were starting out as roughnecks in the Beaumont, Texas, oil fields just east of Houston. Now, many of those roughnecks were filthy rich and overnight millionaires. These stories were recounted over and over but were electrifying each time I heard them.

Andy Thomas, the banquet head waiter, could really spin a yarn, often about how Red Adair, the famous oilrig firefighter, whose group later put out the oil fires after the first Iraq war, would line whiskey bottles up on the front of the bar and the bartenders would duck on the floor while the roughnecks drew their pearl-handled revolvers and shoot all the bottles until they were all shattered. "Hell," said Andy, "who was going to say anything when the owner of the

Shamrock Hotel at the time, Glenn McCarthy, was right in the thick of things with them—he was the law at his hotel."

Every holiday was extra special at the Shamrock: Mother's Day, Easter, Valentine's Day, all of them. St. Patrick's Day, of course, was an annual city blowout, to which throngs of Houstonians would come for the revelry. It was so hard going back to high school in the days that would follow work. At work I appeared very mature for my age, but at school I was still a gangly teenager. I even thought about quitting school, but I knew if I did, my dad would never let me work another job. To me, the money was only secondary to the glitz and the glamour, but it did follow. As a waiter, my pockets were always full of money, and lots of it; fives turned into twenties, then hundreds. Soon, I had my own safety deposit box with double-E bonds and my first credit card from Foley Department Store, while my peers carried their mommies' store cards. When it came time to buy a car, I had the latest.

The assistant principle at my high school once asked me why I worked so much, especially at a hotel, when he thought I really did not need to work for any particular financial reasons. I would tell him about how magical it was to work at the hotel. I would describe a luau out by the cabanas, where a Polynesian, grass-skirted male native would dance for the diners; how, in unison, the lights would dim except for the votive candles while, around the pool, dozens of tiki torches would magically ignite and a crescendo of mystic island drums would set a stunning climax. I would describe how the diners would stretch to see flames emerge on top of the pool's three Olympic diving boards, then on cue and in sequence, a group of flaming divers, myself being one of them, would perform an aerial swan cascade that would gracefully enter the shimmering black water without a splash.

All these years later I can still picture myself there, preparing the guéridon and presenting the guests with fresh fruit, condiments, exotic liqueurs, and a bottle of a hundred-year-old Remy Martin-Louis XIII Cognac Grand Fine Champagne before beginning my magic by igniting the Sterno and dazzling them by building two Shamrock specialty Irish Coffees, dripping a three-foot stream of flaming cognac from one crystal flute to another while caramelizing the sugar-cinnamon rims. Then I would add the Jameson, crème de cacao, Arabica coffee, and a dollop of heavy whipped cream and finalize the enchantment with fragile shavings of imported Dutch Droste chocolate and a drizzle of crème de menthe. Finally, I would insert a freshly baked caramel pirouette into the delicacy and top it with a fresh sprig of mint in each. It was all so magic, and all so memorable.

After several lengthy "conferences" to discuss my grades and attendance, the assistant principal finally got the nerve to ask me how he could get hired on at the Shamrock, "just for the summer."

CHAPTER THREE
Conrad Hilton and the Bus Boy

"We are successes in the Art of Living."

Conrad N. Hilton

I first met Mr. Conrad Hilton in the Charcoal Terrace restaurant at a very early morning breakfast. It was still dark out, but he was sharply dressed in a full suit, already at work, sitting with papers spread out over a large round corner table set for eight to ten people. He acknowledged my presence because of my youthful appearance and my several interruptions to serve him and a group of financiers. I would often see him with his family at the hotel and at my family's church, St. Vincent de Paul, which was just down the street from the Shamrock. When I would see him at church he would smile at me like any other young man, but as time went by he connected the dots and realized that I also worked for him at the hotel.

From the moment Mr. Hilton connected the dots he would acknowledge me and carry on short conversations. Instinctively, I would let him initiate any small talk, as there was always a head waiter, restaurant manager, or alert coworker who would spread unwanted rumors around. Sometime after this, around 1965, I saw Mr. Hilton having early-morning breakfasts with Wayne Newton, right after Wayne and his brother Jerry had performed on *The Jackie Gleason Show*. Wayne was only a couple of years older than I was, and my coworkers did not like to wait on him because they thought he was totally arrogant, whereas I thought he exuded a tremendous amount of confidence. I watched him sing "Danke Schön" to the fluttering hearts of Houston's elite ladies in the Cork Club, and I thought he was a great entertainer. Many years later, I would see him in Vegas, performing his patriotic-themed show, which brought tears to my eyes for several emotional reasons.

But my love of the Shamrock didn't end just working there. Later, when I was twenty-one years old, my new bride, Gloria, and I would spend our honeymoon night in Suite 610.

I clearly remember the announcement when Mr. Conrad Nicholas Hilton Sr. died, in early January 1979. It was just before my thirty-first birthday, and at the time, I had just been unanimously elected, out of a thousand-plus members, to be the incoming president of the Houston Restaurant Association. It was my sad, but indeed great, honor to give a short and fitting eulogy to him at our beloved Shamrock Hilton Hotel.

STARTING A HOTEL & RESTAURANT COLLEGE

Just like NASCAR racing evolved from bootlegging moonshine and rum-running in the South, many successful restaurant and hotel brands can trace their roots back to the Prohibition era of the late 1920s and '30s. The rum-runners were the forerunners of stockcar racing; they eventually organized formalized rules for racing and became NASCAR. Likewise, thousands of mom-and-pop hotels and restaurants were opened by owners without formal training, education, or any official standards of practice. These were families of grit, where generations pooled their monies, often with Great-Grandma's recipes from the old country. Armed with cash in pickle jars and secret non-written recipes and formulas for success, they all banded together to raise their children and put needed food on the table at the same time.

One such family during the Great Depression was mine, and stories such as those of my great-grandmother slugging a copper before stepping into a horse-driven paddy wagon to be hauled off to jail for serving alcohol in the family's speakeasy saloon were common.

Two of my great-grandparents families serving food, beverage and lodging.

A generation later, my great-grandmother's saloon would evolve, with her grand-nephews' help, into Vargo's Delicatessen and, eventually, to the Black Angus and Vargo's Restaurant in Houston, Texas.

Before I grew up in the family business, only a handful of formal hotel-and-restaurant education and training facilities existed in the world. The Ecole hôtelière de Lausanne, in Switzerland, was established in 1893. Later, the School of Hotel Administration at Cornell University in Ithaca, New York, was founded in 1922 as a specialized business school for hospitality management and was the first four-year intercollegiate school devoted to the field. Going to that school and Cornell was a goal of mine since my early days at the Shamrock.

Soon, normalized Hotel Restaurant Management (HRM) college programs were moving south and included the School of Hotel and Restaurant Administration at Oklahoma State University, which was established about 1944.

It was only natural that as other college locations were considered, Houston would be on top of the list, with a metropolis that was burgeoning with such major activity as the Houston Medical Center, NASA Space Center, and the world's first indoor air-conditioned sports arena, also known as the Eighth Wonder of the World, the Houston Astrodome.

Looking back, I think the genesis of the Conrad N. Hilton College was the confluence of a dynamic city; a very motivated Dean in James Taylor, who sought out a noted brand-worthy benefactor to lead an emerging school into a full-fledged college; and the efforts of the local and state restaurant and hotel and junior hotel associations. The impetus was provided by Eric and Barron Hilton, two of Conrad's sons, who recognized the need for such a program. The college was finally brought to life by a visionary and a benefactor in the form of Conrad N. Hilton, who would live to see the finalization of his fitting opus. In 1969, the Conrad N. Hilton College of Hotel and Restaurant Management opened at the University of Houston. In perfect harmony, Mr. Hilton had made two dreams come true: his dream to build the college and my dream to attend it.

CHAPTER FOUR
From Hippy Hair to a Baldini

My brother, Mark, and I were the best of friends until he left for the seminary in San Antonio in the tenth grade. Mark was eighteen months older than I, and my mother trusted him explicitly over me. Somewhere between Cub Scouts and Boy Scouts, we were old enough that we were permitted to strike out on our own for sheer adventure in our small township of Bay Village, Ohio. Mark was always the leader and always got blue clothes because of his blue eyes, where I always got what I thought were frumpy-looking brown clothes because of my hazel-green eyes. Little did I know then that it would not be too long before I would finally have a completely green wardrobe to match my eyes.

My brother Mark and I, Easter 1959.
Shortly after this photo was taken, those new suits would be ripped to shreds, as boys will be boys.

Mark and I would go hiking to such exotic places as our church, the school, the public library, and the post office, where he would always pick up and bring home all kinds of applications that could lead to all kinds of exciting careers all over the world. At church he always picked up the questionnaires for joining a seminary, and at the library I would look in the back of the magazines and copy the addresses of military academies such as Valley Forge and Virginia Military Institute to mail away for admission forms. It seems that even at that young age my brother always saw himself in a priest's tunic and collar, while I saw myself as nothing other than the six-and-a-half-foot-tall cardboard Marine Corps sergeant on display in the local post office.

The cardboard-cutout sergeant was regally outfitted in the Corps traditional dress-blue uniform, with royal-blue trousers and a red stripe screaming down each side. He had a proud chest adorned with several medals, his massive jaw was square, and his eyes were transfixed with determination. Mark and I would go to the post office every Saturday morning—after chores, of course—and I can remember telling my brother, "That guy would look great in our bedroom."

We both agreed and concluded, "They'll probably throw him out anyway." True to my prediction, one Saturday afternoon, Mark and I went to the post office, and found the sergeant gone. When I asked a postman at the post office where they had put my Marine after I saw he was "missing in action," the postman looked at me like I had three green eyes.

Week after week, month after month, Mark and I filled out applications and requested information. But the more postcards we sent out, the more mail Mark received in return, including complete information packages loaded with pamphlets from the Jesuits, Maryknolls, and Oblates, which were all foreign missionaries. I always thought it was amazing how the mailman or the registrars' offices evidently knew that my family could not afford a military academy boarding school and the recruiters always knew that I was too young to join the Marine Corps, because I never got a thing.

Mark and I would trek excitedly to the library each time a package came so we could locate and match up on the map the possible countries that we could go to. The year 1959 was a very exciting time compared to today, and the world was still a relatively young and simple place to us, with plenty of new adventures. Looking back, I realize now that Mark was always destined to help the needy of the world. He succeeded in doing just that, as, in just a few short years after all of our library trips, he would be stationed in India, Bangladesh, and Thailand. I, on the other hand, never received any correspondence but still retained a burning desire to be that Marine Corps sergeant dressed in the royal-blue trousers with the red stripe down each side and a chest full of medals.

I do not feel very old, but I do remember, in the early days of black-and-white television, when the dancers I envied, such as Jean Murray and Fred Astaire, wore tuxedo slacks with elegant, shiny black-on-black stripes. I guess by then I already knew that I wanted to be a sergeant and a gentleman dressed in that beautiful uniform and respected. I could never imagine the gravity of the situation that would lead me to earn those stripes the hard way. As far as all those military academy applications I mailed in, it would be about twenty years later, in a mother's sordid confession, that I would learn the bittersweet but horrible truth: it hadn't been the postman, the registrars' offices, or the recruiters who had thwarted and ruined my goals of being a sergeant; it had been my mother, who had been my unknown personal gatekeeper. My goal of being an academy cadet and a tall, blue-uniformed Marine sergeant had been intentionally sabotaged. But despite this, my goal of being a Marine was realized sooner than my mother or I could ever have predicted.

ST. THOMAS HIGH SCHOOL

When my family moved from Bay Village, Ohio, to Houston, Texas, I was in seventh grade and Mark was in the ninth. By the very next year, he disliked the environment at his high school so much that with our parents' blessing, he went to the Oblate seminary in San Antonio. I had lost my best friend, and in an effort to replace him, I traded a saint for a sinner.

I ended up trading Mark for my black-sheep cousin Gary back in Ohio, a military brat whose father had been a WWII Army major who was always stationed out of town or out of country on duty. Gary had been in and out of trouble so many times that the last judge he saw had politely asked him to leave his jurisdiction, or else. It wasn't long before three of the older Vargo brothers decided that Gary, who was my brother age, was to be implanted in my bedroom in Houston. The idea was that he was going to have a good moral upbringing in a stable environment, straighten out his act, and follow me. Of course, just the opposite happened. Instead of me being a good influence on him, he was a terrible manipulator and ended up being a major disaster for my success in junior high and high school.

Gary was placed in Marian High School, which Mark had attended before he had left for the seminary. Gary was quickly expelled by the good Incarnate Word sisters...for life. My dad and uncle had to keep him busy until he was sixteen, when the two older brothers—my dad and uncle—put him to work as a busboy in their restaurant. It wasn't long before he was into my dad's liquor closet and stealing the waitresses' tips and cashing them in at the cigarette machine. Of course he coerced his booty on me, and it didn't take long for my grades to go straight downhill, as it was hard taking an algebra or Latin test tired, half-drunk, and with a cigarette hangover.

In the early 1960s, of course, smoking was not a bad thing yet. In fact, at St. Thomas, we had the infamous "green slab," where boys from freshman to senior could bribe the pious brothers and priests by dropping quarters into their favorite saints' donation jars sitting on each of their desks. After a properly accepted "donation," the student was permitted to go outside the school to a 100' x 100' green-painted cement slab and take a smoke break. Back then, it was just a sign of manning-up at a Catholic academic institution.

With a couple of hundred students milling around at lunchtime, the slab was also a scene of young testosterone strutting its stuff. At least once a day, two preppy titans would push, shove, and curse each other until a gauntlet was thrown down. As it was too gentlemanly to actually throw a fist on the slab, an immediate appointment would be made between the factions of friends who were egging on the combatants to meet after school at nearby Jackson Hill. The genesis of the friction was usually over something trivial like schoolwork or something as important as a girl, mostly some girl.

After I was in enough fisticuffs—wishing it was Gary instead of my fellow students I was hitting—and after the final grades I had produced in school, it was no wonder the good Basilian priests at St. Thomas asked me—more like told me—to leave, posthaste. Looking back at my cousin Gary, I realize he thought he had "street cred," but in reality, he was just a "street crud."

MARIAN HIGH SCHOOL

By then, the die was cast and noted in the family. Gary was signed up for and sent into the service at the earliest possible age. My brother, Mark, went back to the seminary, and I was condemned to academic hell at Marian High School, where the Irish nuns of the Incarnate Word were waiting for me. Although I wanted to turn the corner and turn a new leaf, by this time, I had fallen so far behind academically that I just never caught up. That was all my fault.

I would voluntarily go to mass every morning, and even to week-long retreats at my brother's seminary in San Antonio. I guess the Incarnate Word sisters were in communication with the Oblate priests, for I was singled out on these retreats at breakfast to eat my cereal on my knees on an uneven brick floor while they chanted the Gregorian. Lunch was endured with a savory watery split pea soup, but I did thank God for real mayonnaise-and-ketchup sandwiches for dinner before vespers. I honestly do think the priests, brothers, and nuns were trying to help me, but I was just so far behind and felt so overwhelmed that I just gave up. It also didn't help that I had two fairly traumatic incidents that exacerbated the situation: I had one extended stint in the hospital because I had somehow developed gangrene in my intestines, and another because my appendix exploded and had to be removed and I almost died from the resulting infection.

It was shortly after my spiritual and physical awareness that I adopted the behavior of running away from my problems by overworking myself to distraction Why, I am not really sure, but I still maintain that habit to this day. That is why I targeted the Shamrock Hilton Hotel, because it was dangerously and sinfully glitzy, a twenty-four-hour, seven-day-a-week institution close to home and on a bus route. Of course in those days it was never given a second thought for a kid to hitchhike home, even at midnight. A hotel was also a good place of employment for a burgeoning workaholic and a mixed-up kid who was running away from his problems.

I was totally confused and torn between my good, pious brother and my evil, vindictive cousin. It would take a war to set me straight. What a hard lesson to learn. The war in Viet Nam and the draft were both escalating proportionately at that point, and if you were not going to college, you were immediately drafted. If you went to college and flunked, a military bus was basically waiting just outside the campus on report card day for your speedy exit to boot camp.

I took a hard look in the mirror, and I looked at my grades and my options. I didn't like what I saw. I reasoned there was no way I would ever pass algebra or graduate and I would not be saved from coming home in a body bag, as I had made seven straight F's. I also knew that if I did go to 'Nam and came back, I could get my education back on track through the GI Bill, where I could control 100% of my destiny, with no priests, no brothers, no nuns, and no parents, only me. I decided to join the Marines and set my sights on becoming a sergeant. It would be another thirty years before I would take another hard look at myself like that and make another difficult decision to change my life and who I was.

JOINING THE MARINES

"Some people live an entire lifetime and wonder if they have ever made a difference in the world, but the Marines don't have that problem."

Ronald Reagan

It was about a month after my graduation-less graduation ceremony that I decided to join the Marines. At that time, Gloria was barely a sophomore in an all-girl high school. I had decided that because we were still so young, we should just do what we both needed to do for now and, in two or three years, if we still felt we were meant for one another, we could get married. It didn't hurt that both our fathers had got together and mutually decided that we needed to separate and that I should go into the Army and far away to Germany.

But no one tells Claude Vargo what to do, so it was the Marines, and I proudly, but admittedly nervously, left for boot camp on June 23, 1967. I was barely nineteen years old.

After surviving the Incarnate Word sisters, the Basilian brothers, and the Oblate priests browbeating me for years, I was pretty relaxed with my drill instructors at boot camp, and I felt at least a little ahead of my peers in dealing with the initial shock of boot camp. My drill instructors did not do anything to me psychologically that the nuns, brothers, and priests had not inflicted on me and others.

I stood more than a bald headed foot taller than my head drill instructor (platoon commander), Staff Sergeant Lowery, but I looked up to him. He was a great teacher to me. He ruled with an iron fist but was fair-minded, if that was possible under the circumstances of boot camp. I really liked this man; he trained us well, and everything he showed me would eventually help to keep me and my platoon alive. The only thing he ever did to me that I really resented was for some indiscretion on my part one day, when he grabbed me by my collar, crushed my Adam's apple and climbed on my kneecaps, screaming bloody murder down at me while bending me like a longbow. I got over the resentment, though, and I couldn't know it at the time, but just a few years later, he and I would cross paths under more positive circumstances. We would have a very warm and wonderful reunion...because we were both still alive.

During Christmas of 1967, I was at Camp Pendleton, California, and was given five precious days off by my employer, the United States Marine Corps. I had just joined that June, but with six months' worth of the infamous and grueling boot camp, Infantry Training Regiment (ITR), and tank school at Del Mar, I was ready to defend my country. Before our brief Christmas release, we had each signed our last wills and testaments and actual death warrants that said we would not exceed a 500-mile-radius travel limit. A couple hundred miles extra to go home to Houston was no big deal, I figured. Well, maybe it was closer to 700 miles out of jurisdiction, but as just a nineteen-year-old pimpled and lanky teenager with the prospect of going to war looming, who really cared?

I had a great time home on leave, never sleeping but instead walking around like a proud peacock, as most Marines do on their first leave home. After leave, on the way back to camp, my luck being what it was, when my flight landed on the evening before I was due back on base, it was not in Los Angeles as scheduled. We had to make an unexpected landing in Las Vegas due to a very bad fog. The stewardess cheerfully told all the passengers that we were lucky that the airline was putting us up at a multi-star hotel until the fog lifted. This was to be a seminal moment in my life, because we had been told that Marines missing from their outfits that were shipping out to war zones would be shot the next day at sunrise, per the aforementioned death warrants we had signed. In Marine jargon, it was called "missing a movement." There were absolutely no excuses and it was taken deadly seriously.

I desperately tried everything to get back to Camp Pendleton: bus, train, even a private helicopter. Finally, I started hitchhiking the 300-odd miles left to the deployment center for processing. Naturally, I was a dollar short and an hour late. My outfit had already left. I was condemned and resigned to my fate with a personal firing squad in less than twenty-four hours. I was sure glad they had made us make out our wills before the Christmas break to save time.

I checked in and was immediately put in shackles; my status was now changed to deserter in a time of war. This was a severe military matter, but I had convinced myself that some other unlucky turd had got my seat on the plane over to Viet Nam and I would go on the next available space, no problem. I did not think that the Marines really wanted to make an example out of little ol' me for being a couple hours late. I was wrong, again. This was really serious stuff.

While I was chained to a brick wall in wrist and ankle shackles, I conversed with the officer of the day, who was sitting at a desk, rubber-stamping a stack of papers. The new "brown bar" second lieutenant wasn't too crazy about his assignment and was about as excited as I was about me being latched to the wall. He initiated the conversation by jokingly asking me who I had murdered and was relieved to find out I was just another tardy teenager. We continued small talk, I think mostly because he felt my captivity looked like overkill for my crime against humanity. After a few more exchanges, I found out he was from Cleveland, Ohio, and had actually distantly known my second cousin while at Case Western Reserve College and that they had become closer while in Officer Candidate School (OCS) in Quantico, Virginia. Thankfully, it wasn't long before my dossier was rubber-stamped and I was on an olive-drab dark green school bus headed to 'Nam.

CHAPTER FIVE
Semper Fi or Die—Khe Sanh

Our flight from San Francisco to Anchorage actually slid in sideways on the runway upon landing. I had thought that was the worst flight of my life, until the flight that landed in DaNang. We flew right over the world's busiest airport and just dove straight down in a corkscrew to miss the enemy flak. I never knew, or even considered, that a commercial Boeing 707 could dive so steeply, like a dive bomber, straight into DaNang...with my stomach just ahead of the plane. That pilot was amazing, but I guess we were also just lucky that we were not hit by any flak or surface-to-air missiles.

It wasn't long before I was processed in and reported in to our tank battalion headquarters in Phu Bai, South Viet Nam, about halfway to the Demilitarized Zone (DMZ) from DaNang. Once we were in the DMZ, life was all about filling sandbags with monsoon mud, battling constipation and diarrhea, and getting used to being in a war zone. Nothing actually happened for a couple of weeks, until the Tet New Year Offensive started and all hell broke loose all over the country. Then I was quickly headed to the front line in the proverbial Year of the Snake.

Everyone could tell I was a Freaking New Guy (FNG) because my utilities were still vibrant camouflage-green, my boots were still black, and I was limping and dragging one of my legs because of an anti-Hepatitis A gamma globulin horse shot painfully received between my hip and my butt. I think Nurse Hefty had used both fists to cram that spike into my hip. I had heard her grunt just to inject the extra-thick serum, which had the consistency of napalm and Dep hair gel, but I had known better than to cry out.

When I arrived in Hue City, which had been overrun and was under siege, one of the first things I noticed was the incredibly smelly "Perfume River," which ran through the city. It reminded me of the solid waste treatment plants back home, only a lot stronger and more toxic. The locals all had clothes lines in their backyards, but instead of freshly washed clothes hanging there, dried and rotting fish and shrimp were waving in the gentle breeze.

As I was in Hue without a tank assignment yet, I was swiftly drafted into the infantry. I found myself assigned to a hastily formed provisional infantry unit, running behind a tank and carrying a brand-new M-16 with Cosmoline still glued to the weapon, and two hand grenades hung from a just-out-of-the-box flak jacket. It was a cold, almost-freezing January on the other side of the world, and I now had my nose stuck up the dragon's ass. It was a fifty-two–ton, thirteen-foot-high monster whose exhaust of 750-horsepower belched out diesel fumes at an enormous rate, while it intermittently hurled 3'6" rounds onto a stubbornly entrenched opponent. I finally evaded the tank's ear-blistering, unannounced explosions and constant machine-gun chattering when a group of us switched dragons for the back of a "zippo" flame tank, which also added the smell of napalm and burning flesh to the stench covering the area. I ran over pools of blood and wondered whose body parts had been scattered around us as we made street-by-street advances.

The central business district of Hue City had been recently overtaken by the North Vietnamese Army (NVA) in the first major Tet Offensive of January 1968 and the first siege of the war. We could see the enemy flags fluttering in the wind but could not rout the embedded troops in the citadel because we were not permitted to carpet bomb or fire indiscriminately on the ancient city, for political reasons, so we just went from street to street, firing point-blank at targets. But politics surely did not stop the enemy from shelling and sniping at us anywhere and everywhere. As we recovered precious military real estate in the middle of the antiquated metropolis, major enemy offensives broke out all over South Viet Nam. Tanks became hot-ticket targets in which crewmen were dropping like flies, but I immediately volunteered for a tank for the protection I thought it would afford me. I would soon find out that, once again, I was wrong.

For my next thrilling military flight with my stomach shoved up into my Adam's apple, I was choppered into Khe Sanh, next to the DMZ, via a couple days at Camp J.J. Carroll. About twenty-five of us were packed in like cattle aboard a CH-46 Sea Knight chopper, or "Phrog." We hovered in the cloudy fog that hung over the plateau for what seemed like an eternity. Finally, the back loading ramp magically opened and a mist drifted in and out, much like our guarded and shallow breathing. There were slowly blinking red lights behind the crew cabin, warning us of the impending danger at hand.

The pilot shut off the engines, and there wasn't a sound except the wind whistling through the cabin and our hearts pounding. We hit the ground and did a dead-cat bounce, and the jet engine turbines on the CH-46 screamed back to life louder than the mortars, artillery, and rockets that were pouring in underneath us and all around us. Adding to the confusion was a blaring bullhorn yelling for everyone to depart orderly but quickly. Was he freaking kidding? It was now every man (and boy) for himself. After the initial recoil from the jets being restarted, the chopper's front end lifted, and all of us newbies fell out on top of one another, like Yahtzee dice on a table. The chopper hit its afterburners and was gone in an instant, leaving us to fend for ourselves.

I left my duffel bag, along with my lunch, right there on the tarmac, somewhere a couple of miles from North Viet Nam. I didn't ask questions, instinctively diving into the first trench and bunker I could find. The walls were corrugated metal, damp from constant moisture; the lights inside flickered as the gas generators strained to keep up with the electrical demands of war. The odor reminded me of a cross between my high school biology lab and the French Quarter in New Orleans—very noxious and damp, with 99% humidity.

The two punch-drunk ghouls inside the bunker were dressed in half civilian attire, with no visible rank, insignia, or identifying service patch but were calm as cucumbers and passing a joint between them. I smoked cigarettes just like all Marines but had never smoked marijuana. If those ghouls had passed it to me, I would have sucked that whole joint down in one drag to calm my totally shattered nerves. Once the shelling abated and I had started to collect my wits, one of them chucked a packet of C-ration (C-rat) toilet paper at me, ostensibly to clean myself up, then starting laughing profusely. The other said, "Welcome to hell!"

As I hastily left the bunker, I turned and saw a sign that read:

Graves Registration
Please take a number.
You might be next!

Already moving into action, several men were dragging the most recent screaming wounded and the dead, either to graves or Charlie Med, the hospital in another dirt bunker. Some of the guys I had just been on the chopper with were, just that quickly, casualties of war. This was the first time I had ever heard human beings screaming in agony, and it all seemed like a surrealistic dream, far from the life-sized Marine posters in the post office at home.

On or near the tarmac were Corpsmen and Army medics dragging bodies onto stretchers and carrying them toward Charlie Med. Behind them were another group of troops quickly repairing the rocket-laden blast holes in the twisted-metal tarmac. It all looked methodical, choreographed, and rehearsed. These were the Navy "Seabees" (Construction Battalion, or CBs), and these were absolutely some of the bravest men I have ever seen. They never knew when one rocket or artillery attack would end and another would start but would do their jobs, riding forklifts and Caterpillars with their unit's flags proudly flying aloft, like it was an ordinary day at the job site back home.

One guy I saw had a red target painted on the back of his flak jacket and was running around, yelling at the adjacent mountain peaks. As I looked out from my hiding place in a trench alongside the runway, standing in ankle-deep water with baby rats paddling, bobbing, and floating all around me, I heard the NVA snipers pinging at the scurrying and zigzagging Seabees. My bladder was full, and my urinary tract was burning. There was no sign for a "head" or anywhere else to piss, and I didn't know whether to let it go in the trench, find a nonexistent tree, or run around to try to find a damn head somewhere. This was definitely something they had not taught us in boot camp, infantry training, or my specialized training, tank school.

Khe Sanh, like all military encampments, was divided into different colored sections so dumb-asses and FNGs like me would know where they were going: North was blue, gray was east, and red was west. But I didn't know where I was going. If someone back at Camp Carroll had told me where to go when I got here, I sure as hell could not remember at this point. I just ran perpendicular to the arc of those freaking missiles, and I didn't give a damn which sector I was running to, only what I was running from.

I must have missed the class back in basic training when they had discussed the rockets, missiles, artillery, and mortars now raining down on me. Or when they had described the divisions of tens of thousands of battle-trained and hard-core equipped enemy called the NVA regulars assembling as close as one hundred meters outside our perimeter, ready to close-in and lock horns with us. Later in the siege, it would be confirmed that several Russian tanks and aircraft had been spotted adjacent to the base. That's when the scuttlebutt began that President Johnson was arguing with some of the Joint Chiefs of Staff about having the nuclear option, just in case. I just never thought of myself as an option or a just-in-case.

But on my first day in Khe Sanh, I was sprinting blindly, clutching my duffel bag in front of me, when suddenly I felt something hit the duffel bag...hard. I felt like I was Jerry Ellis holding a punching bag when Mohammad Ali let loose with his best punch to my solar plexus. There was an explosion that I never heard, and amazingly, it probably had my name written on it by some gook on a Co Roc mountainside just inside Laos. The round hit so close in front of me that I ran right into the hole in the ground that it had just created. Thankfully, the only wound I had was to my pride. When I dropped my duffel bag, I saw it was shredded like a gutted stuffed animal, and everything was falling out of it, including my skivvies. I picked all my stuff up out of the mud with both arms and ran away as fast as I could, cradling the remains of my bag like a thirty-pound unwanted tumor. There would be no Red Badge of Courage, no Purple Heart, and no body bag for me on this day...but the war wasn't over yet. For me, it had just begun.

"They are in front of us, behind us, and we are flanked on both sides by an enemy that outnumbers us 29:1. They can't get away from us now!"

Lieutenant General Lewis B. "Chesty" Puller, USMC

The Khe Sanh Combat Base (KSCB) was about the size of one of the new super regional malls that were springing up back home from coast to coast, which usually had four national anchor tenants. I figured I ran past Foley's, Sears, Montgomery Ward, and J.C. Penney, then all the way out to the last car in the parking lot before I asked directions while the rocket attack abated and my bladder trouble began again. But I decided it was all just burning fear and just another short squirt away.

I ambled all the way back to the west end of the base, the gray sector, where the tank park was located. I got there just as another barrage started up again, and I ran to the tank command post, which was designated by three large, empty ammo boxes covered with a poncho. A haphazardly etched sign read "Bravo Company, 3rd Platoon, Third Tank Battalion." The first thing I noticed was that the tanks were right in the line of fire to those screaming and screeching rounds flying through the air, and the dirt and metal each explosion produced. I was in a mountainside monsoon of light rain and heavy artillery fire with a large red-and-white bulls-eye suspended over our position.

I had arrived on a Sunday, without going to church, and wondered if I was going to hell or if I was already standing in it. A Gunnery Sergeant (Gunny) took my orders and in return gave me three boxes of C-rats. Instead of the delectable Spaghetti and Meatballs or Beans and Wieners, I got Ham and Mothers (lima beans), Ham and Mothers, and one more Ham and Mothers. Before I was assigned a tank, I was shown an underground bunker and an elevated shelf nearest the ceiling that was my intended sleeping spot.

I thought my day had already been a nightmare, but didn't know the nightmare had only just started. These were bunker's hours, not banker's hours. I was lying on my back with my nose a little less than an inch from a wood beam that I could barely see. The only light was a flickering diesel lamp set up in the middle of a dozen guys coming and going 24/7 from duty on the perimeter of the base. As there were only three tanks to guard an airstrip and an entire command post (CP), they were always busy in direct-fire support of a very aggressive opponent always watching, always probing.

I clutched the three cardboard boxes of C-rations next to me while the night's barrage of screeching missiles landed over and under our position, when the acid burning in my stomach kicked in. In between the offensive and defensive volleys of artillery, the only sound we heard was of the squealing rats scurrying on the beams above us, when someone in the dark told me to keep my .45 ready. "Ready for what?" I wondered.

Then all was quiet…I thought everybody including the rats had left the bunker, but as I felt a hundred eyes looking at me, I decided this was no Disney movie. In the next instant, I heard a pistol shot and saw a muzzle flash not but a few feet from me, and a dead rat the size of a large cat and his offals landed on my chest and face. I was so close to the flash that I got face and neck burns from the gunpowder. Whatever I felt that was wet, I did not want to know. My first tank commander (TC) had just shot at point-blank range the platoon mascot that had been eyeballing both my C-rats and me. When the sergeant stepped out of his umbrage, he thought he was cute by blowing the smoke off the barrel of his .45. He jerked his head quickly to the right and said in his drill-instructor-imitation voice, "Topside, Private," for guard duty on the perimeter, I ascertained.

When I saw Gunny Martin again a day or so later, my stomach was growling, with each rumble greater than the previous pang, blaring for some meager degree of nutrition. I asked him when he was going to pass out another round of boxes. I also told him I wasn't too keen on the chef's special of ham and lima beans but would take them if he didn't have anything else. He looked miffed, laughed, and asked me if I had already eaten them all. I told him, "Yes, yesterday, Gunny—breakfast, lunch, and dinner."

He shot back, "Yeah, but they were for Monday, Wednesday, and Friday," and with a shit-eating grin, he said, "Check back with me next Sunday, Private!" It was a very long and very hungry week.

In January 1968, Khe Sanh was an unheard-of outpost, with an airfield defended by a couple of thousand Marines of the 26th Regiment. Shortly after I arrived there, my brother, Mark, the seminarian, mailed me a copy of Bernard Fall's *Hell in a Very Small Place*. Ironically, included with it was a note asking me if I knew where Khe Sanh was. In his note he told me that Jeanne Dixon, a noted prophetess and author of *A Gift of Prophecy*, had correctly foretold and warned then

President Kennedy of his impending assassination. Mark further wrote that Ms. Dixon had also predicted that U.S. Marines would be overrun at Khe Sanh...exactly where I was standing. In Fall's book he gave a chronology of how the French had been driven out of Viet Nam after they had been slaughtered and almost annihilated at the battle of Dien Bien Phu. There was such similarity between the enemy garrisons at Dien Bien Phu and Khe Sanh, they were almost indistinguishable. The same General, Nguyen Van Giap, was also in charge of Viet Nam's battle plan for Khe Sanh, and now a lot wiser on how to defeat his second world-class superpower.

I don't think I had even finished reading the first chapter before a friend of mine named Dale Sandifer stuck his nose into the back cover and immediately ascertained these similarities. He was an incessant reader who quickly wanted me to tear the book in half so he could read it at the same time so we could exchange each other's halves later. Before we could do that, however, the scuttlebutt about my book had spread so quickly that in no time, I was sent to the CP bunker and was standing tall in front of "the Man," who asked if he could borrow the book. Who was I, a private, to say no?

The battle for the hills surrounding Khe Sanh started before the Tet Offensive or my second set of back-to-back offensive siege of Hue City and defensive siege at hand. The hills surrounding Khe Sanh were named 1015, 950, 861, 881 North, 881 South, and 64, based on their corresponding elevation in meters. They were called hills but were really jagged mountain peaks with intermittent jungles surrounding them.

In the hills surrounding the "plateau of death," the mist and the clouds hung around the tops like doughnuts on sticks. We only had five tanks at Khe Sanh, three in the main compound and two on Hill 64, the "Rock Quarry," which was where I would be stationed soon. The lack of tanks had occurred because the NVA had "eliminated" the mountain road bridges and then methodically surrounded us with a couple divisions of troops and a couple more divisions (approximately four units of 11,000 men each against our 4,000 total troops) in reserve. The siege was on, and we had to work with what we had.

I remember discussing the battle tactics with a couple of my buddies, Bob Dougherty and Joe Harrigan, not long after and asking, "If you were the North Vietnamese general in charge, where would you attack next?"

They both replied, "Well, the lowest hill, surely not the highest."

We all felt sick as I replied, "Yep, that's what I figured as well."

We then ascertained very quickly that we had better get ready. We were on Hill 64, the lowest and the most vulnerable of the hills.

"John Wayne" Vargo in front of the dirt cave.

A few days later in early February 1968, we were hit hard and partially overrun on Hill 64, in what would turn out to be one of the heaviest single days of fighting in the heaviest battle engagement of the war. We spotted different colored sparkling flares and quickly used one of our tank's radios to call the CP and determine the meaning of the different colors, as this was no birthday party. Next, I distinctly heard the NVA bugles over our wire in the background and knew exactly what they meant. As a young man I had played trumpet in the band, but in the Scouts I had blown a bugle. I could "Name that Gook Song" in three notes, because I knew exactly what those staccato notes and that crescendo meant in any language—*CHARGE!*

We had been assigned and attached to the First Battalion Ninth Marine Regiment, 1/9, respectfully and reverently nicknamed the Walking Dead because of the fierce fighting they had encountered and the number of casualties they had taken. We were constantly at point-blank range and always expected any moment that the NVA's sapper squads and rocket-propelled grenade (RPG) units would wipe out our two tanks. But we held most of our line that day and throughout the siege and never were completely overrun like they had been on other hills such as 881 and 861, or like the French at Dien Bien Phu.

Two hard-core Marine battle tanks,
Rock Quarry, Khe Sanh DMZ.

The commanding officer, Colonel John F. Mitchell, later wrote about that day:

> *"The total KIA of NVA soldiers exceeded 150 on this day. The 1/9 battalion received over 350 rounds of enemy supporting arms fire in their [our] command perimeter."*

In the two tanks on the Rock Quarry, I was a gunner and a loader. That night, I can remember a senior infantry officer who stuck his head into the turret and said, "Good shooting, boys. Change your skivvies and carry on."

He didn't know how right he was, because I again had bladder trouble. But we would not have to worry about changing skivvies much after that, because, one by one, all our underwear would drop out our trouser legs after having rotted off and from us not having taken our trousers or boots off for weeks on end.

BETWEEN ROCKET ATTACKS

After I had been at the Rock Quarry for about two weeks, I was continuously on shitter duty, even after that job should have been rotated, but I acquiesced to get along with living in the dirt cave with several other grungy tankers. I really didn't like the cave for three reasons: the dirt was always lightly falling from the ceiling, which told me it could cave in by itself or with an explosion above; no one could stand up in the cave, especially me; and the cave was on the direct arc path of the incoming rockets, mortars, and artillery from Co Roc, Laos. I didn't feel like dying crushed below a mountain of dirt. The other side of the Rock Quarry was just opposite the arc of incoming missiles, and it was all rock. Other tankers had earlier attempted to dig a cave on the other side with several types of explosives, but to no avail.

I thought otherwise sleeping under a probable mudslide or cave-in was not in my best interest and I started digging into the rock side by hand, using a tank chisel and an eight-pound sledgehammer. To protect the blisters on my left hand, I would wrap the hand with grungy rags, which were really just old rotted skivvies and T-shirts too dirty to wear that could stand up on their own as if they were heavily starched. I tried chiseling with the hammer in my left hand, but that beat my knuckles up worse than the blisters, so I wrapped the skivvies around my left palm and continued banging with my right hand.

After about three to four weeks and after developing new blisters underneath all the calluses, I was able to curl up in a ball and sleep in a fetal position in my newly cut rock womb, uninterrupted save for guard duty. After another couple weeks of chiseling, I was able to almost stretch out my legs without my final teenage growing cramps. Next in my cave, I made a dissecting right turn so a direct explosion outside the cave would not have an effect inside; I didn't worry about my ears at the time.

Another couple weeks went by, by which time I had made a left-hand turn in the mountainous rock and had a descending Z-type configuration. It was at about this time that the other seven tankers on the Quarry also became convinced that the rock side meant a better chance of survival from the rockets and missiles. The first person to ask about joining me in my cave was Dale Sandifer, so I told him we would both dig until we could stretch out. Before Dale was finished with his part of the cave, Larry Basco pronounced, "Three digging is better than two," while jokingly calling me Huckleberry.

About the time Larry came on board, the other tank crewmen decided to dig their own caves as well. As it turned out, before we left the Rock Quarry and our rock caves, the dirt side, which we had by then converted to munitions storage, got hit, and the entrance totally collapsed on top of where we would have been.

When we were digging, the clanging went on twenty-four hours a day, seven days a week. What we did not know at the time was that the North Vietnamese were also digging, but more rapidly, in the soft dirt that led up to our defensive lines and perimeter. The perimeter had a triple strand of razor-sharp concertina wire, which we knew would only slow them down in an attack because they had offensive sapper units and RPG battalions that could melt through our defensive positions like a hot knife through butter.

"We've gotta get out of this place
If it's the last thing we ever do.
We've gotta get out of this place.
Girl, there's a better life for me and you."

Eric Burdon & the Animals

In spite of the dire situation we were in, life in and around the cave was somewhat tolerable, and the camaraderie almost reminded me of being in the Boy Scouts and the Explorers, the difference being that the worst thing that happened in the Scouts was that you could easily get popped with a wet towel on your bare butt. At Khe Sanh you could get your ass kicked or, worse, die.

At night in our Rock Quarry caves, we would listen to Hanoi Hannah on a transistor radio and see by the light of the homemade, diesel-burning lanterns made from C-ration cans. Because we had no ventilation shaft or any way of circulating the oily smelling air from the diesel fumes, and because we had to cover the cave entrances with ponchos because of the blackout, we were always suffocating in greasy soot. After about an hour of diesel light we would have to blow out the lamp, our faces black with soot, and we spit out black balls of oil crud against glistening shrimp-colored granite walls and a black, greasy ceiling.

We had to stand guard every night, with a three-hour shift per man. Guard level was at a minimum of 25% the majority of the time: 25% equaled one man standing guard, 50% was two men, and so on. We were at 50%, 75%, and, at least once a week, 100%, as the NVA were assembling and a close-in attack was imminent, again.

Besides invaluable sleep, water and food were the other most precious commodities. We could forget about ice or toothbrushes. Virtually nonexistent beer went for $5 per can. The treasured hard liquor was $100 a bottle, but for a twelve-bottle discount, the Air Force boys would give us a bargain deal at $1,000 per case. They bought it tax-free in Thailand for $2.40 per bottle—nice guys, what a bargain. It would be a year before we gave those rear-echelon pricks some inter-military branch payback, when we charged them equally exorbitant prices for NVA weapons and stash that we brought back from enemy arms caches out in the field. The Air Force guys probably took the weapons home to make themselves into frontline war heroes instead of flying pogues.

Before I hit 'Nam I had been about 175 pounds having been chiseled by Marine Corps boot camp, but I would end up dropping about fifty pounds at the Rock Quarry over the next couple of months. The more I cut that rock, the more weight I would lose, and the whole time I was chiseling my personal cave, I was always wondering if I was digging own grave.

PURPLE THE HARD WAY

It was at the Rock Quarry in late March 1968 that I received my first of several wounds. There was always so much metal flying and lying around that we could never tell if we were running over rocks or rocket parts. If we were fairly far away from our tank or cave, we had to hustle at double-time, which *Time* magazine dubbed the "Khe Sanh shuffle." I constantly worried about breaking an ankle or a leg from hitting the jagged metal that protruded up from the ground. It was during one of the hundreds of barrages, while I was running to my tank, that I was caught between two mortar blasts that came in right on top of me. As the first explosion hit, I ducked so fast, my helmet came off. When I tried to scoop my helmet up like a fumbled football, the next explosion tore at the left side of my head. As I realized what had just happened, I also discovered that my arms and face were sitting atop burning, hot metal.

I quickly saw other boys hitting the deck and chewing rocks out of fear; the gooks had our exact coordinates and were dropping rounds in on us as fast as they could load. They were "firing for effect," and we were in their crosshairs...sitting ducks.

Larry Basco saw me go down and flew out of our cave as the cinders were still pelting down from the blast. He grabbed me by the scruff of my neck and the back side of my flak jacket and pulled me backwards into the cave. Although very skinny, I was still heavy. But he was strong, and he pulled me into the cave as I lost consciousness. Both of us were in shock: I from my wound and Larry from the sight of all the blood. What I was really puzzled at was that it didn't hurt, not like I had thought it would. The concussion from the blast had blown me up against the tank and scared the living shit out of me.

I can remember screaming at Larry, asking him, "How much of my brains are left?" as I was afraid to feel the left side of my head.

I reached down and pulled out of my right hand a piece of hot, jagged metal that was burning like hell. At the same time I had been hit, our friend Gunz (Ralph Gonzales) had almost lost his right hand when it was nearly severed by a mortar round, and several more grunts had also been wounded and were screaming in pain.

In all the confusion, I can't remember who started yelling first, Larry or me, but we both screamed, "Medic!" until reality set in that Army medics were not in the Marine Corps, only Navy corpsmen were. The Marine Corps does not have corpsmen, chaplains, or anyone else who cannot pick up a weapon and fight. I don't know what hit us both so funny just then, but Larry and I both began to laugh hysterically. I touched my wound for the first time to see what was left of my head. Larry urged me not to touch anything, but I couldn't resist, as the blood had now filled my left eye. I decided to take a chance. It wasn't as bad as I had thought, but my head had still been split open like a coconut.

Gunz and I and a couple other wounded grunts were stacked on a mechanized flatbed infantry mule and rushed to Charlie Med, the base hospital across no man's land, and then into the CP. I think I was more in shock than hurt, so I really felt for the other Marines I knew were worse off than either Gunz or me.

Because of the number of dead and wounded coming in, chaos was the flavor du jour. Someone put a tag on my blouse and scribbled something on it. Gunz and I stayed overnight in Charlie Med, listening to the screaming and puking going on all around us. Everyone knew that no matter how bad the wounds were, no one, not even the dead, could be medevaced, as the NVA gunners were blasting right out of the air anything and everything that could fly.

Gunz and I were reported as missing in action (MIA) because we were not in either tank park, in the CP, or at the Rock Quarry on our tanks. I still believe that Larry Basco should have been honored for his bravery and that because of him I am still here today to write this. His actions saved Gunz and me from further wounds and probably from dying.

While all this was going on, there was no Jimi Hendrix music in the background; Robert Duval was not surfing on the Roo Quan River; and Oliver Stone was not hanging out of a Hollywood chopper, yelling, "Cut!" This was the real deal. Our guys were being cut down, dismembered, and bleeding to death in the ugliest and most grotesque ways that you can see, hear, smell, taste, feel, or imagine.

As the brutal days and long, eerie nights of the siege passed slowly by, we were totally focused on what the next day was going to bring, and we were becoming ever grungier from the elements.

We had to constantly clean our tank weaponry with petrochemical products, and our clothes were covered with months' worth of oil, dirt, grease, and grime. While at Camp Carroll, I developed a rash and it began producing welts and bumps all over my body. I recall they burned and itched ferociously but would not break. When I went to a field hospital, the corpsman covered almost my entire body with calamine lotion and told me to return later. When the boils still did not break, I was later medevaced, and doctors injected about 100 of the boils on the back side of my body with cortisone. This procedure was extremely painful; I bit down hard on the clean rag stuffed in my mouth. I was asked to return two days later, and the process was repeated on my front side.

As I moved naturally in the normal process of my duties, the boils began to break. Dark purple blood and yellow pus was secreted from approximately 200 open wounds over my entire body, all in different stages of bursting, oozing, and scabbing. After each session of injections and breaking, instead of being wrapped with medicinal bandages, the open boils were sprayed from above with a good concentration of Agent Orange (at Khe Sahn, 43,705 gallons were sprayed, and the Rockpile, 110,050 gallons) from our buddies in the Air "Farce." This process was repeated several times over the next couple of weeks and months, with less and less cortisone being injected each time. The doctors and corpsmen were astonished that I voluntarily returned to receive this kind of painful treatment, but I just thought of the alternative—infection.

After the war, I would continue to have large grape- or half-golf-ball–sized boils under my armpits that leaked pus and dark blood intermittently. This continued for nine consecutive years, until I finally sought treatment at a private dermatologist in Houston.

During both my combat tours I was out in the field for fourteen major operations, constantly exposed to the dirt, rain, humidity, sun, and heat of the Asian outdoor environment for months at a time without a shower, and I had direct exposure to a plethora of chemical agents.

Sometime during April 1968, my buddy Dale and I had the great idea to take a shower in the next steady rain that came by. After about three or four months of not showering, we thought it would be great to get the grunge off. While we were ferociously scrubbing and withering in the cold rain, Dale reached into one of the storage containers on the tank's fenders and pulled out a wire brush to scrub himself, and we both busted out laughing.

But in the irony of war, at that same moment, on the knoll behind us, the grunts were placing several of their buddies who been killed in the previous night's firefight onto a large net that was hanging from a line attached to a Sea Knight chopper hovering overhead. When we looked up and saw it, we quickly found it petty to worry about not having had a shower for so long.

With that, our moment of lightheartedness ended and we both quickly hustled to get the soap off and get dressed as the rain subsided. As we were trying to put our other dirty, but at least cleaner, clothes on, the chopper took off over us with its lifeless cargo. As we looked up, all we saw were arms and legs protruding from the spinning cargo netting, and as we watched, we were doused with splatters of red and black blood.

Dale Sandifer (right) and me in front of our Rock Quarry cave.

About the same time, a couple hundred meters behind us and outside of our lines, an F-4 Phantom was splashing napalm over enemy trenches, and my conscious thoughts were drowned out by the roar of afterburners and the agonizing screams of my dying enemies. This is the reality of war—death and payback.

In another mortar attack, our water buffalo on wheels, the main source of water for all of us on the hill, was hit as well, so from then on, water was rationed. It is no wonder that forty years later I am still rat-holing water for insurance, just in case. In one of the subsequent attacks, enemy artillerymen hit our ammo dump, taking it out, along with most of our tank rounds. Before long, everything was rationed, except for us Marines.

Because we had lost our platoon barber to a rocket, our hair was almost civilian-like once again. However, the body lice were plentiful and it was hard to find privacy to shave under the arms and the hairy parts of the body they could latch on to.

The insects in Viet Nam were large, but the rats were humongous, and as someone said, they were faster at opening a C-ration can than a hungry gunny. The rat population was reported to be well over a million, and they would feed on the dead and wounded, regardless of which side they were on. Rat bites were prevalent, so much so that we shot them regularly. But, the word was passed to stop shooting with our pistols, because some grunt had put a bead on a speedy Gonzales and shot his sergeant in the ankle.

Occasionally, one of the tankers would go down from the Quarry for tank supplies and other sundry items like popcorn. The Quarry was sixty-four meters higher than the main CP (hence its official designation, Hill 64) and about the longest quarter of a mile I have ever carried anything. When exchanging and rolling a 300-pound tank wheel that distance, it was a challenge not to dump it over by going too fast on the way down, but it was the trip coming back up that was a real bitch.

One such trip, I'll never forget. I had gotten delayed in leaving the CP for another quarter-mile race up the hill. It seemed like a lifetime before, but it had been only seven months earlier that I had held a trophy in the air after winning the Top Competition Eliminator at the one-quarter-mile drag strip back in Dickenson, Texas. In this race from the CP, I took off rolling one newer 300-pound tank wheel, and my trophy, if I made it, would be the three cans of traded popping corn stuffed into my pockets. Once I was outside the CP, the concertina wire was closed behind me and I was on my own. I was having difficulty rolling the tank wheel, which made my progress slower than I really wanted. But because of the constant barrage of rockets flying overhead and the snipers' pings, I kept moving and rolling that damn wheel as fast as I could.

It was nearly dark by this time, and nighttime always came ultra fast during this, the monsoon season. It got dark so quickly mainly because of the rain clouds and the setting sun, and now I found myself in no man's land in the dark. Any real estate between the CP and the Quarry was considered no man's land at night because both perimeters closed their respective ingress and egress with concertina wires and only let guys in who were coming back from duty on listening posts and had the correct password.

Because I was a tanker and not used to coming and going on foot, I had never thought to ask for the password before leaving. A light rain had now turned into a heavy downpour, and I tried to pump the wheel over my head. When I had been pumping iron as a civilian, I had made the "300 Club" by bench-pressing the "big three," but this awkward, muddy tank wheel was now my grounded 300-pound albatross. When I tried to roll it, the wheel jumped over the ruts in the road one way and then the other, and I had secret thoughts about leaving it and running up the hill without it or a password. By now the mud trench was a running river of red, muddy clay water.

Every night was a complete blackout for both sides, but occasionally we could see a flicker of light on our side as well as theirs. This night I saw no light anywhere. As I progressed up the hill, the thought crossed my mind that I could very easily be shot by one of my own infantry guys or my brother tankers. Or, even worse, I could run into the concertina wire or walk into our minefield. The rockets and mortars were still intermittently dropping in the rain, and the visibility was almost nil, and I walked smack-dab into an infantry mule.

An infantry mule is like a large, elevated flatbed go-kart with a steering wheel protruding above the bed. I thought this was a good chance for me to put that damn wheel on that mule and get a free ride up the rest of the hill. I was wrong; the driver was dead and in the ditch. Worse than that, a couple of minutes later, I heard some Vietnamese men yelling to one another in the rain. I didn't know if they had seen me or not, nor which side of the DMZ they came from, ours or theirs, but I didn't care. I slid into the muddy, watery ditch with the dead mule driver and partially covered myself with the wheel and a lot of mud.

I was shaking like I had palsy in a cold winter rain, with only a pistol and a tank wheel. Whoever they were, they passed on by like thieves in the night while I continued to shake, and I was not going to ask them any questions. Whether they were friendly ARVNs or enemy PAVNs, the odds were 50-50, and I wasn't taking any chances announcing that I was an American. They could have been North, headed South or South, headed North. I didn't care, I just knew that I was on the DMZ between the two, and I briefly thought about my 20th birthday, which had just blown by without any ice cream, cake, or candles.

I stayed frozen in that watery ditch, with that damn tank wheel and the stiff, dead driver next to me, until morning light. I thought it would be safer to stay there till first light, safely hidden, rather than getting shot or stepping on a landmine. It turned out that my buddies at the Quarry had covered for me, thinking I was still at the CP and the CP had thought I was back at the Quarry. I finally accomplished my "short" mission that morning, when I not only rolled that freaking wheel up the hill and into the Quarry, but still had one of the popcorn cans left to share with the guys.

ATOMIC BOMBS AWAY

The siege of Khe Sanh was a never-ending cascade of bombs, artillery shells, and mortars from both sides. The amount of munitions expended during the siege at Khe Sanh is staggering. It is estimated that the North Vietnamese fired over 40,000 rocket, artillery, and mortar shells on American positions during the Khe Sanh combat phase, which were responsible for a large percentage of the American and allied casualties.

Robert M. "Satch" Walkley (KIA) and Dale Sandifer eating a box of precious popcorn, the spoils of war.

Then there were the munitions we fired at them. Our artillery fired back around the clock, 24/7, from Camp Carroll. The big guns fired around the perimeter an estimated total of around 150,000 rounds into NVA positions from inside the base during the siege. Also were the nonstop sorties from carrier-based A-4 Intruders, and the DaNang-based F-4 Phantom tactical aircraft.

Between March 22nd and 23rd 1968, the NVA decided they had a real treat for us and unleashed the mother of all artillery and mortar attacks. During a ten-hour period, a record 1,109 rounds were unleashed and fired on KSCB, for an average of more than 100 incoming rounds per hour.

But the granddaddy of them all were our B-52 Arc Light raids dropping racks of 2,000-pound bombs, each one of which left a crater big enough for a tank or two. According to John Prados and Chaplain Ray W. Stubbe in the book *Valley of Decision: The Siege of Khe Sanh*, "That amounted to almost 1,300 tons of bombs around Khe Sanh, the equivalent of a 1.3 kiloton nuclear weapon, every one of the 77-day siege."

It has also been said that "All the bombs hit their intended target 100% of the time, because they all hit the ground." While we were in our cave during the arc light raids, the bombs were so close that we were popped around in that cave like the corn popped to make our popcorn.

The final push to relieve us and the besieged 26th Marines was named Operation Pegasus. The Army, headed by the 1st Air Calvary, had been staging with the 1st Marines at Ca Lu and arrived at Khe Sanh on April 1, 1968. By the end of that month, the NVA had finally decided they'd had enough of this direct confrontation and would take their four divisions, or what was left of them, to the east along the DMZ. We would now have a great chess move, in that we would be going from a defensive to an offensive position and would be going from the prey to the predator.

Oddly, the first thing a supper gaggle of Army choppers brought in to us was boxes of apples and oranges. We thought this was all too funny but welcomed the fresh fruit that we had not seen in many, many months. Upon seeing the crates of fruit, I immediately remembered from my health class in high school that scurvy was a result of a vitamin deficiency, and I had to chuckle. When it was our turn to take our tank from our Rock Quarry nook down to the CP, we dismounted and ran to the choppers, where we were given a selection of a couple of apples or oranges. The guy in front of me bit deeply into his apple and left half his teeth in it, spitting out the other teeth and dripping blood. After seeing this, when my turn came, I told the guy passing the fruit out to give me two soft oranges. I savored them slowly, slice by slice, as my gums were mushy and my teeth were wobbly. It had been months since I had last seen my toothbrush, which we had used for cleaning weapons.

PRESIDENTIAL RECOGNITION

The 26th Marine Regiment had been reinforced by elements of the 9th Marine Regiment, and, to a lesser degree, various elements from the Army, Air Force, and Navy personnel, and our five tanks from Bravo Company, Third Tank Platoon. Of the approximately 230 Marines in Third Tanks alone, there were almost one hundred medals awarded for heroism, from Purple Hearts upwards, including Bronze Stars, Silver Stars, and Navy Crosses.

Photo Courtesy Jack Butcher
One happy Marine!

The twenty-plus tankers who were at the siege of Khe Sanh, along with the 26th Marines and attachments, were awarded the Presidential Unit Citation (PUC). (See Appendix A.) During the entire Viet Nam war, only eleven PUCs were presented to Marine units—the Walking Dead were awarded two. The degree of heroism required for a PUC is the same as that which would warrant a Navy Cross to an individual, which is second only to the Congressional Medal of Honor. For the 700-plus Marines who died and the several thousand more who were wounded at Khe Sanh I have always thought everyone deserved a little bit more public recognition than just the front cover of *Time* magazine. I have also always wondered what the North Vietnamese received for their part.

The total estimated number of bombs dropped, artillery fired, and mortars tubed during the siege of Khe Sanh exceeded 100,000 tons of ordnance during the seventy-seven day siege. The total number of casualties is very hard to determine for various and obvious wartime reasons, but unofficial estimates put NVA casualties at between 10,000 and 15,000 around Khe Sanh and thousands more in the surrounding trails. Official estimates of American dead at Khe Sanh are put at 730 soldiers, and counting. Because soldiers were medevaced directly from the base to expire elsewhere, it has been difficult to account for them accurately.

Operation Pegasus would officially end the siege, but not the fighting, within the valley or the plateau. The siege of Khe Sanh officially ended on April 11, 1968, when the main supply road, Route 9, was finally cleared and the combat engineers reopened it and supplies began moving through the enemy lines again.

Khe Sanh Combat Base was dismantled and officially abandoned on June 23, 1968.

The battle for Khe Sanh is historically recorded as the turning point in the Viet Nam War and one of the most notable and proudest battles in Marine Corps history, but one for which both sides have since claimed victory.

CHAPTER SIX
Semper Fi or Die Hard

MY SECOND "SEE THE WORLD" TOUR

It was a warm Sunday afternoon along the sun-drenched mountains that bordered the DMZ in South Viet Nam, and so far, a relatively quiet one for the spring of '69. I was on my second tour in 'Nam and based at Camp Carroll, about three clicks below the DMZ. I was just between Con Thien—the "Hill of Angels"—and the "Rockpile," a jagged but beautiful, almost-800-foot–tall piece of rock that overlooked three river valleys and two of Charlie's trails. We used this huge chunk of granite as an observation post and a chopper and artillery base. From here, we mercilessly gave the NVA absolute and total hell in an attempt to force them out of Quang Tri Province and back to the Ho Chi Minh Trail, where we could get a better crack at them.

During the siege of Khe Sanh, "The Rockpile" had never once been overrun (in fact, it was never overrun at all during the war). Now, a little over a year after the siege, this Sunday spring afternoon was supposed to be an especially good day because it was some type of battalion holiday; the officers had all been hyping the all-day team festivities such as horseshoes, basketball, and volleyball for some time. We had some great grudge matches going between the platoons, and we could participate or watch our teams compete; read and write letters; play chess, checkers, back-alley bridge, poker, or acey-deucey. Damn, we could even wash our clothes or take a hot shower!

To top it all off, we were told we would be getting a hot meal of thick, juicy steaks and cold beer—true "pogey bait." This meant there would be an actual day off in a war zone, with the big 175-mm guns at Camp Carroll keeping a watchful eye over the DMZ and our backs. Attitudes had definitely taken a U-turn for the good, and boy, were we ready!

Just before the revelry started, I heard my name called over the company bullhorn, which was never used very often, only for important matters like announcements of "Incoming!" I was summoned to the commanding officer's (CO's) bunker and urgently told to gather my tank and crew and round up another tank, which was specified, and take them both down to Route 9 toward Cam Lo. My mission was to locate an Army convoy that had been ambushed

Lt. Peter Ritch, Bob Haley, Fred Janneck, Bill Eaves, and Andy Anderson. Rank has its privileges in who holds the beer.

with no tank protection. Corporal Larry Basco and his two crewmen, Andy Anderson and Robert D. (Bob) Halay, bolted to their tank as ordered, but bitching all the way.

I was quickly briefed that an Army Duster and the lead truck had been hit and rendered useless and the rest of the convoy was stalled behind them, taking heavy automatic weapons and mortar fire. I was further informed that Army tanks were on their way but still miles off in the rear so we had to get there fast to provide some immediate support and show some muscle in the meantime. "Hell," the CO said, "it will just be a Sunday walk in the park." I tried to tell him that I was really short on my crew, but he cut me off and insisted that I get going: "Di di mau!"

I quickly threw off my Sunday-go-to-meeting blouse, put on my never-been-washed, now very smelly flak jacket, and informed my grumbling buddies of the situation. We immediately (if not sooner) headed for Route 9, leaving a thunderous cloud of red dust behind us. As we barreled out of the front gate, past our defensive minefields and the triple-stranded concertina wire, I flashed back to my first tour of duty and remembered how, around fifteen months earlier, another group of tankers had rolled into a heavy ambush. We were now on our way to the exact ambush site on Route 9.

On January 24, 1968, the NVA had set up a devious and deadly ambush where the road curved sharply on Route 9 and the vehicles had to gear down and slow down to make the turn onto the access road as they returned to Camp Carroll. This sharp turn in the road was where a small Marine convoy and then a second rescue convoy, led by Captain Daniel W. Kent and his unit, had both been ambushed.

The NVA had opened up on the first convoy using recoilless rifles, pounding the convoy as it had slowed into the turn returning to camp, wrecking the vehicles. Mortar rounds, small arms, and machine-gun fire had poured in on the Marines, pinning them down. The outmanned, outgunned Marines had held their own with one quad .50-caliber and gotten out a call for help. Captain Kent had immediately mounted up and led a rescue column of tanks roaring out of the camp, with himself seated in the turret of the lead tank.

This is when the NVA had launched their second ambush of the day in the same spot, as the rescue column arrived on the scene. For this second ambush, Corporal Harry C. Christensen had been awarded a Silver Star for valiantly trying to save Captain Kent's life after the captain had been hit and fatally wounded by the recoilless rifle barrage that had opened up immediately as Kent's group with Christianson arrived on the scene. The Marines had fought back until two helicopter gunships had arrived and finally run off the ambushers. There had been eight dead and forty-four wounded Marines in that previous "walk in the park." The battle had lasted most of the day, with a couple hundred dead gooks and multiples of body drag marks.

Briskly, I cocked my tank commander's cupola at half mast; locked and loaded our .30- and .50-caliber machine guns, our grease gun, and my personal .45; then grabbed some grenades and mumbled, "Yeah...just a walk in the park, huh?" I remembered the months at Khe Sanh during the siege when we had been forced into a defensive position and the hundred thousand rockets, artillery, and mortars they had pounded us with. We were now in an offensive position, and the boot on my foot was looking for some ass to kick. To paraphrase Captain Jim Coan in an article I'd seen in the Marine tankers quarterly newsletter "Sponson Box," "There is nothing worse than several pissed-off Marine tankers with one hundred thousand pounds of steel and explosive force looking for one thing…PAYBACK!!!"

After about twenty minutes or so on a very dusty road, the first thing we saw was a small bird-dog spotter prop plane that was dropping white-smoke "willie peters" on the ambushers' location. We went from a lackadaisical pace to an all out ricky-tic and next heard loud explosions and the familiar sounds of automatic-arms fire. We were met with a few hastily fired but errant RPGs, a couple mortars, and the faint splatters of .50-caliber gunfire on the front of our tanks, where ace driver Lance Corporal Robert (Bob) Mendez quickly buttoned up. As a tank commander, I had several drivers, but Mendez was one of the best. I looked back to see that half our tank tread was hanging off a mountain cliff, with Bob barreling forward. To this day I still get cold chills thinking about those mountain drops. Bob was an illegal seventeen-year-old, but damn fine, Marine!

I figured the NVA had to be firing a Soviet-type DShK .51-caliber gun, because I could hear the heavy splats individually hit the bottom half of our tanks and see them hit the dirt but the splats were too slow for a .30-caliber type weapon and out of range for an AK-47 assault rifle.

We did not know our spotter's radio frequency, so we had no direct communication with him. The spotter dropped three more of the smoke grenades, which, we ascertained, were in the direction the bad guys were moving.

We did have one small problem, though: there were only two of us out of a standard crew of four. We didn't have a loader or a gunner, only the driver, Mendez, and me as the TC, so I made a command decision (ha!) to pick up Mendez into the turret by traversing it to six o'clock to the crawlspace. This must have looked pretty stupid to the aerial spotter, our other tank, and the gooks, because we approached an ambush zone with the gun turret to the rear, pointing at our backup tank.

Once I got Mendez in, I ordered both our tanks to clear out the immediate area by firing several canister rounds each on the left-hand side of the road. This made sure that there were no RPGs or sappers in close quarters and we were then free to fire our mini-dart beehive rounds that were set for a couple of hundred meters further. If necessary, we would then utilize our HEAT rounds for exact target locations.

Larry Basco's tank then moved up and pushed the convoy's damaged lead truck into a culvert on the side of the road, dumping their payload on its side. Mendez and I in our tank pushed the Duster off to the same side. This made room on the road for the remainder of the convoy to proceed without dropping off a short but treacherous cliff on the opposite side of the road.

At that point, the spotter swooped down on the other side of a mountain razorback, where we lost sight of him. When he came up, white smoke was rising well behind him and on the other side of the razor. We took this to mean that the bad guys were still firing with the opposite mountainside crest as cover. We switched several rounds to a time-delay fuse setting and pelted the ridge with both of our tanks. After that barrage, it was obvious that the bad guys were shattered or had retreated. The spotter tipped his wings and headed south. There would be no major ambush on Route 9 this day.

In the meantime, we had heard from the CP that the Army mechanized was on the way and we were to stay put. After a short while, a General Patton-looking Army major came roaring up in a Jeep, with his steel mounted cavalry following. He had a swagger stick, his boots were spit-shined, and he was decked out with everything but pearl-handled pistols. Looking back, I swear I think he even had an ascot, shiny buttons, and cufflinks! Mendez mumbled something hilarious over the intercom, and I lost it; I couldn't help myself, I couldn't stop laughing. Basco and his crew saw what was coming, and all pointed toward Mendez and me to face the oncoming heat from the Army major, who looked like he wanted some leatherneck revenge. I had never seen so many new-looking tanks in my life; they looked like they might have even been waxed. They shimmered like polished turtle shells coming over a sand dune from the high side of the road, avoiding the convoy.

The major climbed aboard my tank, kept calling me captain, and then announced that he was assuming command of the situation from the back of my tank and was directly prosecuting this engagement. He told me to fire a white phosphorous to where the enemy fire had last been seen and his armor would take over from there. After my tank fired a round in the proximity, I told him the shot had been low and about 100 meters to the right. He yelled back that my gunner was a lousy shot and had probably been trained at Disneyland or some such place. I responded by telling him that I did not have a gunner, was overriding the firing with my TC's joystick, and had aimed and fired by eyesight. He angrily told me to back up my Marine Corps piece of crap "right now!" and that's when I told him, "I do not have a driver, either, sir!"

In all the confusion, I never did count all the tanks, which could have been anywhere from 25 to 50—what an absurd spectacle. When they all let loose their fire for effect, I thought I was back in Khe Sanh during the siege. After they had effectively eliminated all the wildlife and anything else that moved in a blinding cloud of dust, Mendez and I both shook our heads and stood with shit-eating grins on our dirt-covered faces, and we both ducked into the turret at the same time.

Just then, the major looked at us and demanded that I stand tall on the back of my tank and give him an instant sit rep (situation report) and account for my "sorry" actions. When I climbed out of the tank commander's cupola, stood, and saluted, he could not believe what he saw—a 6'6" leatherneck wearing only shorts, boots with no laces, and a flack jacket—no socks and no shirt.

I could tell he was Irish, because on his blouse was embroidered O'Something, and I remembered that one of my drill instructors in boot camp had had that same devilish, reddish face. So I knew this guy was either Irish or a man about to have a stroke, maybe both, but I sure as hell didn't care. I, too, was sunburned red, embarrassed, and had scabs on the tops of my ears and on my nose, along with a pretty good smirk on my face. We both must have looked pretty freaking stupid. The major looked up at me and said he was going to bring me up on charges of "conduct unbecoming an officer," or some crap like that, and asked me what kind of chicken-shit outfit this was.

That was when I smiled and proudly informed him that we were the light section of Ritch's Raiders and that I was "but a corporal...sir!"

The major screamed bullshit and grabbed my "com" helmet that was then resting in a full-tilted copula hatch with the radio-connected coiled-cable inside the tank. He grabbed the helmet and just about smashed it in my face, yelling, "See this!" I looked at my beat-up old green com helmet with etched black letters—"Cp" and a worn-out "l." I suppose he must have thought I was a "Cp"—captain—rather than a proud "Cpl"—corporal!

Our mission being accomplished with both the NVA and the Army major, my team started to return to base, but the Army tanks began firing. One of them accidentally put a bead of .30 calibers across the rear of our tank. They were so close that their tracer rounds hit our "forty mike-mike" ammo boxes attached to the back of the turret, which held all our personal gear. In no time at all, the tracers ignited all our skivvies and personal effects, including the extra .45-caliber rounds we carried for our pistols. We headed into the sunset, spraying a fire extinguisher on the flames fanning behind us and with all our ammo cooking off like scorched popcorn until everything burned itself out.

When we got back to the CP we found out that the steaks we were supposed to have were actually stamped cutlets in a watery brown mucilage and the Falstaff beer was warm...as usual. And it would be decades later before I would find out that my Good Conduct Sheet stayed clean after all.

Photo Courtesy of Jack Butcher

Yumbo dehydrated steaks, fit for a rat and skillfully prepared by Chef Lt. Harris Himes!

CHAPTER SEVEN
Semper Fi or Die Harder

THE FIRST WRONG AND A LAST RITE

It was during my second tour that I contracted falciparum malaria, through the abundant and deadly mosquitoes. The NVA, and probably their southern counterparts, too, would fish with hand grenades so the fish would quickly float to the top after the underwater explosion, easy top fishing. But then they would move on and leave the rest of the fish floating, bloated and rotting, where the mosquitoes would lay more larvae in a never-ending cycle. Along come our tanks and infantry, and we got bit and came down with malaria.

These same warriors would eventually forcibly emigrate to Texas and fish the same way in Galveston Bay.

Having contracted malaria I had never been so weak in my entire life, and only one other time since then. One minute I was in a boiling tank turret, soaking up the 110-plus Fahrenheit heat like it was really cool, and the next thing I knew, I could not move even one muscle in my body. I could not move my mouth or my parched lips to summon help, and I could not lift my eyelids, even trying with all my might. I slumped over like I was a bag of mush that had jumped off a forty-story building, only barely aware of my own existence. I heard voices as I was pushed and pulled out of the turret into a blizzard-feeling cold in the boiling month of August.

I fought to remain conscious as I heard the whoop-whoop-whoop of a chopper picking me up with a couple of other wounded as a yellow-smoke grenade swirled over us. Marines wounded, with tags blowing, were twisting erratically about under the wind and dust from the rotors. As my luck would have it, a Corpsman was giving the guy next to me a tracheotomy, and I took more than my share of a backlash of blood.

To make things even worse, after we lifted off and started back to a field hospital, we took automatic fire. Smoke started to fill the hull, and the ceiling was spinning around the room in the opposite direction of my stomach.

Calling in a fire mission after malaria #1, in front of "incoming" and "outgoing" clouds!

This was no dress-rehearsal, and as we hit the deck very hard, the air flew out of my lungs like a B-52 had dropped a 2000-pounder right on top of us. I thought a couple of teeth fillings flew out of my mouth as well. I do not know what exploded, but it was as loud as whenever we hit a tank mine. I could not hear the obvious yelling or the screaming, but I could see the door gunners' shells flying off their machine gun belts. It did cross my mind that all of us were not going to get out of here alive, but then suddenly, unconsciousness gave me its reward.

When I finally opened my eyes, I was no more than a lifeless sardine aboard a C-130; all I saw were plasma units on poles, swinging and rocking back and forth in unison. The next time I opened my eyes, I was in an all-white painted boat that I thought was the big turret in heaven or some such place, it was all so clean and medicinal-smelling, with a faint smell of sea salt. The next time, I was in a crushed-ice bath in a canvas-covered bathtub. It was all so systematic and mysterious. I was barely able to hear anything, except the high-pitched whistling in my ears and head. I do remember the chaplain with a gold cross on his lapel making the sign of the cross on my forehead and saying something half in English, half in Latin.

As weak as I was, I felt embarrassed. This guy was a priest, and he knew I was a Catholic by my ID tags. But I knew he probably had also read my other joke tag that said, "When I die, bury me face-down so the whole world can kiss my ass." I was going to die in shame and most likely in the state of mortal sin and go straight to hell. Those damn nuns had been right; I could not remember the words of An Act of Contrition before I expired. Sister Marcella had foretold this event ten years earlier, when I was in the fifth grade. Out of our whole class, it was me she pointed at whenever *the* word, a guttural "hell," came out of her mouth. Now it seemed so very damn real; her prediction was coming true.

I don't know how much time passed before God sent me an angel in the form of a nurse dressed in that white, tight naval outfit (OO-RAH). She, I would learn later, was Ensign Deborah Nast, and I quickly renamed her in my mind Double Nurse Nasty, for obvious reasons. To add to my embarrassment, whenever she placed a crisp new unperspired light sheet over my nude torso, I was humiliated because she was so good-looking that she really got me going—and she knew it, because she could see everything.

OLLIE'S RIBS

Another one of my most memorable incidents was from my second tour and also occurred in that spring of 1969, when my platoon was sent out on a search-and-destroy mission. As usual, we were accompanied by the grunts on the backs of our tanks. Our unit was a five-tank platoon, which consisted of three tanks in a heavy section and two in a light section. In charge of all five tanks was Lieutenant Peter J. Ritch.

Under normal circumstances, a tank commander would be a sergeant or staff sergeant and the man in charge of a section would be a gunnery sergeant or above. However, as the war dragged on, there were fewer and fewer trained tankers, so now as a very salty, experienced corporal, I moved up to a TC's slot or to command a light section. As I had been in the country almost a year and a half by then, I was intermittently in charge of a light section, depending on how many tanks were needed and how they would be dispersed for a particular operation. For tasks such as protecting convoys, security on bridges, or direct fire artillery support, we would use two or three tanks in separate situations.

Lieutenant Peter J. Ritch, our intrepid leader, was our greatest and most highly decorated field officer. I couldn't help but look up to him; he inspired me. He reminded me of that six-and-a-half-foot–tall Marine in the post office from so many years before. He always did everything correctly, and at the right time. Of course, we did make mistakes and sometimes were in very tight positions, but with his leadership, we always seemed to work ourselves out of a jam. Sometimes he would pull rank and take over my tank, leaving me to go back to my old job as a gunner or loader, but instead of feeling insulted, I welcomed the brief respite from responsibility. On other occasions, the lieutenant would leave his Jeep and ride on the back of the tank to direct fire support in an ambush or firefight.

This particular day, as my tank section rolled out with grunts on the back of both tanks, we were ambushed from behind. Suddenly, from out of nowhere, gooks started hosing down the backs of the tanks with their AK-47s. All hell broke loose. As the deafening chatter of machine-gun fire came from both sides of the road, the grunts scattered to protect themselves and the tank from incoming RPGs and sapper-satchel charges. The firefight was so intense, we had to call in choppers to pick up the wounded from one of the tanks. One of our guys was flashing around a shotgun, trying to direct the situation, but in return for his heroism he ended up on the ground, gravely wounded, and was himself medevaced by chopper.

Almost forty years later, Lieutenant Peter Ritch and I met at a Ruby Tuesday restaurant in Chattanooga, Tennessee. Over lunch, he told me that the brave lieutenant medevaced that day had not been wounded by enemy action but by Peter knocking him off the tank by mistake. The accident happened after the lieutenant jumped over to the opposite side of the TC's controls to manually override the turret and swing it around to the rear in his haste to quickly return fire by eyesight. He couldn't see our guy waving the shotgun at all and had hit him with the turret as he was swinging it around, which had sent our guy flying, breaking his ribs. The lieutenant who had been hit that day like a baseball out of the park was Oliver North. This firefight and these incidents were later recorded in one of his books, *Under Fire*. Both Lieutenant Peter Ritch and Lieutenant Oliver North were later awarded Bronze Stars for valor in recognition of their actions that day.

But my heartwarming with Lieutenant Ritch reunion almost never took place. In fact, as far as I had known before then, that Peter had been KIA. After Viet Nam was over, I had tried to contact him several times: I had mailed him a wedding invitation, opening announcements for my restaurant, and a letter when I graduated from college. I had sent them all to the New Jersey town that I remembered he was from, but the envelopes had always come back stamped "Return to Sender." They were never opened.

Undeterred, and having better computer skills after finally graduating college, I had continued to look for Peter on the Internet. I had located another tank commander, named Tommy, who had heard that Peter had been KIA. Even though it was some thirty-five-odd years after the war, I was devastated when I heard that news.

In the fall of 2008, however, I decided that I would finally find Lieutenant Ritch, whether he was vertical or horizontal on this earth. I knew inside that I just had to; he had not only been a great officer who had helped keep me alive but had written me a letter of recommendation for Officer Candidate School in a way that had touched me ever since. Finally, after several weekdays and a long weekend searching on the Internet, I located a Peter J. Ritch who lived in Huntsville, Alabama, just a couple of hundred miles away from me in Atlanta. I contacted him and was delighted and very relieved to find that it was my Peter. Because I was in Atlanta and he was in Alabama, we met halfway, which brought us to the Ruby Tuesday in Chattanooga, Tennessee. I had thought it would be a thirty-minute lunch, but by the time we finally left the restaurant, it had been hours—it was nearly four o'clock. Peter and I have kept in close touch ever since.

LEAVING 'NAM

While in Viet Nam, technically, I had one complete tour and two extensions. On my second extension, however, I was suddenly and unexpectedly jerked out of the bush while I was commander of the lead tank of a major operation headed down the A-Shau Valley of death. Generally, when someone was a "short-timer," they were given a little bit of preferential treatment, like going to the rear while they waited for their flight date. That was not really my style, nor the way I wanted it, but it would have been nice. Instead, I was summoned and ordered to the rear. I knew from experience that this was not typical, and I was very skeptical. Gloria and I had arranged to get married on November 8th, so I had tried to time my in-country duty so we would have a full thirty days of leave together. A honeymoon with only one person was not what I had been thinking about over the past couple of years. And I knew full well that if I didn't make the wedding and did not come home when I was supposed to, when I did get back, there would be a funeral instead, with my would-be in-laws presiding.

Climbing out of my tank, I slowly and somewhat awkwardly left as ordered. Looking back at my crewmen, Andy Anderson and Bob Halay, I shrugged my shoulders, assuming I would see them later and tell them what happened. How wrong I was, once again. As soon as I got back to the CP, I was told to pack my gear because I was going home right then. I never really got to say good-bye or exchange anyone's addresses, as I had thought I would. I had told myself that I would never forget anyone or where they lived.

I went from out in the bush to DaNang airport so fast, I really wasn't sure if I had all packed all my worldly possessions. The guys didn't even have time to pull any departing gags, like putting a bunch of scrap tank parts in my duffel bag so

I would get stopped by the Military Police for trying to leave the country with contraband. That would hold me up from leaving because not one of the MPs would be able to identify the parts.

At DaNang, I boarded the big, beautiful bird that would take me back to "the world." As I found my assigned seat, I found that my platoon commander from boot camp, Staff Sergeant Lowery, was already in the seat next to mine. He was now a first sergeant, and he grinned from ear to ear at the sight of me. We were both just so damn glad to see each other alive! I didn't know at the time that he had been in charge of deportation and outgoing seat assignments. With a stroke of his pen, he had jerked me out of the bush, right underneath some "bird" colonel's nose. He had done it to get me out alive, to see me again, and to be next to me on my flight home. I was now almost on equal footing with him, as I was in line to be promoted to sergeant. It had been more than two years since he had stood on my kneecaps, but I still retained a tremendous urge to stand at attention in that tight cabin and scream back at him, "Sir! Yes, sir!"

Our first stop, after about an hour's flight, was Okinawa, Japan, for processing. After that, it was about a sixteen-hour flight to San Francisco. En route, First Sergeant Lowery told me about things in boot camp from his point of view and about my personal service record, which I couldn't have cared less about at the time, but I listened intently. Interestingly, he described how proficiency and conduct marks were arrived at by the team of drill instructors and then sent up the chain of command. He told me that he had given me extremely high marks—in fact, maximum—but they had been batted down and returned lower. As the story goes, when another Marine, Lewis Burwell Puller, had taken his training decades before on the officer side, he had been given perfect scores of 5.0, 5.0, and 5.0. He had appeared to be the perfect Marine. When Puller's marks were turned in, they had been bumped, supposedly by the Commandant of the Marine Corps, who purportedly said, "There is no perfect Marine!" Puller's marks were returned as 5.0, 5.0, and 4.9.

Puller turned out to be a legend and an eventual lieutenant (three-star) general in the Corps. He was the only Marine ever to receive five Navy Crosses. His nickname, obviously, was "Chesty" Puller. In a thirty-seven–year career, Chesty was in nineteen major operations. For comparison, I was in fourteen major operations in less than two years and would end up being drummed out medically as a lowly sergeant.

Then, decades after Chesty, along came Claude. My platoon commander told me that my marks had been turned in at 5.0, 5.0, and 4.9, the same as Chesty's. But as divine military intervention would dictate, they had been returned as 5.0, 4.9, and 4.9, because "Claude Regis Vargo is no Chesty Puller!"

ORGANIZATION	DATE	REASON	PRIMARY DUTY	PROFICIENCY GENERAL MILITARY SUBJECTS	PROFICIENCY DUTY	CONDUCT	SIGNATURE OF MARKING OFFICER
RT Bn, RTR CHDep, SDIEGO	30 JUN 1967	Jd	9900 Recruit Trng	/	/	/	Bydir
RT Bn, RTR CHDep, SDIEGO	5SEP1967	Tr	9900 Recruit Trng	50	49	49	Bydir
HqCo, CasSec, 3dBn							

Claude's proficiency & conduct marks, boot camp, San Diego, CA,

A common incantation to end one's day with in Marine Corps boot camp is "Good night, Chesty, wherever you are!" My chant was, and still is, "Thank God I'm still alive."

[I have most recently researched *Chesty: The Story of Lieutenant General Lewis B. Puller*, in which it is disclosed that Puller was in the middle of his class!]

SAN DIEGO MALARIA

When I arrived back in "the world" in September 1969, I took one week of leave instead of the thirty days I was due. This was because November 8th was coming up awkwardly and fast and I was unexpectedly early. It took minimal time during that one week for Gloria and I to fall madly in love with each other all over again; the big day couldn't come soon enough.

On my last day on leave, however, we did have one serious, marriage-deal-breaking argument. It happened when we went to look for a new car. Gloria decided on a beautiful, brand-new, Nassau-blue Chevrolet Chevelle and intended for me to pay cash for it. There was only one hitch: I did not feel that we needed air-conditioning in the car; Gloria was adamant we did. If we were not going to get a car with A/C, we were not getting married. This all played out in front of the cash-itchy salesman. Finally, we let the past two years' tensions explode in front of a showroom full of little people with big ears.

I told her that, actually, I felt great sitting in the car with the windows rolled up in over 100-degree heat and Houston's 99% humidity. She told me I was out of my mind; no person could drive a car like that. I pointed out that we could roll down the windows and blow the air out, which felt almost freezing to me with just the fan on, and that we did not need the luxury or the expense. However, Gloria said, "No damned way. No A/C, no marriage, cheap-ass, or even worse...no honeymoon!"

Inevitably, although I gave it a valiant effort, I lost my first battle and love prevailed. I bought the model she wanted, with A/C, for a couple of hundred extra dollars. Of course we did make up, and that part was worth the last fight of our single lives.

Finally, my week's leave was over. I packed the car, putting my uniforms on the hooks in the backseat, like a laundry pickup from a cleaner, and filling up the trunk with a lot of items that Gloria had received from her bridal showers. I loaded up the car in a hurry and headed towards California with category-five Hurricane Camille's 190-mph winds at my back.

As I hurriedly drove back to Camp Pendleton, California, I should have known something was grossly wrong. Why did it feel more comfortable driving through the West Texas dry lands and the Arizona desert with the windows rolled up than with the air-conditioning running? I thought it was because I was used to being inside the tank in a stifling and overwhelming 120-degree heat.

Because I had left Houston at night, I didn't realize the hostile attitude that people were showing to me as a soldier until the next morning. People were passing me and giving me a one-finger salute and throwing beer cans and chicken bones at me and my car. I yearned for a weapon, if only a couple of hand grenades, so I could just lob one at them and show them what a real bang was. I thought they were throwing the beer cans at the brand-new car sticker on the rear window, but I soon realized they were throwing things at my uniform, hanging on the rear seat hook behind the sticker. I thought about laying the uniforms on the seat, but I was stubborn and wasn't going to lose two battles in a row. I drove on, a little faster, trying to suppress the anger that would eventually rear its ugly head at the most inopportune moments.

The whole drive, I felt survivor's guilt and was under enormous stress. I didn't know then what a panic attack was, but I had tunnel vision, shortness of breath, and a racing heart, all at the same time. I wanted to catch up with those West Texas rednecks and run them off the road. I had to remind myself that I was not driving my battle tank but Gloria's brand-new car.

I drove back all the way through the desert and finally checked in at Camp Pendleton, about three weeks earlier than I was expected. Today, I'm still so glad I checked in then. While I was going through the formalities, I started to shake as if I had delirium tremens. I shook so badly that the duty officer asked me if I had come off a four-week bender. Suddenly, the air-conditioning was making it feel like about 20 degrees Fahrenheit. Something was really wrong.

After signing in, I walked along a path and, seeing a major, tried to salute him. My legs gave way, and I collapsed. When I fell, he too was convinced I was drunk instead of sick. However, I felt the same way I had when I'd had malaria back in the bush. I was carried off by two other Marines, the major yelling at them to take the drunk to sick bay to have his stomach pumped. By this time, I was convulsing and almost delirious. One Corpsman pumped my stomach while another covered me with a pile of blankets. I was still shaking badly. When the doctor came in and took my temperature, he furiously stripped the blankets off me and could tell by the scabs on my nose and ears that I had been in country very recently.

The next thing I knew, they were cutting the clothes off my back and putting me in a bathtub. It was just like before. Again, they put canvas over me and let my head protrude while they ran cold water into the bath at my feet and shoveled mountains of crushed ice in as fast as they could. The doctor was yelling at everybody to hurry, "before we lose him!"

I finally woke up in the naval hospital, where I spent the next three weeks, and started to recover from vivax malaria this time. When I was ready to be discharged from the hospital, I was told to report to the Judge Advocate General's (JAG's) office before I left, to be assigned an attorney. I was being investigated for a violation of the Uniform Code of Military Justice for not taking my anti-malaria pills for at least eight weeks after returning to the States. It was beginning to seem that by going overseas and coming back to base, I was destined for another round of shackles.

During the investigation, there was heated debate over whether I had really checked in when I had returned to the base and had access to the pills, because my papers had not been processed. It was therefore ambiguous whether I was on duty or on leave when I was in the hospital. If I had been in the hospital while on my leave but claimed I was checked in, I could be court-martialed for not taking care of Marine Corps personal property, that is, myself. I was beginning to see the spit-shine, regulated side of the Marine Corps, which I had not known previously. My relationship with the Marine Corps was changing; I was very confused as to whether I wanted to go to school while in service, graduate, and then go to Officer Candidate School (OCS), or leave the service and go to school on the GI Bill.

In the end, I was recommended for a Naval Medical Review Board for several reasons; it was not optional. On the first of November, I flew home, and Gloria and I were married on November 8, 1969, as scheduled. Much to Gloria's mother's chagrin, I had come back from Viet Nam alive. I was twenty-one, and

Gloria was barely eighteen. She was absolutely gorgeous, while I was very, very lean and a much different man.

After we drove back from Houston to Camp Pendleton in a rented truck with almost all of our worldly possessions and all of our new wedding gifts, we had a blissful six weeks alone in a rented trailer house in Oceanside, California, just outside the back gate of the camp.

Sergeant Claude R. & Mrs. Gloria A. Vargo, November 8, 1969.

Shortly after I checked back in, the date for my Medical Review Board appointment came, much quicker than I had anticipated. The doctors didn't take all that long to decide my fate. When asked what I wanted to do, I said, "Go to school." Before I could continue with where I would like to go to school and what I wanted to study, the doctors were stamping my Service Record Book, "Discharged." I had never seen the military move that fast. Within seventy-two hours, I was a civilian once again.

CHAPTER EIGHT
From Leatherneck to Long-Hair

"Education is the best provision for old age."

Aristotle, 384 BC

So, it turned out that getting out of the Corps wasn't as hard as I had thought. The Naval Review Board had at warp speed sent me on my way with a medical discharge under honorable conditions. They were only too happy to bypass my health problems that they would have to ultimately support, because they knew those conditions would continue for the rest of my life. The review board had all the records from all the previous wars at their disposal, so they knew what was going to happen to me, and approximately when. It's like the odds in Las Vegas: statistically, the house always wins, and in my case, like many others, it was a sure bet that I would medically double-down for life.

When the doctors had mentioned "percentage of disability" to me, my only question had been "How fast can I get out of this outfit?" And I remembered the old Texas saying that goes, "There were sure a lot of questions that I should have asked before I hired on with that outfit." But by then, again, I had gotten all the answers, and then some.

When I went home and gave Gloria the news, she took it really hard, crying herself to sleep in my arms. She wanted us to be alone and away from our parents for as long as possible; this didn't seem possible if I was unemployed. But for my part, I was far from being disheartened; I felt the world was now at my feet. I wanted to get on with our lives, and pronto! I had unlimited energy now and a renewed, positive outlook on life. I would go to school, graduate, and make a zillion dollars! In the meantime, we would work hard, make babies, and save our money, not necessarily in that order.

As Gloria drove us out of the back gate of Camp Pendleton for the last time, another door closing behind me, my mouth was bloated and I was screaming with pain from the twenty-two cavities that had just been filled, without Novocain, in my last two days of military service. After at least 700 shots of cortisone in my boils, including some in my face, I had not wanted any more injections. I had served my country honorably and could hold my head up high to society...or so I thought.

We headed east to Houston, against the grain of the California fortune seekers heading west in the late '60s. It was the day before Christmas Eve, 1969. I had already missed most of the restaurant busy season; I wasn't about to miss New Year's Eve, too. I had made several calls in advance and could get on with a couple of old employers, and maybe a new one or two, as well. I was not going to lie around, like a lot of vets. I was known as a hard and energetic worker, so we drove home in thirty-two hours, and within four hours after hitting the Houston city limits, I was working at a new-concept steakhouse called Steak and Ale. I considered it a fast-food steak joint, but it would do to get started and get my civilian attitude back. Within a few days, I was working three jobs a day and knocking down the equivalent of a month's Marine wages in a single day.

In spite of my success at work, all was not well at home. I was upset at Gloria, who had not yet unpacked her suitcase after more than a week. She was displeased with me because I was always gone working. It was not what she had imagined that being married was all about. She did go back to her previous employer, Associated Credit Bureau, but was still unhappy at my schedule. I was now working breakfast, lunch, and dinner at restaurants, hotels, and country clubs. I worked as a bartender, waiter, cook, and any job that paid and trained me well. When one job played out, I had my choice of two more waiting.

I was tending bar at one club when I met a vice president of Union Carbide, who was a happy-hour customer. He needed a few janitors from midnight to six in the morning. He was half drunk, but my empty pockets were now burning, so I went to work there that night and got home at daylight. Gloria was frazzled, at her wit's end, waiting at the door, not knowing where I had been. All I could do was smile and say, "Don't pay the ransom; they let me go!" She didn't know whether to shoot me or kiss me or both, because I had another fistful of dollars!

I always thought I did the work of three, and, boy, was that good short-term money. Whenever any employer said to me that we needed more help, I would retort, "Pay me their half, and I will work twice as long and three times as hard. If I am not successful or you don't like my work, then you better line up three more pronto, because I am outta here!"

When the play was over at Union Carbide a few months later, an opportunity knocked in Galveston, sixty miles away. It was only on Saturdays, at a convention restaurant facility called Gamboa Cay. But now I had four paychecks and cash tips coming in, plus Gloria's salary.

There was no limit to the work I could do, but Gloria was still complaining about us not being able to spend any time together, except under the covers. I figured that because we had been apart for the better part of two years, this time was very tolerable...she didn't. Instead of quitting some of my jobs, I did the next best husbandly thing I could think of at the time. I found her a job as a salad girl and eventually as a cocktail waitress at the place where I was working as a club manager. Now we were bringing in six paychecks and lots and lots of cash tips. With no time to go to the bank, the checks, cash, change, and blank deposit slips were literally falling from our newlywed kitchen table, onto a very dusty floor. Life was good, and all appeared to be on schedule, or so I thought.

Finally, after nine months of grueling work, in September 1970, we had saved enough money for me to go to college and not have to work for at least the first semester. Boy, was I ready. If anyone thought I was ambitious working a job, they should not have gotten in my way when I hit the books. I longed to go to Cornell or the Hilton College, which had very recently opened at the University of Houston, but I decided on San Jacinto Junior College in Pasadena, about forty miles away, for a warm-up and gradual start. I was very conscious of my poor performance in junior high and high school and wanted to reverse all of my bad grades. My biggest wish was that they would all fade into oblivion. I didn't realize then that my past would always follow me, along with my physical and mental health as well. I wanted life with both hands and feet, and I took it in giant steps.

I drove Gloria's old Volkswagen Beetle to school every day to save on gas while she drove the new car. Since I am almost 6'6", it was a little snug, but at least I wasn't packed in with three other screaming crewmen and no one was trying to kill me. I could carry a drink, eat a snack, and even fart at my own leisure without getting slugged or kicked. And I did not have to take a dump in an ammo box or wipe my butt with cardboard or burlap.

The first semester at school, I did not work a job at all, concentrating totally on studying and my books. Studying was a mindset, and so were classes. I slowly began to realize that the other students, faculty, and staff were always intently watching me, but I couldn't understand why. It didn't take long until I realized it was my age. They picked up right away that I had been in the service and, worse, was a Viet Marine. I had "baby killer" written all over me like a scarlet letter, and there was no escape. Rapidly, the word was passed.

Almost all of the former military guys, regardless of service, rank, or job description, congregated under a large camouflaging willow tree before class, which muffled our bitching about our new mutual enemies. We were in a league all our own with special needs and problems—mostly problems. These gatherings were a good way of keeping up with the military scuttlebutt, and the vets who had been there the longest would pass along free advice. What we heard was not good. A common thread was that no one in the entire college really wanted us there. We were poisoning their medicinal, academic environment.

Usually, we were seated in the back of the class and ignored, until it came time for a teacher to embarrass one of us in front of the class. We were given special assignments, usually with an underlying message that would expose our war-tainted past. One such assignment that was doled out to me was a report on the Second Amendment to the U.S. Constitution, gun control. Another example might be atrocities during war, including rape, because by then, the Mei Lai Massacre was in the headlines every day.

As soldiers and Marines, we were given lower grades, I mean the lowest grades. A's magically turned into biased C's, and B's turned into slanted D's—that is, if one did not drop or withdraw, having drawn an F for a C. Whether we were graded objectively or subjectively, the teachers always seemed to bring out the worst in each of us. One GI went full-time for five semesters and was still classified as a first-semester freshman. I didn't see him again after that semester.

I hung in there for three straight semesters before I figured out that at the current rate, it would take me a couple of decades before I would graduate, and then again, I would be at the bottom of my class. There was too much money to be made working, and Gloria turned up pregnant, as well, so I left school. Like everybody else, I told myself that I would just stay out for maybe a semester or two. Like 99% of them, I didn't return.

CHAPTER NINE
From Diapers to Depends®

"When you men get home and face an anti-war protester, look him in the eyes and shake his hand. Then, wink at his girlfriend, because she knows she's dating a pussy."

Lieutenant General James Mattis, USMC

I have known Gloria as long as I can remember. Her brother and I were best friends in the same elementary school, our families were at the same position on the socioeconomic family ladder, and our dads were sporadic golfing buddies. On occasion, our parents would play card games together, like canasta and bridge; those are the things our parents did after World War II.

I can't remember the exact moment when Gloria and I both realized we would get married, maybe because it never really happened like that. I think we both just always knew in our hearts that no matter what, we would spend the rest of our lives together. The years passed by wonderfully slowly as we matured.

When I was in overseas, Gloria wrote me every day for almost two years, even if it was just a sentence or two. I always had a sense of connection with her while I was there, and that made all the difference in the world to me. Sometimes, for one reason or another, we Marines wouldn't get mail because we were out of the field. Of course, there were also those times that I was medevaced or in the hospital, and then letters were rerouted and rerouted again. Writing, sending, or receiving a letter in a moving war zone was laborious. In the monsoon season, the paper was always wet and the ink often bled, making it impossible to read the words. Other times, the gum on the envelope would be wiped away, and of course Scotch tape was not readily available to reseal it.

G-L-O-R-I-A

"Like to tell you 'bout my baby, you know she comes around,
Just 'bout five feet four a-from her head to the ground.
You know she comes around here just about midnight,
She make me feel so good, she make me feel all right.
And her name is G-l-o-r-i-a."

Van Morrison ~ 1964

My letters took between two and three weeks to arrive back home in Houston. By reading the dates that Gloria would send hers, I saw it took about the same time for me to receive them from her. When she received a letter that had been damaged, she would sometimes mail it back for me to see. It would have an ambiguous slip of paper attached to it that would say something like, "This parcel was unexpectedly damaged en route," which really meant the envelope and letter had been hit by shrapnel or burnt up by some chemical or some other type of flying metal.

Occasionally when we came back from the field from an ambush, a firefight, or a major operation, I would receive ten, fifteen, or twenty-plus letters, usually more than the rest of the platoon combined. It was common practice that friends would let each other read their letters from home. I would do this on occasion, but only with my closest friends. I was very selective in the letters that I would let them read; of course, they were highly personal.

When the senior enlisted Marine passed out the mail, it was the highlight of the week. Before we opened our letters, everyone would try to guess what all the acronyms on the backs of the letters meant. For example, ILY meant "I love you," ICWTKY meant "I can't wait to kiss you," and then it generally went sexually downhill from there, with longer and longer acronyms. The senior noncommissioned officers had a ritual of smelling the perfume on each envelope, guessing the perfume's name, reading the acronyms on the back, and then teasing the guy that his letter was from his mother!

The heart rate of every tanker in my outfit would rise in anticipation of getting a letter from home. I never had to worry about not getting mail. When I received a stack, I would carefully place the letters in chronological order to get the full value of their loving contents. Photographs, newspaper clippings, graduation announcements, and miscellaneous information were special treats, but they were also especially hard. They would make me realize that as we sat in a mud cave on the other side of the world, unshaven, unbathed, with rationed food and water and being used for target practice, our loved ones were all dressed up, having fun at enjoyable occasions with friends and family. As I looked around at the other young men, most of whom had just graduated high school, I would think about how some of them would never attend another festive occasion. Maybe including me. The only events in their futures, the ones that they would never even know about or see, would be their own funerals. What if I was next?

I would clutch the stack of envelopes a little bit tighter. My lips would narrow, and my eyes would water; I'd turn my head away from the group, just as others were doing. This was a time of emotional ups and downs for everyone. Several guys in my platoon received the dreaded "Dear John" letter. Other guys had girlfriends or wives who just stopped writing for one reason or another, which I guess was an easier way out of the relationship. As time went on, the guys who'd lost their loves became more upset and bitter at life. At Khe Sanh, it was more than scuttlebutt that some would irrationally stand up or walk into Indian country just to be sniped off.

WAR MALADIES—PTSD

"As memory may be a paradise from which we cannot be driven; it may also be a hell from which we cannot escape."

John Lancaster Spalding

I could be the poster Marine for post-traumatic stress disorder (PTSD). This is the primary reason that I always push myself so hard and always stay above 120 mph in everything I do in life. The harder I work and push myself and the more I do to overwhelm my brain, the easier it is to stay two steps ahead of my demons.

In retrospect, I guess this compulsion actually really ended up helping me in college. My PTSD started cultivating during Khe Sanh, and continued afterwards, while I was out in the bush. But it was massively triggered by the fall of South Viet Nam in March 1975. That event set off some kind of five-year delayed-anxiety attacks that I could not explain. The attacks were brutal and got worse and worse the more I thought about what we had all gone through over there...for nothing! It got so bad that I could not make simple decisions, down to choosing which shoes to put on in the morning, without just shaking in a petrified state. I was afraid of anything and everything, totally disoriented and confused.

Finally, Gloria and my dad took me to the old veterans' hospital in Houston, which appeared to have been built before the Civil War. This only made things worse. Back when I was in the service and on leave, I had once had developed a super-sore throat, probably due to some type of infection, too much air-conditioning, or too much smoking. When I had checked into the VA hospital, a nurse had asked me what the problem was, so I had leaned back and opened my mouth to show her that my throat was all red. Maybe it was strep throat. I never did find out, because in place of the tender, loving care I had thought I would get, I got the shit slapped out of me by the nurse, I guess for exposing her to something, whatever. Since then, I had always been hesitant about going to the VA hospital, and I really did not like the idea at all.

But in 1975, by the time my wife and dad got me to the VA hospital, I was having back-to-back panic attacks so bad, I did not know where one ended and the next one started up. I was immediately taken to the third-floor lock-up ward. Once there, someone promptly gave me the once-over verbal questionnaire while my head was reeling around like a junior-high drunk. When the nurse asked me if I was going to hurt myself and next if I wanted to inflict pain on anyone else, I paused and stuttered and was swiftly put in a straightjacket. Then I got real upset and began jumping and jerking around until I was quickly shot from behind with some type of heavy medication, which promptly put me down.

Regaining consciousness, I remember, I had trouble lifting up my arms, just like when I had had malaria, and I did not need a straightjacket thereafter because the drugs kept me lifeless. I was in my own cuckoo's nest right before the movie came out.

After a series of shock treatments, I was weaned with controllable medications and was allowed to have visitors, including Gloria, who came alone without our first daughter, Christina, who was saved from my embarrassing condition. I was diagnosed and labeled as severe shell-shocked. After about seven weeks of "treatment," I was released as an outpatient and was scheduled for even more experimental therapies and continued medications. I guess I was one of the guys they wrote about in all the medical journals.

At the time, we shell-shocked guinea pigs at the hospital were subjected to all kinds of different experimental treatments such as electroshock therapy, stress therapy, combat therapy, and relaxation and breathing sessions. But my panic attacks still continued to varying degrees. Anything, at any time, could set off one with the same symptoms, just from different triggers.

My mind would race every time a trigger was activated. It was a one-way ride into Dante's Inferno. I could peak in any one of his nine circles of suffering before a freefall would occur. Three decades later, I can still look at the Mercedes Benz icon on the front hood of a car and immediately turn it upside down into an inverted hippie sign. Upon hearing Jimi Hendrix's guitar music in the background, I can feel my mind take off on a one-way roller-coaster ride, straight downhill in a purple haze. If the Mercedes happens to be a diesel model and I smell that exhaust, I can get to the bottom circle of suffering in a flash. To this day, I can look at an absolutely breathtaking, lush landscape of vegetation and, in an instant, vividly point to all of the ambush sites in the horizon.

The symptoms of PTSD are usually the same, although some come faster than others. My nine circles of hell are racing thoughts, hypertension, tunnel vision, hyper vigilance, dry mouth, claustrophobia, imbalance, choking for air, and suicidal thoughts. These can come anytime, day or night, and last longer and longer if left untreated. I can usually tell when an attack begins and how deeply I will descend. I probably only average about three a week now, but with the new medications, I can have an attack and still go about my business somewhat effectively. If my attacks are left untreated, I can have immense mood swings, survivor's guilt, feelings of being surrounded, severe indecision, and depression, any of which can last for weeks or longer. When the attack subsides, it can and often has the opposite results—euphoria and false expectations. Sometimes I can't figure out what causes an attack, because a lot of the triggers are subliminal, I guess.

With plenty of new medications, along with the tips and tricks I learned from Tony Robbins, my life began to be somewhat tolerable again, and where I am able to have some kind of normalcy, whatever that is.

CHAPTER TEN
Light Years Later—Deciding to Go Back to College

The first and biggest step toward going back to college, which can absolutely be the hardest one, is to actually make the decision and the commitment to do it. People have a lot of reasons and excuses for not going back to college, and it's a lot easier to just keep using them. If you don't change that pattern of thinking and get rid of the excuses not to go, you never will.

My decision to start back to college and start from zero again was not an easy one; it was a thirty-year–long, hard and painful process. In mid-January1997 I sat down and wrote down all the "pros," positive reasons why I should go, and all the "cons," negative reasons why I could never do it. The negatives far outweighed the positives. In the end, I came up with nine major headings, which matched Dante's circles of suffering and included more than one hundred negative reasons against only five positives. The main reasons I felt I could not successfully go back to college were my age, time constraints, my finances, my health, my marriage, family and friends, my mental issues, feeling that I was dumb and dumber, and just the entire school environment, which I had been conditioned to feel very uncomfortable in.

EXCUSES NOT TO ATTEND

So, I had my laundry list of what were very sensible and logical reasons not to go back to college. But in the end, it turned out they were all nothing more than excuses to rationalize not going back. The first and most obvious excuse not to go back to school was, of course, my age. Pushing fifty, I had simply missed my shot altogether and was just too old; I could be pushing sixty and Social Security (or retirement age) if or when I ever graduated. I told myself there were just not enough years left, the time was not right; I should have done it years ago; it had been too long since high school; I hadn't finished then, so how would I ever finish now; etc.

My age was the biggest negative, but the longer the list got, the more I could think of additional negatives to add: I don't need this aggravation at my age, it'll age me faster; my own daughter took the same curriculum and it took her six and a half years to do (because of an accident). I also figured that I would be too old to be hired afterwards; I would be denying my family, my wife, and my friends the time they fittingly deserved; and I would be denying myself personal pleasures, replacing them with endless pain.

Next, my personal finances were a big problem at the time and a major excuse not to go. Although I was making money, I was still putting my kids through school, so there was no way I could really afford to go to college. My GI Bill had expired, I could never get a scholarship with my horrible transcripts, and in Texas, I couldn't borrow against our house. I had no IRA, no 401(k), and no savings. It would be a waste of money, and there would be no way that I could ever finish school and financially recover from it even for a reasonable return on the investment. Also, I just knew that no one would ever give me a student loan at my age.

My health, especially mental, was another serious concern. It would be too much stress, too many panic attacks accompanied by too much depression. I'd probably have a stroke or heart attack. I had severe arthritis, bursitis, plantar fasciitis and neuropathy in my feet, besides having cold feet. My eyesight was getting worse as I had two major eye surgeries already, my memory was not as sharp as it once had been, and I still had severe tinnitus in my ears from countless explosions. That was only the start of my medical problems. The decision was leaning very negative.

Under the Marriage heading, I thought about the strengths and weaknesses between Gloria and me. I thought it might make us grow apart, that we somehow might not be compatible after I finished. Then I thought about how my mother-in-law was constantly telling her daughter, Gloria, that after college, I would divorce her for a younger, graduate-student model. The decision was now –7.0 on the Student-Vargo scale.

Under Family and Friends, there would inevitably be undue pressure and gossip, and if I failed, all I would hear from some of them would be, "We told you so!" That pressure would also add to my panic attacks and depression. If I failed I would feel shame from many people. As I wrote down all the negatives, it became clearer and clearer that it was a high-risk move on many levels, that I should even contemplate such a life-altering change.

Then there was the challenge of being out of my comfort zone. I would lose a lot of sleep, the university was too big and too hard on me to walk, and we might have to move to another city after graduation. I would have to take out-of-town internships and we wouldn't be able to take vacations. Why struggle with all the late-night and weekend studying?

Under the heading of Dumb and Dumber, I convinced myself that I didn't understand the Internet and I didn't know how to use a computer very well. I'd rather die than speak in public to a bunch of giggling girls, and even if I could pass all my other courses, I could never pass algebra. I was the dumbass in my family; everybody else in my generation had at least one degree.

Under the School Environment column, I had a lot of excuses: The university is too big and too far, I don't have clothes, I won't fit in, students will laugh, and the professors will think I'm a know-it-all or, worse, think I am stupid. I asked myself, "What if they make me take gym? My body is already falling apart; the extra strain of keeping up with kids less than half my age will make it even worse."

In spite of my list, or, rather, lists, I was still trying to think positively about it, because I really ached to make it happen and go. I started thinking that maybe I should consider another major or an easier business degree. I thought maybe just an associate's degree, or something like one of the new and easy online courses, or maybe I should just wait and go next year. Procrastination was always a good friend of mine, and I knew just how to put this whole idea off by listing more negatives.

It was then that I analyzed my friends and out of five friends, one had committed suicide and another had died of a heart attack, slumped over a prostitute in Mexico. Ironically, the one who had been found in Mexico was my sponsoring real estate broker and a deacon in our church—go figure. The others were partners of mine in various real estate ventures, where I was the only one specializing in hotel restaurant real estate.

The harder I worked, the more deals I closed, and the more of my money the partners wanted. Later, when my three remaining partners' money ran out as they were working less and fooling around more, they claimed they were due a greater percentage off of my hard work. I figured between them and their wives, girlfriends, kids, and pets, I was supporting a platoon of deadbeats and moochers. When I offered them a cash take-it-or-leave-it settlement, they refused, wanting even more. I responded by giving them all a one-finger salute and left our office for good. They sued me, and in the end, they lost; I won.

This was apparently not the group of friends that would help turn my life around. I needed to find more positive reinforcement and a new, better circle of associates.

POSITIVES TO ATTEND

I compared my positive column to the negative one, but it was virtually empty; it had a total of five items listed. I was staring at the floor and the ceiling, struggling to find more positives. It felt like I was having writer's block, another senior moment, and a brain fart all at once. But I also had an ache in my heart, a burning in my stomach, and a lump in my throat every time I conjured an image of me graduating, maybe even with honors, and receiving a degree from some kind of dean or chancellor.

I thought about how graduating would be a monumental achievement and effectively erase my past educational woes. I could be a role model for my children; I could make better money, have a better job, and live happily ever after. And I still had an insatiable desire to learn. I already knew a lot through the school of hard knocks, but I couldn't connect all the dots, and that was extremely frustrating. It was something like hearing people speak a foreign language in front of you, while you stand there stupefied. Not being formally educated has its own form of self-hounding and persecution. Contrary to popular belief an education is not just a piece of paper.

To help me make my impending choice and decision, right then and there, I took what I feel was the biggest and most important step for anyone going back to college at later age: I made the firm decision that it was now or never; I was going to go back to school. I would jump into this with both feet and get it done, right now, or never let the thought of school enter my mind again. I wanted to put the final decision on Gloria, but she wouldn't have any of it. I would have to decide this for myself, because I would have to live with my decision the rest of my life, regardless of the outcome.

THE FINAL STRAWS

"Most great people have attained their greatest success just one step beyond their greatest failure."

Napoleon Hill

As I was starting to settle on the decision, a few events happened at work that would help push me over the edge and make it clear what I had to do. The restaurant I took over then was Odd' R in Seabrook, Texas. It was about 15,000 square feet and seated about 500 people. It was somewhat like a Dave and Buster's and had games, novelties, and amateur gambling, such as blackjack for points, but was geared for the whole family. It had been in business for less than a year, and

I had been there for the past several months in a turnaround situation, which I knew was hopeless. The Kemah/Seabrook channel between Clear Lake and Galveston Bay was full of shrimp boats, with the Kemah side made up of American fishermen and the Seabrook half, ironically, made up of Vietnamese. It was always understood that the American side was the filet-of-fish side, while the Vietnamese side was the head, bones, and tail side.

At the time, the two factions of fishermen were literally at war with one another. The newly replanted Vietnamese fishermen didn't play fair according to U.S. law or customs. They would drop their nets at night like they had in their old country, which was totally illegal, and they also fished with electricity, dynamite, and grenades so they could just scoop up their catch off the top, as the fish were either dead or numbed and an easy catch. Eventually, the guns broke out and dead bodies started showing up.

Finally, one day I came to work and found a stiff under the bay-front stilts of our restaurant. I called the police, and the corpse was removed. This was the last straw and way too much déjà vu for me, and I was not going to have any more of it. The Texas KKK had already been involved in incidents earlier after Le Bin Son acquittal for the murder of three American fishermen (later memorialized in the Bruce Springsteen song "Galveston Bay").

Since I had started working there, I had watched the Vietnamese men crouched in a very familiar seated position in a circle, playing card and bone games such as *tienlen*, *xito*, and *gomoku*. I had seen them in the same crouched position, playing these same games, many times before in 'Nam, but then everyone had had a weapon. Now it was no longer any different here. I reasoned I could go about my business and play like nothing was wrong or I could address the situation head on. Nervously, but determinedly, I chose the latter.

I took two unopened bottles of Johnny Walker Black Scotch and joined the circle in a Viet crouch, opened one of the bottles, took a double burning-chug, put it on the ground, and waited. There were several uncomfortable moments of silence as dark, dead, steely eyes darted coldly at me, like a scene in a movie. Finally, one of the men picked up the bottle and drank. He jabbered something in his dialect, and I repeated a short and dirty joke I remembered in broken Vietnamese. They all laughed and then began to drink heartily. I told them I had been a tanker at their Ta Cong (our Khe Sanh) during the siege; they all had instant recognition, and in their opinion, I had to have eliminated "beaucoup" Viet Cong VC and NVA. After that night, the shootings still continued between the two warring factions, but there were no more bodies ever found under my restaurant. In fact, I felt like they stood guard over my environment and my personal perimeter.

After we shut down the restaurant game-room facility, to preserve my income for a little bit longer, I rented a box truck and sold the small, medium, and large stuffed animals at vacant gas stations around town. It was the kind of roadside stand with a rope strung from pole to pole and various cheap items dangling from clothespins...how humiliating. I used to go unshaven and unbathed, with unruly hair so no one would recognize me. I got a baseball hat and would crimp the brim and pull it down when I would see one of my customers, friends, relatives, or neighbors, as I was completely ashamed and embarrassed. This was a defining moment in my mental decision to attend college, but next would come one of the last and final straws

One of my sons had painted a huge sign for me that read, "Giant—$25, Large—$15, Small—$10, 3 for the price of 2," which I would point at the oncoming traffic. When the cars passed by, I would wave the stuffed animals in front of them, hoping to catch someone who wanted an impulse item for their kids. Of course, there were always the cars that would pass by and shout profanities or toss empty cans, bags, or boxes with half-eaten lunches. After a while, I became immune to the razzing and would jabber back at the hecklers. A car full of apparent college students would come by and give me a moon. I would scream back as they passed, "Why don't you give me a pressed ham or a redeye, you jerks!"

Then one day, in the parking lot of a closed-down bank where I had set up my wares, a beat-up old station wagon filled with dirty kids passed by, then turned around and pulled over. Mom was riding shotgun and smiled with most of her teeth. Papa got out and snapped his suspenders to show that he was coming not to wheel and deal but to rob and steal. In a thick Mexican accent, he asked me, "Hey, *vato*, wut ju got?"

"Beautiful stuffed animals for your children; how many do you want?" I responded.

"Where du getz deez? Day hot, man?" he asked.

"No, they are from a big game room I had," I answered him firmly, getting leery.

"Gimme four pequeno and a beeg snake for me ole lady; she likes beeg snakes," he said with a crotch pull.

Now, totally annoyed, but wanting to make the sale and get rid of this guy, I told him, "Great, that will be fifty-five dollars, sir."

"Fity-fi dolares ees too mach, *ese*. I only got thoidy-two, you vant it all or nut-ing?" He grinned.

"I guess I'll take it. My family has to eat too," I replied. I smiled inside that at least I had thirty-two dollars more than he did now.

A couple of days later I had another altercation, this time with a carload of gang-bangers. They drove by slowly, stopped, and got out with their megawatt sound system still blaring, then started to strut vacuously, toying around, trying to impress one another.

One of the punks came over and asked me, "Hey, grandpa, you got change for my C-note if I buy sumteen?"

I responded by telling him, "It depends on how much you buy."

Immediately he got the typical gangbanger attitude. "Hey, wot's ju problem, man? Dares four of us, pops; wot ju gonna do?"

The bangers were on all four sides of me now, toying with me. One of them bran-dished a straight razor and fanned it across his empty wallet, which was attached to a chrome chain clipped to his belt. I knew he was trying to tell me something that was not positive. He asked me if I wanted to fill it up.

I looked at these clowns, all dressed up in their little gangbanger costumes with their white tee-shirts and do-rag bandannas, and a rage started building up inside me. Not one of these little turds could have lasted a single week in the Corps, let alone a single day in a war zone. They had no idea who I was, or what I had gone through to survive in real fights.

In total survival mode now, I looked at them with a dead stare straight from the war zone and said icily, "Well, hell yeah, but first, why don't you get back in that punk-mobile and make like a tree and leave...bitches!" I meant it, and a part of me so wanted to have any excuse to wipe out those pukes. I quickly walked over to the truck, pulled my shiny chrome .45-caliber pistol out of a stuffed bunny's butt, pointed it at them, and said, "Better yet, why don't you all just walk down that street behind your fucking car...and keep on walking until I say stop!"

As I slowly aimed my pistol from one face to the other, I was sure glad I had the only gun in a knife fight, as I was not about to let those four gangsters get back to their wheels. I could only imagine what firepower they may have had in the trunk, and I did not care to be another South Main Street statistic on the ten o'clock news.

They started walking backwards, and I happily walked forward, pushing them back, until I was even with their punk-mobile. It felt so good to blow the front tire that I decided to do the back ones as well so they definitely could not follow me. I packed my bunnies, bears, and snakes and left posthaste.

It felt good at the moment, but then I realized I actually felt like a complete failure. I was facing unemployment again, just like the punks who were looking for trouble. I had gotten to the point where I felt like I never wanted to own or manage another restaurant or food enterprise the rest of my life, and my wife and children surely didn't like my work schedule or following my shrinking avocation.

This was the last straw, and I knew I had to do something to change and improve my life, for myself and my family.

CHAPTER ELEVEN
A Tortuous Decision—Taking the Plunge

"Action is the real measure of intelligence."

Napoleon Hill

The decision of whether to go back to school became a 24/7 obsession without end. I had learned my negative list by heart, and it had become my personal mantra. It was playing loudly over and over, like a bad song that was stuck in my head, with no relief. I could hear it clearly, even though my ears were still ringing from the decades-old explosions—I have tinnitus and damage to my tympanic eardrums, all permanent—but even through that ringing and pounding day and night, my negative list still came through loud and clear.

I wanted the better things in life for my family: better employment, decent non-restaurant hours, and a single shift, instead of seven days a week at double and triple shifts. At one point, I had worked nine years without a day off; the next time, it would be seven years in a row, interrupted only by hospital visits for ulcers, high blood pressure, and panic attacks and the like. I wanted this all to stop and was willing to do anything to achieve this goal...well, almost anything.

I sometimes picture myself in a surreal vignette, going through life as I do when I am in a cafeteria-type restaurant. Right now I am at the end of the line, near the cashier's cubical. I was raised in full-service restaurants where a menu was always presented, so it was easy to pick out everything you wanted on your plate and in what order to balance the entire experience. Whenever I take Gloria and the kids or some other friends, nieces, or nephews to the cafeteria on Sunday after church, I am always the last in line, and Gloria is the first. I watch the staff and the setup—the efficiency of the operation, the display and the service, etc.—with one eye—and watch the people in the serpentine line, as it wound through various turns, with the other. I also watched my entourage and what and how they chose.

In life, as in the cafeteria-style line, the least of my concerns was how I was going to balance the meal. After from through each meal section such as salads, entrées, vegetables, dessert, beverage, and accompaniments, I would get to the end of the line and look at my tray, and it would typically not be what I really wanted. The meal wasn't balanced, and I would look back and see other items that I should have gotten, so I would exchange the items or, even worse, give the cashier my entire tray and start over back in salads.

As I contemplated going back to school, it was almost like each dish on my tray represented a major decision in my life and that from the very beginning, I had not made wise choices. Now the cashier of life was upon me and it was too late to change my mind this time. I couldn't go back; I had to go forward with what I had on my plate. The only thing to do now was to make a wise and educated choice. This hypothetical moment was another turning point in my life; everything was coming to a head, and I could feel it.

Another pivotal turning point in my life came unexpectedly when my wife's cousin Alvis was diagnosed with brain cancer and then died, all in just a few short months. Dr. Alvis McConnell was only a few years older than I and had been in 'Nam just a year prior to when I arrived. We had missed meeting each other overseas by a matter of days, if not hours. At that time, Alvis had been an Army officer, with five Bronze Stars already, and I just an undecorated private, but in the end, we shared that common bond of military service in the same war. Another bond that we developed after I returned home was that of dentist and patient—he was a dentist and I was one of his steady patients, with lots of dentistry problems.

Before Alvis died, he made me promise that I would file the necessary papers for medical relief from the maladies that I suffered from being in-country, if not for me, then for my family. Alvis had been in the reserves for about twenty years and had obtained the rank of major but had been booted out after he started filing grievances against the Veterans Administration and the Army for his brain cancer. This was about the same time that the government was forced to admit its complicity in the Agent Orange debacle. I didn't understand the legalities of the bulletins that were being sent to me then, but I had certainly known firsthand, when we had been constantly sprayed in the field while they killed all the foliage around us, that something was not right.

Alvis knew all about my military service, my medical records, and the twenty-two cavities that had been filled in those last two days of active service by what I had thought were sadistic Naval dentists. Alvis routinely treated these cavities, as there was a constant nuisance taste in my mouth of deteriorating metal from the numerous cheap government fillings. Up until the day he finally succumbed to his cancer, Alvis was a good friend and confidant, and after he made me vow that I would file papers with the Veterans Administration and seek help, I could not let him down. On top of the intangible bonding, he rebuilt my entire mouth for a pittance of the cost.

When Doctor Major Alvis McConnell died from Agent Orange brain cancer, he was only fifty-two years old. It made me look at my own life very differently, and it helped me take stock and, I feel, actually helped me put my life in perspective and made my choices seem easier in comparison. At least I was still alive to have choices. I still had a young and beautiful wife and four strapping children who needed a father. I began to look at myself differently and realized that I too could be dead in a matter of months and would have nothing to show for my life. Suddenly, I felt very vulnerable and afraid, because Alvis had left a stunning young wife and two of his children behind.

Like many veterans who were sprayed with Agent Orange, Alvis had children who had been born with various cancers, and others we knew had deformities such as spina bifida. Alvis' first-born daughter had died of brain cancer as well. My second-born had not come to full-term. It was all adding up; the importance of the Agent Orange bulletins were soaking in, and it was making sense that something was really wrong medically with the troops who had had boots on the ground in 'Nam and, additionally, with their children.

I lost a lot of very good friends overseas, very good men, and many more afterwards who have since died of numerous residual medical causes, some unfortunately including suicide. But the loss of Alvis hit me the hardest because my own immortality had been touched. I was determined that I was going to do something with my life before it was too late.

It was late on a Sunday night when I couldn't sleep, shortly after Alvis died, that I stumbled onto an infomercial by Anthony Robbins preaching how he and his course could change my life. I had heard this type of hype many times before and had looked into and taken several self-help courses, with little or no results, but his looked different, and I decided to try it. I was always chasing goals that never seemed to have a success, not the kind that I wanted. Tony's course was indeed different, and it touched me in a way that made sense. It was a thirty-day course, which I finished in about half the time.

I was listening to one of the cassette sessions of Personal Power II while I was driving, and Tony told me to do something, right that instant, toward a goal that I was contemplating....Something...anything...just do it now! If I was driving, I was supposed to pull over and do it! So I pulled over to make a call at a phone booth because my cell phone had been recently cut off again and I only had a couple of dollars but no change. I doggedly dug under my car seats to find enough change. Finally, I found a quarter under the driver's seat. That quarter, that coin worth just 25 cents, found on the floor under the seat of my car, would change my life forever. I could have gotten change for the bills, but the symbolism of that moment has never been lost on me.

I called the University of Houston registrar's office with that quarter, as I wanted to fulfill my commitment to Tony to take action and do something. But as in the cafeteria line, I approached it in a clever way so I could easily change or back out of it at any juncture. I was lucky enough to get a nice-sounding man who genuinely wanted me to register. He informed me that registration had ended the week prior; I was ready to hang up when he told me that late registration was still ongoing but it would be over the day after next. Then he asked me for my name in order to set a time to come in to register.

When I told him my name, he surprised me by saying cheerily, "Claude! This is George, George Nolan. I know you from Nanny's, the restaurant across the street. I'm sorry it had to close. I know you remember me and my wife, Phyllis. We came in a couple times a week. You were always so gracious and would buy us an appetizer or dessert on occasion. OK, now it's my turn to buy you lunch. Let's meet for lunch tomorrow, and be sure to bring all your papers; we'll get you all set up."

I was stunned, and in shock; he had totally caught me off guard and when he asked me for my phone number, of course I acquiesced. He told me to meet him at Barron's Restaurant at the Hilton Hotel on the UH campus.

I hung up the phone not once, but twice, and harder the second time and mumbled under my breath, "Why didn't I hang up earlier? Why did I make such a foolish commitment? Now he has my home phone number, and I can't back out. If I meet with him, he's going to know my terrible academic track record." I felt like such a phony. How could I have put myself in another negative, no-way-out box situation? No matter which way I went, this was going to lead to embarrassment and disappointment...mine.

I talked it over with Gloria, and after a couple panic attacks during the night, I wished I could meet Alvis horizontally, sooner rather than later. But Gloria told me that I should go and reassured me that the worst that could happen was I would see an old acquaintance and get a free lunch.

After another sleepless night, I met George for lunch and was glad he could return the favor from the past. After some small chitchat about our wives, family, and the vacillating Houston weather, he finally got around to the reason we were there. He asked me if I had brought any papers—transcripts, diplomas, and the like. I had to be upfront and honest with him and let him know the sordid details of my past education. I told him I had gotten kicked out and been asked to leave St. Thomas in ninth grade, I had never graduated high school and never taken the SAT exam. I almost gave up and just told him that I really couldn't do this, but thanks for lunch. Instead, George only reassured me and suggested that I just take a couple of classes the first semester and we would overcome the hurdles, step by step, together. This was another educational turning point in my life.

George had one of his assistants look over my ugly transcripts and papers. My transcript from San Jacinto Junior College was just enough to barely get in. That transcript had been sealed for almost thirty years, but it was still sealed tight, as required. The courses I took amounted to a lot of D's, F's, I's, and W's. But ironically, and very luckily for me, the three hours that finally put me in were from a flame-throwing class I had had to take in the military. It had been a class for military flame tanks, not for "Tableside Cooking," as the assistant gave me credit for. George and this assistant were only two of the many people who would give me a lot of help in the near future.

When I thanked George before leaving, I asked him why he had never lit the cigar that had always appeared in his mouth after he had had lunch at my restaurant. He would carefully guillotine the end and always savor the aroma when it was fresh out of its classy glass tube but would never light it up, even though his regular lunch table at Nanny's was in the smoking section of the club. George responded by telling me that he was waiting for a special occasion. Then he surprised me by saying, "I'll tell you what: When you walk, I will personally come to the ceremony and light it up to toast the occasion."

I smiled in a tenuous agreement and said, "Thank you, George," Then, shrugging my shoulders and with a slightly tilted head and a raised doubting eyebrow, I said, "If I do and you do, I'll light it with a fitting gold Dunhill lighter."

Within the next couple of hours I was registered at the University of Houston, and I naturally picked hotel and restaurant management (HRM) at the Conrad N. Hilton College of Restaurant Management as my major, and for my first two classes I selected political science and English. I walked away feeling like Robert Redford did at the end of the movie *The Candidate*, when, just after being elected as a very long-shot senator and realizing he had really won, he looked at his advisors and said something like "Now what do we do?"

Between closing another restaurant, enduring Alvis' passing, and getting a final push from Gloria and George Nolan, I was finally ready to take the plunge into college. This time there would be no turning back.

"Your life changes the moment you make a new, congruent, and committed decision."

Anthony Robbins

PART II

ACADEMIC REDUX

CHAPTER TWELVE
First Spring Semester, 1997—The Big Splash

CLASS BEGINS

Now that I was in, I was determined and I was ready to give it my all. But in reality, I was not yet mentally prepared for the change, and to be honest, my first day in class felt more traumatic than my first days in a combat zone. There was one exception, however: in college, I could quit any time I wanted, and while I sat there that first class, I stared at the exit sign and my watch with a big lump in my throat. I had arrived there early, very early, and paced the hall with a dry mouth. "My God," I had said to myself, "what am I doing here?"

By the time everyone had filed into the auditorium, I noticed the other students all had backpacks, most with bottled water. It was against my constitution to buy water, but I would have given someone my credit card, if I only had any credit left, to stave the parched cavity I now possessed. The only moisture I could feel was on my palms and the now-receding hairline on my forehead. My daughters had recently teased me about doing the comb-over, and I felt older.

I took only the two classes I had signed up for, political science and English, then sickeningly found out the HRM curriculum was a science and not a liberal arts degree. That meant the Bachelor of Science degree required four math courses instead of the two I had thought I would need. I should have known better, because my oldest daughter had graduated with the same degree a couple of years earlier. I hadn't been paying attention, but now it was personal, it was me who had to take those classes. Why hadn't I checked it out before I had committed? I knew only that I had to take algebra, I would never pass it anyway, and then I would drop out. No, I would not think about it any more. I had a parched throat; wet, sweaty palms; and more cold feet.

As an incoming first-semester freshman, I was assigned a parking lot almost halfway back to my house. During the summer it was mostly weeds and dirt, but in the month of January it was usually muddy in a cold rain. Sometimes it seemed like I had walked through less mud in 'Nam. Of course I quickly caught the flu, and Gloria bought me a pair of L.L. Bean hunting boots for my feet and a branded pair of jeans so I would loosely fit in with the kids. Gone were the days of having to sleep in the elements out in the bush, but also gone were the days as a restaurant owner, with valets who would bring me my keys after parking and wiping the dust off my "ride" daily.

I really don't know how I made it through the first two weeks, as I was in total social and cultural shock. After the first several classes, my English professor told me to report to the English department head, where I was informed I would have to take the Test of Standard Written English (TSWE) before I could continue with the English course. In a nanosecond I knew I could never pass it and this was probably my way out of college. Being kicked out, or being asked to leave, was something I could rationalize the rest of my life, and that would be the end of that, an easy way out.

I really felt there was just no way, after thirty years, that I was going to pass an English grammar, reading-comprehension, and writing test. I had only signed up for two classes, but already I had been put in a position to forcibly drop one and possibly flunk the other. I had already made an agreement with Gloria that I would not drop or add classes like I had decades before. But much to my astonishment, after tutors, practice tests, and the teacher's assistance, I actually scored a forty-three, which was three points over passing, and I stayed in the English class by the skin of my teeth.

My political science course was not going all that well, either. The first book I had to read was *Leviathan* by Thomas Hobbes, which was written in 1631 and established the groundwork for Western political philosophy. It read like Old English. I could read a whole page and not be able to tell you one iota of what the author was trying to say. It was like reading ancient Greek upside down. I had that much understanding of its contents.

HARD ATTACKED

My first test in political science was on a Thursday after a long week. I studied really hard compared to any previous test in my education, and to say I was anxious was an understatement. I read my textbook, answered all the end-of-chapter quizzes, read over my notes, studied the abbreviated notes, replayed the tapes I had made of the class lectures, and was finally ready to take my first test.

My stomach itched like acid hell and was spreading more and more the closer that I got to my first test. I had Gloria look at my stomach to tell me if I was having another Agent Orange flare up or, even worse, maybe shingles. She got the salve we had from the VA and rubbed it in and, while I was still scratching furiously, gave me a peck for good luck.

I arrived early for the test, sat in the front row, as usual, and continued to study while the rest of the class started filling up the auditorium. I was keeping to myself when a girl tapped me on the shoulder and asked me, “Hey, Pops, why do you always sit in the front?”

I turned a little to acknowledge her and her girlfriend and replied, “I sit here because I always tape the lectures, and I don’t hear so well.”

She shot back, “This is test day, Pops. This is when you’re supposed to sit behind everybody. Ya got it?”

The two girls giggled, then she wiggled and whispered to her friend and continued her questioning with, “Like, how old are you, anyway? Are you, like, married?”

“Now that’s pretty forward. Why do you want to know?” I replied, amused.

“My mom’s about your age, divorced and looking. She’d be a sure thing…any interest?” she blurted out, and both girls started giggling louder.

I twisted my wedding ring around and told her that I needed to finish studying. Then it suddenly struck me that they were sitting behind me because they wanted to see my answers.

The pre-PhD lecturer and his student proctors entered the room, and the whole place went quiet at once while they immediately passed out the exams to nervous freshmen, including me.

What I had not done to prepare was take my medications. I wanted to have a clear head during the test...big mistake. The second word on the first question was *Leviathan*, which literally jumped off the paper at me, causing instant tunnel vision, and I had an immediate Richter-nine panic attack. As I was trying to catch my breath, I slid to the ground to immediately do my breathing exercises and try to bring myself back into a calm state, while not realizing where I was. Then my rash began really flaring up and I started to scratch crazily.

One of the giggle-girls screamed, “He grabbed his side! He’s having a heart attack, call an ambulance!”

After the melee, and to my total embarrassment, I went to see the professor, and he told me that it was a pretty lame excuse to get out of his exam. But after I explained a little of my background and we discussed several options, he really helped me by suggesting I take my exams in the Disability Testing Center on campus. He further suggested that I get some support from the Veterans Center, which I immediately did.

I had to submit a lot of papers and sealed letters from the Veterans Administration Regional Office and the Veterans Hospital to the Disability Testing Center, which I fast-tracked. The professionals at the testing center were terrific and very accommodating. I took a teacher-modified test over and really thought I got a good grade, but it came back a D–.

To make matters worse, my first English paper was returned without a grade. My English professor had not wanted to embarrass me or have me walk out and quit, like many others she had seen before me give up. So she wrote a note and asked me to see her in her office. She asked me how I was researching, outlining, and writing, and she encouraged me to go to the English tutors at the university to improve my basic grammar and writing skills.

Then I had another setback, which would be just another of many to come. What both my professors didn't know, besides my lack of basic skills in reading, writing, and arithmetic, was exactly how seriously I was also battling lack of concentration, PTSD, panic attacks, depression, and a few other physical maladies, courtesy of war in a combat zone. In the first month of class I felt like a miserable failure again and became immensely depressed; here I was in another position where I wasn't going backwards, but I couldn't find a way to go forward successfully.

I asked my English professor if I could resubmit the paper that had a lot of nosebleed–type red ink on it, and she agreed, to my surprise; on its return it came back a D+. Now I had a set of double D's, which would have been great if I had been a high-school senior prom queen or a college sophomore sorority sister. But I was sandwiched in between them as an incoming freshman. When I called Gloria and gave her the news in that way, she switched subjects real quick, I guess to get my mind up out of my gutter. She quickly asked me what I would like for dinner...I told her to fix me plenty of crow.

There had to be a way for me to pull this off, and I was going to find it, no matter what it took and no matter what level of perseverance or pain it would take…mostly pain. I started going to the English tutors for writing and even hired a personal student tutor who was in my class. I made him a deal he couldn't refuse: money and beer...most of what every male college student wants.

I had watched *Rudy* many times and had been really inspired by Rudy Ruettiger's accomplishments, especially his academic persistence. If he could go to Notre Dame, I could go to Cornell. At a convention in San Diego a couple years earlier, I had heard one of Rudy's motivational speeches in person. In the movie, this guy was "five-foot nothing," but now in real life, he was an older guy just like me, but a world-renowned motivational speaker. So I began to look for other role models in my life to see how I could turn all the lemons facing me into lemonade. I thought about other speeches that moved me—personal friends, family, books, and tapes—and I began to put together my own plan.

I had read many personal improvement books over the previous decades and books on personal human achievement, and I looked through my bookshelves again to see which ones I had really enjoyed and wouldn't mind reading again. Books that I had reread and drawn inspiration from were *Think & Grow Rich,* by Napoleon Hill; *Catch Me if You Can,* by Frank Abagnale, who inspired the feature film of the same name starring Leonardo DiCaprio and directed by Steven Spielberg in 2002; and, of course, the Personal Power II tapes by Anthony Robbins, to name a few.

BOARD OF DIRECTORS

I decided to create my own personal Board of Directors to help direct me. I borrowed Napoleon Hill's "Invisible Counselors" idea and placed imaginary inspirational people I knew in a Board of Directors-type environment, where I would crunch one of my pressing problems between all of us. Initially at my director's table were a collection of five awkward individuals, all of whom were positive thinkers or bullshit artists. Eventually I would have almost a dozen, consisting of people on both sides of the table, including positive thinkers as well as doubting Thomases.

Napoleon Hill had aristocrats, noted politicians, financiers, and world-renowned historical figures such as Emerson, Paine, Edison, Darwin, Lincoln, Burbank, Napoleon, Ford, and Carnegie as his invisible counselors. My group started with Anthony Robbins, Rudy Ruettiger, Sylvester Stallone, Frank Abagnale, and Staff Sergeant Lowery, my platoon commander in boot camp. In comparison to Napoleon Hill's group, mine was obviously shallow and limited because of my education. I decided to add better, stronger members as my studies, knowledge base, and sessions increased.

If my imaginary director had a skill, attribute, knowledge, or talent I needed, I would add the person after researching him or her thoroughly on the Internet. I would also replace someone if I came across another with a better or stronger talent or attribute. In short order, I would replace Sergeant Lowery with Colonel Oliver North and add someone like Napoleon Hill. Napoleon Hill, of course, had all his counselors behind him that I could, in turn, leverage with mine.

Just like Napoleon Hill's, my sessions were typically at bedtime, and to start, they were problem-solving sessions. For example, I could get an English tutor, but political science was a different story, so I used my invisible counselors. At the same time I was using English tutors and imaginary counselors, I was weaning myself of going to the veteran's hospital for group therapy and I was replacing old warriors with imaginary scholarly directors. I was also then replacing my limited number of uneducated friends in the real world with a more educated circle of associates at the university.

This was the start of my complete educational makeover. It was at this juncture that my life playbook went from defense to offense and I turned things around for the better. In retrospect, I realized this was an essential step in moving forward and changing my life. It can be in yours, too. You aspire to the level of the friends you have and the company you keep. You really are who your friends are. Surround yourself with people who will challenge you and help you grow.

I took Anthony Robbins' goal-setting workshop again. As Tony reminded me, Thomas Edison tried ten thousand experiments before he was successful, and I reminded myself that if that's what it would take to achieve my goals, I would do exactly the same.

Researching new members to add to my imaginary Board of Directors was an education in itself. I found out things about these people that really surprised me that a lot of people don't know. A lot of what I discovered was very inspiring and motivating and often left me feeling that nothing is impossible if you just keep trying at it hard enough and never give up.

In researching Sylvester Stallone, I learned that although Rocky was a fictitious character, he was based on real-life boxer Chuck Wepner, who had earned tremendous respect for "going the distance" with the champ in his underdog title-shot fight against Muhammad Ali and had been the only boxer to ever knock Ali down in a fight. Stallone's life, his attitude and his success, are very similar to Wepner's story, as he was struggling to break into writing scripts for film at the time and was a real underdog, fighting against the big boys to get his scripts read. He wrote the original eighty-page "treatment" script for *Rocky* in a small New York City apartment in one week, then worked tirelessly with his agents to get it into production, in spite of the studio. His script and his movie would earn three Oscars in 1977, including the coveted Best Picture Oscar.

Sylvester Stallone is a real-life rags-to-riches Horatio Alger. I admire him, and I was determined to do the same as Rocky and Sylvester.

I learned from Rudy Ruettiger that the physical and mental hurdles on the gridiron and in the classroom were very similar and can both be overcome in the same way, also that, in comparison, his first step, Holy Cross College, was my Houston Community College, and that his dream goal of Notre Dame was the same as my Cornell goal.

From Frank Abagnale, I learned that even a bullshit artist could turn things around until smelling like a rose. I had heard Frank speak at a Houston Restaurant Association meeting decades earlier. I always got a kick out of his closing trick, when he would say, "Everything is not as it appears," then pull the kerchief out of his upper suit pocket to show that it was a pair of women's panties. He would then reason that the panties were cheaper than men's kerchiefs and were much more startling.

From Pappy Boyington, WWII fighter ace, Medal of Honor recipient, and leader of the infamous Black Sheep Marine Squadron, I learned to be shrewd and a huckster to get what I needed.

Finally, last, but not least, from Claude Regis Vargo, I took my own personal strengths of being a survivor, my tenacity, resourcefulness, efficiency, organization, and networking, which I would hone to a new level of precision. These were the best tools I had in my bag, but all were very rusty and needed an immediate dusting, cleaning, and polishing.

Nothing could stop me now, and nothing would! All of this introspection and self-analysis had helped me realize that I had already learned the most important skills and strengths in life from myself. One of the most important strengths I have, the one that has saved me all my life and would indeed get me through this, too, was that I had learned to be a survivor.

LEVIATHAN

With a redirected set of goals, armed with brushed-up tools in my toolbox and a new perspective on life, I went to my political science professor and asked him how I could improve my grade. He very much surprised me, in a way I hadn't expected at all. He told me to get a CliffsNotes book on *Leviathan* and other readings that were included in his course syllabus. Next, he told me about an off-campus tutoring outfit that specialized in a somewhat gray area of test tutoring. These businesses operated under the guise of tutoring, but in reality were test takers. Even though I thought they were a little questionable, I decided to give them a try anyway because he, after all, had recommended them. He also suggested creating flashcards for the numerous political terms I needed to know. Then he gave me some extra-credit assignments to help me bring up my grades. These would prove to be invaluable guidance and essential keys to adjusting my approach to succeeding in college.

But most surprisingly, one of my first assignments turned out to be writing a letter of recommendation for him so he could complete his PhD. Initially, I felt that writing a letter for him was inappropriate, considering my academic standing, though I was still happy to do it. I immediately understood why he asked me, after he explained that to complete his PhD, he had to have letters of recommendation from three students he'd taught. But how would nineteen-year-olds write him great letters? As I was the only mature student in the auditorium and was used to writing business-type letters, it was a no-brainer for him to ask me, and not a hard request for me to fulfill as he was personally editing his letter along the way. This doctoral candidate would be one of the many people who would help me achieve my goals. He was not just a good teacher, he was a great one, and a soon-to-be professor. It is very important to always look for these kinds of opportunities to establish collaborative and symbiotic relationships, and sometimes even partnerships, with your professors.

Another major turning point was when I was guided to the university's Veterans Administration office. I checked out the assistance available to veterans, and I was amazed. An ex-Army sergeant by the name of Sean Graves was the Veterans Service Coordinator and gave me a book titled *Student Veterans Survival Guide*. Sean and I would become close friends, and that survival guide would become invaluable to me.

When Sean asked me if I had any of my GI Bill coming to me, I explained that my term limit had expired decades earlier. He then told me about a little-known veterans program in which veterans under special circumstances could have their GI Bills reinstated as "Chapter 31exceptions." He also told me how to go about getting this process started. I was now getting assistance from the Veterans Office at the University, the veterans' hospital, and the Regional Veterans Office. Things were definitely looking up.

Back in English class, I repeated the process of going to my professor and asking the same questions that I had asked my political science professor, most importantly, "What can I do to bring up my grade?" I would repeat this process in every class where it even looked like I might just get a B. No exceptions, even if my first test grade or first paper was an A–. However, I quickly learned to rephrase that question to "How can I learn more in this class?" My English professor recognized that I was extremely serious about digging myself out and assured me I could achieve the grade I sought if I worked hard enough. I did pull one little trick that would turn out to be a major eye-opener for me.

Being a Marine, I have never been one to save or hoard a lot of items, because we were always on the move and therefore had to stay lightweight. But for some odd reason, I had saved that term paper I had written on the Second Amendment and gun control at SJJC during my first try at college almost thirty years earlier, which, of course, had come back a D–. Gloria simply retyped the yellowed paper for me verbatim, and I turned it in for my English class, and this time, much to my surprise and delight, it came back as an A!

This experience glaringly showed me how badly I had been screwed out of my grades back then and that I wasn't anywhere near the failure I had been made to feel like by my junior-college teachers. I didn't even want to think about how many years I could have saved, and the fact that I may have graduated thirty years earlier if I had received the grades I had deserved back then and stayed in school. I honestly don't know if I would have had the same drive and commitment to making all A's back then, but seeing that A made me furious and made me a total believer in myself again at the same time. I was more determined than ever to make all A's in every class I took.

With a newfound confidence and total resolve, I prepared in earnest to get back up to speed in English basics. First, I gathered up all the English books I had ever bought for all four of my children. These books were from approximately third-, sixth-, ninth-, and eleventh-grade levels. Whenever I wrote a paper, I would check each and every book to make sure I had used the correct spelling, grammar, and structure for each word, sentence, and paragraph in the paper. I would then take each paper to two English tutors, one after the other, until the paper was flawless. It was painful at first, but I gradually began to catch on to thinking and writing in correct English.

Before every soldier, sailor, or Marine goes into military service, they will usually get a lot of advice from anyone who has been in the military, with the first and number-one piece of advice usually being "Do not, under any circumstances, volunteer for anything." This includes things like answering when the drill instructor asks who has their driver's license, with those who answer yes winding up driving a wheelbarrow full of manure. I was different—or maybe just stupid or stubborn—as I volunteered for everything! Although it had nearly gotten me killed or wounded a few times, I had survived, and I believe I am a better person for it. I therefore decided that in my new academic environment, I would do the same. I volunteered for extra-credit projects, speeches, papers, additional work, and acted as an instigator, starting and leading a lot of study groups.

My Hilton College counselor was Kevin Simon, who was a returning student himself. He helped give me a better picture and insight into drawing out my goals, as well as ways to achieve them. Kevin gave me a great perspective on college life as a nontraditional student. After several impromptu meetings, I asked him what the highest I could hope to graduate was, considering my past college try. He already had my transcript in front of him and knew all too well my miserable past attempt. He was also a pragmatist and reminded me that the HRM degree was a 132-hour science degree with four math courses. But then he also told me that although my course credits had transferred, my miserable grades had not! A bell went off in my head as I realized that I had just gotten an educational reprieve and a new start in college. I now thought of myself as more of a nontraditional, first-semester undergraduate than a returning student.

Kevin told me not to set my sights too high, but he didn't laugh. In subsequent brief three-minute impromptu meetings, I asked Kevin the maximum number of credits I could take in one semester, and he informed me it was eighteen hours but that there were special problem classes that I could work at the same time by talking to different professors. He also told me that I could take additional outside classes at other colleges as long as they would be accepted by the university. This turned out to be the pivotal information I would use to reformulate my entire approach to going to college, enabling me to accelerate the process and graduate much more quickly.

Taking outside classes opened up a lot of possibilities; most importantly, it meant I could take more classes at Houston Community College and elsewhere. I had decided to use every edge I could find, and this was a huge one. I was not interested in learning less but was totally obsessed with cutting time, my newest enemy. I never told Kevin that I had already set my private personal goal as graduating number one in my class by May 1999 and graduating summa cum laude. If he had known that, he probably would have laughed aloud.

But for every week I went without a full paycheck, I would have to work two or more to make up the lost time, so I now had 120 or more hours to go, and I gave myself just twenty-four months to complete them. Now that I had set that goal, I began looking further ahead. When I heard about a meeting for potential students at graduate school, I promptly attended. At the meeting, the professors who were hyping the masters program had us fill out a questionnaire asking basic questions like when we would expect to matriculate, what our backgrounds were, how many years we had been in industry, and so on. It was obvious looking at my questionnaire that I was not a good graduate candidate, seeing as how I was just a first-semester freshman and struggling with my grades.

Toward the end of that first semester I came up with another trick to help my future grades and speed up my learning process. I asked to sit in on the classes that I intended to take in my next semester, just to observe and take notes. I was now looking and learning ahead. By this time I was seeing other things I had not previously noticed, such as the fact that most of the professors were interjecting their personal thoughts into class, which was a good thing, because I valued personal experience. However, their thinking was more often than not a liberal point of view. Not that that was a bad thing, but if I were to get along with all the professors, I would have to express my own political opinions more moderately if asked about them. Although this was most obvious in the political science course, I found it was almost universally necessary for me in the academic environment.

I got a kick out of my first political science professor, because the two bonus questions on the final exam were about how we would classify him politically—was he liberal, moderate, centrist, or conservative? A Republican, Libertarian, Constitutionalist, or Democrat? As I did not want him to know that I saw through his veil, I chose not to answer the bonus questions. Maybe because of this, I made an A– instead of an A on the exam. Rather than answer the questions directly, I wrote him a pithy and succinct personal thank-you note.

I was very glad that George Nolan had advised me to take only two classes that first semester so I wouldn't reach a quick burnout and quit. I recommend this initial approach to everyone, to get acclimated and used to college life. My first semester had been a transitional one, in which I had made the psychological and strategic turning point in my college career. It was full of self-doubt and numerous hurdles, but I managed to overcome each one, with bruised, black eyes, but successfully. By the end of the first semester, I had brought my grades up from the double Ds and achieved an A– in political science and an A in English.

It was then that I made my most important move of all. I promptly registered for twelve hours during the summer semester at the University of Houston, Hilton College, Houston Community College, and the Hotel School at Cornell University and sent my brand-new two-class UH transcript to the registrar's office at Cornell. With Frank Abagnale talking louder in my ear than my tinnitus and conscience, if all went well, in a couple of weeks I could be in Ithaca, New York, attending class at the Hotel School at Cornell, my lifelong goal!

CHAPTER THIRTEEN
Cornell at Last—My First Summer Semester, 1997

A LIFELONG DREAM

During the next few weeks, late in the spring of 1997, I called the registrar's office at Cornell so many times, they knew me by my voice and my first name. One of the many questions that I really wanted answered was which professor was going to teach the Hotel School class so I could call him and talk to him about his class. The registrar's office personnel were only too happy to call me when the teaching assignment was made, just so I would stop bothering them.

When I obtained the professor's name, I promptly did a cumbersome 1997-level search on the Internet for anything that I could learn about him, including his dissertation. I used a couple of the early Internet search engines like Bigfoot and WebCrawler, which were relatively clumsy at that time. Even so, I located a short executive summary of his dissertation. It was about forward-looking loan commitments, which I had some experience in, through restaurants that I had mortgaged, so I felt like we had something in common to discuss.

I promptly called the professor and was fielded by his administrative assistant, or gatekeeper, who kept me at bay for at least two days until she, too, gave way, unable to handle my constant questioning. To schmooze, I sent her a modest bouquet of flowers. I decided to wait to meet her in person to see if she liked chocolates or maybe some truffles—I never forget that the word secretary starts with "secret"; they usually know where all the bones and golden door keys are hidden. Then, just like the registrar's office, she called me at the most opportune moment, when I could talk to the professor, who had just walked into his office with a fresh, steaming cup of coffee and I could ask him just a couple of questions.

My professor, Dr. John B. "Jack" Corgel, is not only a gentleman but a true scholar. He is the recipient of numerous teaching awards and has been published, with almost eighty papers to his credit in some of the most critical research publications in his field. He would also shortly become the most prestigious Baker Chair at the college. After several of the phone calls that I initiated, he must have picked up on my enthusiasm and yearning to learn. I mailed him my resume and a pristine cover letter and called to ask if there was anything I could do prior to taking his class. He said, "As a matter of fact, there is. I have just completed the second edition of my real estate book. I will send you a copy of the final draft and manuscript for your critical analysis and to check for errors."

Lo and behold, at 7:30 the next morning, the manuscript arrived, all 1000 pages of it. The professor had inserted a note in the package, asking me to proofread the manuscript and make standard editorial markings. I almost fell over right there, as to do that, I would first have to find out what those marks actually were. It was an honor and a privilege, and I was expected to proofread the thousand-page manuscript of a tenured full professor from an Ivy League university in about ten days. After all, he would expect me to have made some corrections by the time the class started.

After punching holes in the papers and separating them in two or three binders, I felt like the Texas A&M Aggie who quit hitting himself on the head because it felt so good when he stopped. Then I browsed the pages and almost felt sick when I saw that it looked like another *Leviathan*. Instinctively, the first thing I did after binding the pages was make flashcards from the glossary. Next, I made additional flashcards from the conclusions of each chapter. These both totaled almost 400, and I still only had about ten days before I was due at Cornell.

The manuscript had arrived just before my final test in political science, and my final English term paper was also due. Now, yet again, I had dug myself into another deep hole. This behavior would need to abruptly change. I would have to work on this problem with my Board of Directors.

ARRIVING AT CORNELL

I arrived at Cornell for the very first time late on a chilly Thursday night toward the end of May, 1997. A foggy mist was floating in the air along with a very light rain, but that could not possibly dampen my spirits. I don't think I had ever felt so excited in my life. I lugged my trunk straight up a very steep hill, along with almost fifty years worth of emotional baggage, and saw a dimly lit stone archway with a gigantic gate and big, beautiful metal letters arched across the top reading, "Cornell University." My heart was pounding so hard I thought it was going to burst right out of my chest. There was no band and no fireworks. It was the end of May in Ithaca, but it was the Fourth of July between my ears. I dropped my trunk and promptly did a Rocky victory jump, lost my footing, and immediately slid halfway back down the hill in the slippery grass and mud. I quickly thought to myself that fifty-year-old men did not act like this. But fifty-year-old freshman, first-semester students, did. I had arrived!

It was Thursday night, and my class did not start until Monday, but I had a lot to do in this short time, with the university and college offices closed on the weekend. I'm glad I had that time in between, because I could not sleep, simply because of my almost immature excitement. I checked into a room in the attic dormer of a 100-year old, five-story house. I had trouble standing in the room, even in the middle. It was another cave that I would have to dig out of, mentally this time.

The next morning, a Friday, I went to the bursar's office and double-checked to make sure that they had received my money, my account balance was zero, and my status had been adjusted from pre-registered to registered. While I was standing in line, the young student in front of me was arguing with one of the cashiers. He wanted a copy of his transcript, which was not forthcoming because his parents had not paid all his tuition and he had not paid some parking tickets. The amount they were discussing was staggering and made me think about the cost of my first three children's educations, with more than seventeen years each, plus ten years on my fourth child, Amanda, up till then, a total of sixty-one years worth of tuition. No wonder I was broke. I began to feel like the guy in front of me, and I was working on another panic attack, because I had Amanda's remaining eight years of school, plus mine now to go....I would just have to make mine shorter, that's all.

It didn't me take long after this scene and the accompanying financial visualization to slip into a depressed state. Leaving the bursar's office, I walked quickly across the Cornell campus, walking a fine line between relishing every bit of being here and panicking and feeling like I had made the biggest mistake of my life. I was about to lose it. But that Friday evening was particularly spectacular outside, and as I walked, I passed by a huge tent where a massive beer and wine festival was going on. There was a large crowd of people of various ages, many of them my age, and they were all holding cups of beer and by now feeling no pain. I was smiling with envy when one of the guys yelled out to me, asking, "Are you a five or a nine?" I really didn't know what he meant, but I quickly remembered that I was still forty-nine years old, so I yelled back, "I am a nine!"

What I didn't realize until a little while later was that the five and nine he was referring to were the two graduating classes, 1965 and 1969, that were celebrating their respective class reunions, thus the beer-fest. I joined the party. We all drank a lot of beer that night, and I had a great time feeling like I was part of something traditional, although, in my mind I knew I was still a broke freshman and I just barely had one foot in the tent. But like the camel's nose, I was a big guy, ready to move in with all four hooves and both stubborn hands and feet.

The party and the camaraderie I felt helped my panic pass over the weekend, and I carefully studied the professor's manuscript, because this was going to be the book that the entire class was based on and I was lucky enough to have an inside, sneak preview. I flashed my cards, even though I didn't know what they all meant, and was still proofreading and trying to find the mistakes and typos that the professor wanted me to correct.

Classes lasted longer in the semester at Cornell than they did back at the University of Houston, and I had arrived there just as Cornell was letting out. Cornell was a destination campus, unlike the University of Houston, which was a commuter campus, so students were still leaving their dormitories, packing and exiting the university. The hustle and bustle was exciting, and I quickly felt the buzz and picked up on the energy the kids were exhibiting.

This was an especially exciting time for me because I didn't have any commitments aside from my education. Any problems I had, including potential financial ones, I had now finally set aside and let myself feel and be as free as a study-bird, as I knew Gloria would temporarily take care of the home front. I would really have to make it up to her somehow, though, after I was a college graduate.

That Sunday before classes began, I was walking over the Cascadilla Gorge, on the Cornell campus, when I stopped to take it all in. I happened to overhear two beautiful, drop-dead gorgeous young ladies talking about previous suicides that had occurred there at that exact time of the year. As I inadvertently eavesdropped on their conversation, they were talking about the latest pre-med student who had not been accepted into med school and then jumped into one of the moss-covered jagged-rock gorges indigenous to that part of New York. It took me but a second to wonder, with my PTSD and panic attacks, if I didn't pass this upcoming course, could I get that distraught? This was another all-or-nothing part of my life, and I was risking everything, including my sanity. I knew what the odds were. The next jumper could be me. I went back to my room-cave and studied until well after midnight, nervously shaking between pages in the manuscript.

My first day of class at Cornell, I woke up at four in the morning and couldn't go back to sleep. I just still couldn't believe where I was. That first day of class went great, and finally meeting Dr. Corgel was extremely rewarding. I thought him to be about three to five years younger than I but found out later we were both the same age, although we had very disparate backgrounds. To say he was smart was an understatement.

In the restaurant business I had met many people whom I had thought were brilliant, who made tons of money, or who wielded lots of power. The Black Angus Restaurant was located next to River Oaks, Houston's premier and most expensive subdivision, which attracted the wealthiest oilmen and the most prestigious astronauts, doctors, astronauts, and attorneys in the area, plus United States Presidents 41 and 43, George H. W. and George W. Bush. Most all of these people, at one time or another, had come into our restaurant. One thing was for certain: Dr. Corgel was in this league of people, and he didn't waste any of his time or ours at the going price of tuition, nor did he deny anyone a chance to learn at a fast clip. His class was run like a machine; twenty-four desks seated eighteen undergraduate and six graduate students. The impression I perceived during my first class was that if you did not like your seat, there were two or more people outside the door waiting for it if you stumbled. I was going to fight for mine, no matter what it took.

The professor wasted no time and quickly asked who the graduate students were in the class and how many were coming off Wall Street or from other Ivy League schools. My heart sank, as I knew that I was in a class with a bunch of brain-children about to flush out the only confederate in the room, me. Professor Corgel was methodical in delivering his course materials and was equally precise as he confidently presented himself. I was duly impressed. I clutched the manuscript that he had sent me and quickly darted my focus around to each of the other students' desks, to see if anyone else had a copy. They didn't, and I felt triply privileged.

During my college career, Professor Corgel would be one of many PhDs I would watch, "go off on the board" and give a quick synopsis of an impossibly complicated problem or model on the first day to shake off any borderline, nonserious students. He asked everyone in the room to get out their Hewlett-Packard HP 12c calculators and see how long they could keep a multiple-step problem within it. As I did not even know what an HP 12c was, I quickly looked around and put it on the top of my items to buy at the bookstore. At the end of the problem, he asked who in the room had kept it within their calculator, and then he paused and looked at me. When I responded, "No, sir, I am still just trying to keep down my breakfast," everybody started laughing, including the professor. They thought I was joking....I wasn't.

I took this course very seriously and studied eight to twelve hours a day, after our three-hour class. By Friday, after the first full week of class, I was feeling pretty good about everything, until Professor Corgel gave the class a little weekend problem that made a Rubik's cube look easy. He said, "Most of you won't even attempt it. Out of the half of you that will, almost half of you will give up and one or two might come up with an answer that may or may not be correct." It was Friday around noon, and I quickly calculated that I had approximately sixty-two hours left to complete the problem, save for sleep. It would be a long, non-sleeping, eye-opening, eye-burning weekend.

After much to-do about everything, I learned how to use my new HP 12cC in another baptism of fire. True to the professor's forecast, most of the students did not attempt the problem, and those who did gave it up for the summer-weekend life. A female Army captain and I were the only two who finished the problem, and I was the only one who got the correct answer. Of course, the professor asked me how long it had taken or how long I had spent on the problem, which was a loaded, double-barreled question. If I answered that I had spent fifty hours on it, I would look like a fool to the other genius students, but if I told him a couple hours, I would be a Texas braggart. What I answered was, "It was over lots of cold pizza and some straight Scotch." I said Scotch because it seemed a little more fitting for my age.

The reality was I had not had a Scotch since I had quit smoking years earlier. I knew most of the class was still guzzling beer and knocking down exotic drinks like Cuba Libres and Sex on the Beach. When everybody chuckled or laughed, I knew it was *with* me, not *at* me, this time around. I knew I could hold my own if only I studied harder and harder and kept ahead of my younger peers. I definitely had more at stake. I quickly dismissed a flash of the Cascadilla Gorge waiting for its next victim.

Among that summer crop of brilliant people in the class were highly serious and well-bred students from Harvard Business School, Princeton, Wharton School of Business at the University of Pennsylvania, and the University of Chicago, all working on their finance degrees and related curricula by picking up a fill-in summer course to round out their student transcripts and resumes. There were also two students from the military, both captains: the one female from the Army and a recently severed captain from active duty in the Marine Corps. Professor Corgel had welcomed them warmly, and I mentally noted the young man's rank and service. Even though he was half my age, he was a captain and I had only been a sergeant, so I looked up to him, his rank and his education. He was a graduate student and I was still just a freshman. In this harvest of intellectuals, I knew I was truly in over my head.

The captain's name was Tom Lewerenz, and I could tell after talking with him several times that he was a strong leader and dedicated Corps commander. Tom and I would end up getting to know each other quite well because I immediately asked to study with him, which we did frequently. I also immediately asked several other students to study together in a large group. This was an offensive move made mainly to offset my defensive fear, because aside from benefitting from their knowledge, I could find out where their confidence lay, and much more useful reconnaissance information.

Aside from my "moment" and epiphany the first day of leading the study group, I also became fascinated at the differences in how I compared to them and how their backgrounds contrasted with mine—not necessarily in a bad way, though. In fact, it was a positive difference for all of us, as we all brought different strengths to the table. Where my fellow students had the academic knowledge, I had the practical knowledge, and both my "groups" moved forward together. My fears were allayed as I got my "teaching legs," and at least my emotional roller coaster came to an end, as I got to know everybody as just plain human beings.

Professor Corgel's class was exhilarating, and leading the study group made me feel confident, but what meant the most to me was that I could tell, possibly because of my feeble but admittedly funny jokes, that Professor Corgel seemed to respect me...and my opinion. He would sometimes look to me to confirm what he said, from a mature financial sense and an operations point of view. Even when I sometimes did not have clue what on earth he was talking about, I would nod in agreement. The thought of a bobble-head doll came to mind. But I was not mocking him as much as I was in awe of the way he was conveying his knowledge. It was one of those student-teacher relationships that just clicked. My confidence was growing, the knowledge was coming easier, and I was looking forward to each and every day instead of dreading it.

I would automatically get up at four in the morning because of sheer excitement and study until six. Then I would fast-walk to the cafeteria, where the food was always outstanding. There was no giving my tray to the cafeteria cashier in this chow hall. Cornell has always been known for, and is consistently rated number one or close to it for, college culinary arts. These chefs were all as good, if not better than, the professional chefs who had worked for me in the open market environment.

One of the first days after I arrived, I had purchased a meal card on a tenuously thin credit card, because I did not relish the thought of eating dog food out of a trash can or C-rations if I ran out of cash. The first thing I did in one of the cafeteria restaurants was tip the chef, Fritz, a quick, but very precious, $50. Afterwards, whenever I was in the back of the line, Fritz would always personally acknowledge me by waving his hand and motion me to the front of the line. He would personally prepare my breakfast with a little lagniappe, and as I would be at the front of the line, I was saving a bunch of valuable time. If he had time, he would kindly interrupt my reading over breakfast and discuss some of his problems or the advantages of "cheffing" for education, versus a private for-profit restaurant or hotel or country club on the "outside." Our discussions were often very challenging and sometimes heated, as Fritz was almost as stubborn as me. Life was getting better, and I was starting to relax in my new ivy-cloaked environment.

After the midterm exam, which came up rather quickly in a summer class, I was in the computer lab at the Hotel School one day when an associate dean and a dean from the International Labor Relations (ILR) College approached and set next to me and in front of me. It seems that they were baffled at some of my answers to one of the many questionnaires I had filled out along the way. I immediately thought, *Uh-oh, this is it, they are going to ask me to leave.* The only thing that flashed in my mind was whether I was going to get my money back. I then thought maybe I had blown the exam or, worse, they had found out that I had never completed high school.

The dean from the ILR College and I had talked several times before, as his computer lab was closed during the summer. But the conversation on those days had always been light chitchat and just curiosity in one another, like about what two middle-aged men were doing in a computer lab every afternoon during some of the most gorgeous Finger Lake-area summer days and cool, firefly-laden evenings in recent memory. But what he had gotten out of me was that I was on my, as he stated, "third career."

I'm glad I didn't volunteer and blurt anything out just then that would have gotten me in trouble or given me away when they sat down. It turned out that I had told them in one of the questionnaires that I would like to teach. They told me that with my thirty years of experience in food service, I should think about teaching in their Professional Development Program (PDP) during the summer at Cornell. One of them said they didn't need any more professional hotel academics but needed teachers with deep restaurant operational experience. I gathered that they thought I was doing a fill-in class for my master's degree. I don't think they had any idea I was still barely a first-semester freshman.

I was making good psychological progress and found out that I had made a solid B on the midterm, so now I was getting even more confident, almost cocky, and I volunteered for a graduate-level project in class, as well as working on my undergraduate individual project at the same time. Of course, Professor Corgel told me that it would be ungraded but that it was most welcome, and I wanted the challenge, the knowledge, and the opportunity to see how high and fast I could now fly.

The only thing that held me back in class was my lifelong nemesis, algebra. But the other students, including Tom, knew that I had been away from school for thirty years, and it was obvious and acceptable that I would be rusty. My dirty little secrets were still safe for a little while longer. I continued to flip through my flash cards night after night, and I was still unknown to the campus night life. I relentlessly used a regular calculator to verify the results of the HP 12c. By the time I left the course, I would not need the regular calculator.

Around this time, I tried to call Gloria one night and found that my cell phone had been cut off, and when I tried to use the pay phone, my credit card did not work either, so I resorted to quarters dropped into the phone every three minutes, just like we had done decades earlier, between San Diego boot camp and Houston, with my shaved head and our broken and racing hearts.

Gloria was by this time borrowing from one credit card to pay the other and kiting credit, the total opposite of what we were learning in class on the efficiency and time value of money. On the financial front, things were not going very well. I started contemplating getting some type of job outside of the Cornell campus, such as waiting tables or tending bar, to make some quick and easy cash. Then, just when it didn't look like things could get any worse financially, everything changed. Professor Corgel announced, somewhat sarcastically because he didn't think it was a sound financial idea, that the house-poor homeowners of California would be very pleased that they could now borrow against their houses on second or third mortgages. The *Wall Street Journal* had just reported that the federal government had enacted a new law that would supersede any state laws regarding second mortgages.

It didn't take me two seconds to figure out the ramifications of what that meant to Gloria and me. Texas was a homestead state, from Spanish influence dating back to when Texas and California were founded. They had always preserved the equity of the house to maintain the family, centered on the wife and her dowry, regardless of a philandering or dead husband. This meant that the equity we had in our house, our only asset, was now free for Gloria and I to borrow against. I asked the professor for clarification, which was positive, and immediately after class, I searched the Internet to obtain further information.

As I called Gloria from New York, my heart was again pounding because we could borrow the needed funds for me to continue in school. I had projected how long it would take me and how much it would cost, but when I got hold of Gloria, she was already more excited than I was, about another huge stroke of luck we had. We were both talking at a hundred miles an hour, not making any sense to each other. She said, "But I've got great news!"

To which I replied, "No, I've got tell to you tell you something better!"

She said, "No, you have got to listen, I've got tell you this!"

Now, I was thinking maybe one of the children had come into something good, we had won the lottery, or somebody had left us an unexpected inheritance. Gloria blurted out that a Mr. Perkins had called and the Veterans Administration Chapter 31 program that I had applied for months earlier had been verbally awarded to me; I would get the written letter shortly.

I literally almost fell out of the phone booth. It flashed through my mind that we would not have to borrow against the house because I would be receiving a monthly check to go to school. The Chapter 31 program wasn't just money from heaven, it was more. First, it was tax-free money, and with my small disability check, they both amounted to almost $1,000 a month, plus all my books, fees, parking, supplies, and tuition were reimbursable expenses. With Gloria's check we could make it. Why had I not heard of this program before? Why had I let the original ten-year GI Bill lapse without taking advantage of it? How could I have been so stupid?

The cashier at the end of the cafeteria line was now giving me money, and I was able put my wallet away.

Then I told Gloria about the change in federal law and that we could borrow against the house. She too was amazed. These events erased any lingering doubt about our financial hemorrhaging stopping shortly, and I could continue my education with almost no financial worries.

For the next step, I had to immediately fly back to Houston for a personal interview for the Chapter 31 program. I met Mr. Perkins, who had interviewed me months earlier, and he asked how I was going to finish, because the fail and dropout rates were extremely high. The Chapter 31 program was not easy, because it was closely monitored. Although about sixty veterans had recently started, he told me, only a few would likely graduate in easier programs. Mr. Perkins asked me to think of him as my probation officer because if I slipped, he would jerk my chain...extremely hard. He was representing the Veterans Administration, who wanted to know what my plan was and where their money would be going. It was their investment in me. It had to be in writing, factual and true. I told Mr. Perkins that I would go to school twelve months a year until I finished—proud words coming from an old newbie against a mountain of other negative statistics.

We also talked about me possibly taking additional courses at Cornell. After a couple months of monitoring my progress, Mr. Perkins eventually went to bat for me and got approval for me to have my tuition paid at Cornell, as well as the Houston Community College. He knew I was dead serious about completing the program. What he didn't know, just like my counselor Kevin, was that I also planned to graduate at the top of my class.

Next, I was assigned a caseworker whom I would have to see on a regular basis. I had to get letters from the university, the college, and any other colleges I was attending. I would also have to get status reports from the veterans hospital's various clinics, especially the mental health–PTSD clinic. They would closely monitor and manage the financial, mental, and educational facets of my life. Mr. Perkins also informed me that my room and board would not be paid for at any college. But, he continued, "If your grades are high enough, you could apply and receive scholarships to offset the cost."

On the Monday morning following these big events, Gloria had my cell phone reactivated, and I could call her. The arrangement of the Chapter 31 program had not just put us in a position of financial parity but comforted Gloria, which pleased me to no end. Now I could totally concentrate on my studies with even more vigor.

The only other financial change I made at the time was to move onto campus, into the dormitory nearest the hotel school. Because of my age, they were kind enough to upgrade me to Sheldon Court, which was a graduate facility, as they thought I would be more comfortable away from immature freshmen. Maybe the opposite was true.

To get through the next twenty-three months and reach my goals, I would have to cut every known corner, right down to milliseconds. For example, I used mechanical pencils and found out that the thumb-push style was faster than the top-plunger one. With a thumb-push mechanical pencil, I could keep on writing without pausing when ejecting the lead. And of course I used a stronger .07 instead of .05 lead. Also, when I took tests, I would have an eraser always in my left hand and ready to make a correction. I reactivated the skill of using both hands from my bartending days.

I had an amazing algebra tutor from Russia who taught me how to write with my left hand so I would not get tired and because two pencils are faster than one. I got good at it but I never did get to where I could simultaneously write mathematics equations upside down like he did. But another couple months and another couple semesters, and you never know.

I would need to become a learning machine. Just like the Outback Steakhouse slogan says, "There are no rules, just right" and, like the Energizer bunny, I would need to "just keep going and going." Every movement, every step, every thought had to be an educational process in which there could be no idle time: nada, zip, zero.

I was having a great time, but working very hard for it. The professors did occasionally apply some undue pressure on me, challenging my thoughts by making me synthesize the material instead of simply regurgitate it from rote memory. They could tell by then that I was a human flashcard. For instance, one time the professor asked the class what a CMBS was, and I blurted out in front of everyone that it was a Commercial Mortgage-Backed Security, which I knew from my cards, yet when he asked me to compare and contrast the difference between it and its residential sister, I groped around like "Ned and the First Reader." Thankfully, he always caught me before I mentally hit the ground. Before day's end, all twenty-four of us knew what a CMBS and a RMBS were, because of his teaching methods.

Sometimes the banter in class would be playful, to help lift the summer doldrums of the class. Sometimes Dr. Corgel would impulsively ask me something intuitive and a side-step away from his teaching point. I would make the class of younger students burst out laughing, because I always had a somewhat smart-ass answer. For example, he would like to ask me, "So, Mr. Vargo, how long have you been in the restaurant business?"

I would answer, "Well, I was a busboy at the last supper."

Or he would ask me later, "How did you make a million dollars in the restaurant business?"

I would respond, "I started with two million!"

I had such a great time, I wondered why in the world I would ever want to stop these feelings of accomplishment. It would be years later that Dr. Corgel would confide in me and pay me a very high compliment by telling me, "You made the class into a community."

While I was still in class late that semester, in the beautiful Finger Lakes area of New York state, Gloria and Amanda flew from Houston to Cleveland, Ohio, where three of my aunts lived. Once they were there, my aunt Marianne was kind enough to lend Gloria her minivan, and Gloria and Amanda drove over to Ithaca. From Ithaca, the three of us drove into New York City for a holiday, where Gloria had traded her vacation prize from her American Airlines Christmas party for a free three-night stay at the Four Seasons Hotel. It was while we were staying there in the city that I found out that I had made a respectable B+ for my first class at Cornell. The feeling was exhilarating.

ALGEBRA

But then, to turn my joy into drama, it was time to finally face my arch nemesis...algebra. I had a perfect record when it came to algebra: I had flunked it each and every time I took it, including summer school. The ninth grade at St. Thomas High School was the first try, Marian High School was tries two through five, two additional tries at San Jacinto High School during the summer were numbers six and seven; all were perfect and straight F's. Try number eight was at San Jacinto Junior College, and now I was faced with number nine at HCC, an easier community college. My fear of fears was the fear of algebra itself, because I now had thirty-five years worth of negative programming to reverse. Just the thought of XYZ was enough to trigger a Richter-nine panic attack. I double-dosed my medications to get through my first algebra class at HCC.

Having survived fifty minutes of pure mental white-knuckled torture the first day of class, I looked for the nearest bulletin board for a paid tutor. The first raggedy slip of paper I pulled off the board had a very Russian-sounding name, Alex Romanoff. True to my expectations, he had a very thick accent and had been a math major at the Moscow School of Mathematics and Navigation. Almost all male college students in Russia at the time were being drafted into the Army and sent to someplace like Afghanistan to serve as cannon fodder, much like our Viet Nam albatross. Alex had instead decided to seek fame and fortune in the United States. He had three things on his mind: mathematics, money, and finding an American bride as quickly as possible.

He negotiated his hourly rate by asking how many daughters and nieces I had. Alex was so adept at math, he would sit across the table from me and explain the problem that was upside-down to him so I could follow it, while he continued on a calculus problem, also upside-down to him, with his other hand and another pencil. I knew this was my guy. I also went to the free study labs provided by HCC but still continued to struggle. I just did not think in abstract terms, although I was starting to make progress. When my final grade came in at a D+, I was devastated. It was a lousy three points from a C, but a D meant I could not transfer the class credit to the University of Houston and all of this had been a complete waste of time and money!

I decided to take that same course at UH and hope to make at least a D, regardless of how it screwed up my GPA, because if I did make at least a D at my home university, it would count. Then, I further worked myself into an A+ panic attack with the realization that on top of the algebra, I would have to take three more maths, from a choice of calculus, finite math, statistics, logic, or differential equation. Again, I had very real and very severe doubts about whether I was college material and if I ever could or would really pull this off at all.

In the last half of the summer, I took courses at HCC and at the CHC. All totaled, I had racked up nine hours at three colleges, with a 4.0 semester GPA and one big black eye in algebra that wouldn't transfer. No matter how bruised my ego was, nothing was going to stop me now but my nemesis, algebra, which chewed on me day and night for months.

C.H.E-Being Taught to Teach

Another one of my counselors at the University of Houston, Dr. Stephen Barth, had actually taught my daughter in hospitality law a few years earlier. I was really looking forward to taking his class instead of looking down the barrel of the four-math shotgun. Dr. Barth instantly became a good friend and confidant, and he helped me immensely. I hadn't forgotten my conversation with the two deans from the ILR college at Cornell, about teaching in the PDP there, so in one of our discussions, I told Dr. Barth that I would really like to take the practical knowledge that I had gained in my many years of restaurant and hotel operations and obtain the necessary knowledge to teach at the Hilton or the PDP at Cornell. He then told me that, ironically, there was a class coming up later in the summer that would teach me how to teach hospitality in college. *Perfect*, I thought.

It was the Certified Hospitality Educators (CHE) class and certification course, and was sponsored by the American Hotel and Lodging Association. The course was only given a few times a year, in select cities all over the world that had major hotel colleges, such as Paris, London, Singapore, and Los Angeles, and it had now somehow landed right in my lap in Houston.

I immediately knew I had to take this class, and the double irony was that Dr. Barth was certified to teach the upcoming class. Whereas other teachers and professors who took the class were reimbursed by their respective schools, I paid my fees on my own. I don't think there was a professor, teacher, student, or counselor who didn't think that I had made millions of dollars in the restaurant business prior to going back to college and was only toying around in school with nothing else to do. I pre-registered for the course, which happened to be scheduled perfectly between the last class of my first summer semester and the first day of class in my first fall semester. It was too perfect; I fully expected my registration to be dumped, as I did not have a PhD, a master's, a bachelor's, or even a high school diploma, but it wasn't.

When the intensive classes began, there were seventeen PhD professors and me, seated at a U-shaped table. I put my hands in a prayer-like position between my knees so no one would hear my knees knock. I asked myself what I was doing there, but I continued to hang in the class that I had paid for. I quickly learned that the pass/fail ratio of professors that took the course was about 50:50. This, I was told by my counselor, was because some old dogs do not want to learn new tricks. Those stubborn professors who did not go along with the program flunked. I quickly assumed that I would be in the nine who would not make it and would have wasted several hundred dollars. But I would give it a college try and my Marine Corps all.

By age and experience, I was equal to the people in the class, only having a terrible imbalance in education. As we were all about the same general age, most of the people from other countries and universities did not know the difference, or that I did not have a doctorate. The reason this class was so important to five or six of the attending professors was that they were from the Hilton College, which meant they had to pass this class as part of their contract with the college. Their paychecks were tied to passing, and if they didn't pass, they would have to chase the course wherever it was given next, even overseas, to take it again and preserve their paychecks. I assumed this would be at their own personal expense. So, for the Hilton College professors there, this mandatory course meant their jobs and paychecks, their self-esteems and futures. All eighteen of us were now on equal footing.

The course itself was a two-week–long, very intense class, and it opened my eyes to things I had never known existed in education. I had thought that lecturing a class for forty-five minutes was an easy venture; I was mistaken. Like Mark Twain said, "Easy reading was darn hard writing," I quickly began to see that preparation was 90% of the class, and afterwards, I immediately applied these techniques to my student approach to learning. We learned that with pure lecturing, students would typically only retain about 11% of what they were taught but if taught properly, using the techniques taught to us in this course, our students could retain over 90% of the material they were taught. I was learning to teach at a college level, and from now on, I would know how to teach myself at that level as well.

At the end of the course, we had our final exam. When starting the class, I had thought this part would mark the end of it for me...a fast guillotine by a grade.

The professors were used to taking so many courses in rote memorization that it was very easy for them, and the whole group got along together well. By the end of the course, I was very relaxed, but prepared to be one of the nine who did not make it, as I was already preprogrammed to failing. To my amazement, I passed the first half of the class.

However, I found out that over the next six months, we would each have to make a film of ourselves as a professor in front of a classroom, applying our new set of skills to a class. This would be 50% of our grade and was where most of the professors who did not pass flunked in the application of what they had learned. So all I had to do within the next six months was borrow a college classroom and film myself applying what I had learned during the course by taping myself teaching an hour-long class. Of course, I had Dr. Barth and Dr. Agnes DeFranco as global certifiers to help me along.

I arranged with a friend of mine who was the A/V manager at the college to tape my hour-long tutorial with my outline in hand. I also found out how and when the other Hilton professors were doing their taping and on what subject matter. This was just ordinary reconnaissance of the competition, not infiltration or cheating. I found out that the others were doing their subjects and topics on the specialty courses they were already teaching. I also soon heard the news that a few of the Hilton College professors that had taken the course had not passed. This would later turn out to be a major problem for me, which I had never anticipated.

As I thought about what I would teach for my own film, I instinctively knew that students would rather be presented with something they could touch rather than just learn another theoretical concept. This is not to say that the students did not like finance, real estate, or accounting but that they would rather do something that excited them. While most of the other professors were trying to make finance sexy to a bunch of twenty-one-year-olds, I put together an outline about tableside flambé cooking, skills I retained from my days at the Shamrock Hilton Hotel.

I was very worried about my presentation, the outline, and the outcome of my class, but when I practiced with a study group from the foods class, they didn't want my class to finish. During the actual taping of the class, I simultaneously built and flamed an Irish coffee and flambéed a Bananas Foster dessert. I felt very much at ease, much like I had back working at the Shamrock years earlier, and I was loaded with youthful exuberance. The students' reception of what I presented was extremely good. When the A/V manager stopped taping the class, it went on for another hour and a half, with the majority of students still there in the dynamic foods kitchen/laboratory, until I was thoroughly exhausted. This teaching was not as easy as I had thought, but it was thoroughly rewarding.

What I saw in those kids' eyes when I was teaching them and telling them about how I had learned how to toss Caesar salads with ten ingredients, de-bone fish and chicken using French service, flame Steak Diane and European Pepper Steak and masterfully carve a Chateaubriand, all in front of the guest table was that I had 110% of their attention. When I showed them how to, and actually let them, start from scratch with ingredients and flame an Irish coffee themselves, they went wild.

After the class was taped, the film was sent to the AH&LA Educational Institute to be graded by a panel of judges, each grading different aspects of my abilities: conduct, student interaction, question answering, how the students in the class questionnaires were graded, and students' knowledge retention in the short run.

I would soon find out, much to my real astonishment, that I had completed and passed the prestigious CHE course. I had taken it as a freshman and was awarded the designation as a sophomore in college. I was totally thrilled and excited and immediately went out and had student business cards made at Kinko's with my new designation, CHE, proudly embossed after my name. I had put the cart before the horse one more time, and oh, what a mistake I had made!

Now my real problem was the Hilton professors who had not passed the CHE whom I would have to take classes from. Because the professors knew from my business cards that I had passed, these would be classes that I would have to work twice as hard in to get half as good a grade. I then found out again the difference between objective and subjective grading. When I asked Dr. Barth which professors passed and didn't pass, he told me that, ethically, he couldn't tell me. I completely understood that and respected his opinion, but in the end it didn't take me long to figure out which professors they were. On the first day of class, I could tell, and they could tell I could tell. One professor did not give me my course completion for more than a year after the class was finished. Another professor actually dropped me from his class without my knowledge, although I had not gone through drop or add. As Gloria and I both agreed, that one was out of my control. It naturally dented my progress toward my goals, not to mention my pride, but it didn't stop me in the least; I just dug in like never before.

A couple of years later, I was asked to interview at the Cordon Bleu, to teach a tableside cooking class there. When they asked me to submit my resume, I instead sent the only copy I had of my CHE tape, to show them a true example of what I could do. The tape is now in their curriculum every semester.

CHAPTER FOURTEEN
First Fall Semester, 1997—Hitting Full Stride

DAMN THE ALGEBRA, FULL SPEED AHEAD

Even with the first summer's D+ disaster in algebra at HCC, I registered for eighteen hours at UH for the fall, which was the maximum allowed per semester. I then went through an office-manual "drop and add" and added one more class without any drops, kind of a sneaky way around academic regulations, I guess. The schedules that the colleges post are probably not meant to prohibit a student from taking too many hours, but they do. With other college courses plus 21 hours at UH, I completed a full sophomore year of work in one semester, in the fall of 1997.

My classes were divided evenly between the university basic courses and major courses that I needed in HRM. With my ninth toe being hit with a hammer in algebra, I decided to bypass the subject again for one more semester. At the same time, I took basic courses at HCC, which were more in the evenings and on Fridays.

The new spring semester was extremely exciting. I hadn't noticed the excitement in the previous January's 1997 spring semester at UH or in the half-empty summer campus at Cornell, but in my first fall semester of 1997 it just seemed full of campus life, which was probably just because I was now relaxed enough now to notice it. Every August and September there was always a new crop of freshmen coming in, and the professors seemed to take baby steps in their explanations of the classes and university procedure. There would be a huge influx of new students rushing around. The University of Houston had about 33,000 students at the main campus, and it seemed everyone drove two cars; I could tell because the parking was twice as crowded and because of the wolf packs of tow trucks circling the university streets like sharks with easy prey.

In this fall semester, I also experienced things I had never expected to, including the fraternities and sororities on campus, rush week, and fraternity life. I was asked to rush in at least two organizations and thought it was great, until I got home and told my wife that I was going to join a social fraternity. My youngest son was a sophomore at Texas Tech and was in Kappa Sigma fraternity, so I had thought it would be kind of cool. He did not, nor did my wife. She said, "Oh I get it, they want somebody to buy the beer." I promptly put that idea on the back burner, but it gave me an open door in our marriage from there on out to keep kidding Gloria about the boys and girls. Her retort was always the same: "If you really want to join a fraternity, go start one yourself with students of your own age or interests."

Starting the new fall semester was exciting, because I was beginning my major classes, which seemed entirely different than the university auditoriums full of up to 400 students. That semester I eventually booked thirty semester hours, and afterward, I was a proud junior and ready for the worst...algebra. Most, if not all, the HRM classes were audio taped and seemed choreographed between professors, research assistants, graduate assistants, and technicians. Also, the kids at the Hilton College appeared preppier and better dressed than their counterparts on the university side, because most HRM students were already working in hotels and restaurants as servers and bartenders and were more extroverted and full of personality, especially those lovely coeds, Ooh-Rah!

The environment was also much more enriching. The buildings were newer, there were smaller class sizes and student-to-teacher ratios. The atmosphere was also more professional, as the professors seemed more interested in the knowledge that they were imparting. Some classes were even taught in test kitchens and laboratories, so we all spoke the same language, foodie and hotelie, and all but a few professors were certified hospitality educators. I could hardly wait until I was taking only my major classes. One class that I was looking forward to in particular was Foods in Space, as the University of Houston and the Hilton College were located near NASA and had contractual obligations with one another.

Besides the classes becoming more interesting and thought-provoking, I began to catch on to and accelerate in my academic life. Every day was an adventure with something new to learn. Besides my imaginary counselors, I had tangible counselors, tutors, study labs, and study groups, and I was accumulating the tools I needed to work with. I was using every available means to learn a massive amount of information ever quicker. And of course at home, I could depend on Gloria.

It was during that first fall, or "sophomore" semester that I had serious thoughts about transferring full time to Cornell. There were those damn pros and cons and again; I reduced them to paper. The indecision chewed on me almost as much as making my initial decision to go to college had.

After that first summer semester, I knew I wanted to take several more courses in hotel and restaurant real estate finance at the hotel school at Cornell University; however, registration for classes at both the University of Houston and that class at Cornell was difficult, and I could not coordinate the two efficiently. I called Professor Corgel, and after we talked, he agreed to work something out during the upcoming Christmas break, when I could take a course from him. After he checked with "his people" and I checked with "my people," he called me back to say that the paperwork from the "Veterans people" was too difficult on his end, so we further discussed a course during the spring. I also offered to pay the professor directly out of my pocket, but the bursar's office balked, as they wanted their customary college and university cut of fees if I was to receive credit transferable back to the University of Houston. The professor and I agreed to wait until the spring semester.

Again, after much to-do about everything, late in the fall semester of '97, I registered for my second Cornell course that was a graduate/senior course. As I was already in the Cornell computer system, I was good to go. I guess no one again checked to see if I was actively enrolled, but I was not asking questions. Professor Corgel, who set up the class, referred to it as a "poor man's long-distance course," because of the logistical problems of taking classes in New York and Texas, he would videotape his classes for me and I would travel intermittently to Ithaca when needed. The professor arranged with his A/V department to do the VHS tapes and send me them as needed.

It became a kind of Netflix forerunner; he and I constantly had tapes and lots of long-distance office hours going back and forth. Sometimes I would make audio-only reproductions of the video tapes, because we were under instructions that I could not duplicate any VHS tape. However, I had become used to bending the rules from my days in the Marines, and anyway, I needed only the audio portion to lock down the course material at test time. This was a hard way to take a class, especially at an Ivy League college, but on spring break, I would spend the entire time off up in Ithaca, studying at the feet of the master.

OLD WOUNDS ARE HARD TO HEEL

I had already missed several chances to reconcile my bitterness toward the students from South and North Viet Nam. But by the fall of 1997 I would be faced with a bigger challenge in the form of a classmate in a sophomore English Diversification class at HCC. I had thought the course would be a mixture of writing genres: prose, short stories, poems, etc. It was the complete opposite, and I was very surprised when it turned out to be nothing like the course listing or syllabus had stated.

The teacher told the class her entire life's history in the first ten minutes of the first class. She even shed some tears regarding her no-good husband of thirty-plus years, who had turned her into a raving lunatic and middle-aged lesbian...a real man-hater. After surveying the class, her fixation was on me, the stereotypical man who always cheats on his spouse and then abandons her for a younger model. She knew the type well and must have known my mother-in-law.

She announced to the class that everyone was required to keep a daily writing diary seven days a week until the course was finished or they quit, whichever came first. I reasoned that she got paid for starts not finishes. After the priests at St. Thomas, the nuns at Marian, and the drill instructors in the Corps, I felt I could handle a little writing course. The teacher went on to say that, through our diaries, she would get to know each and every one of us intimately: our strengths, weaknesses, and innermost thoughts, where we came from and where we were going. Whenever she finished a point, she would glare at me like my Sister Marcella had in fifth grade.

I tried to warn another Tex-Mex veteran brother about what I thought was going to happen. When the vet turned in his diary, he had written about his tour in Panama and his distaste of Spanish-speaking people, whom he felt always put him down because of his imperfect Spanish with stuttering. The teacher without delay asked him to stand face-to-face with a cute Mexican girl; they were instructed to ask one another questions. The teacher had known from the girl's diary that she didn't like mixed gringo men because she had been molested by one. In this way, the class found out what the teacher's meaning of diversity was going to be for the rest of the semester. By the end of the term, among those who were still left, everybody had developed and displayed a distaste of everyone else in the class, based solely on personal feelings that the sorcerer had sucked out of our daily logs.

One day, after the veteran finally walked out in the middle of the class in a huff, I was up next and was pitted against Nyugen (pronounced "When"), a young man from Viet Nam. We were like two rabid pit bulls in an arena primed for action. She let the class know that the younger man was from Haiphong (in the North). She wanted him to tell the class about their customs, family, and morass. It sounded innocent on the surface, but she knew that my blood was boiling over the young man's braggadocio.

I was looking at my enemy's son, who was now taking advantage of our American liberties, privileges, and freedoms that I had paid for dearly with my sanity, my body, and my blood. The professor also knew that my outfit had been responsible for killing many North Vietnamese and probably had many medals to show for it. She made sure the young man knew it, too. Nyugen ended his diatribe by finishing his last thoughts in Vietnamese and spitting on the ground. I responded by cursing him in Vietnamese and also spitting on the ground. He responded in addition by giving me a cutthroat gesture. Class ended, but the war was back on, and the professor was grinning.

She was an underpaid, unprofessional, and insensitive community-college-level, professorial lunatic. After taking her class, I decided to start interviewing professors whenever possible before taking their classes. I would evaluate her as having achieved her PhD from a diploma mill. She was a vicious, swagger-stick carrying, man-hater, a real bitch and a total manic. How she had ever got a job teaching anyone at all, let alone at the college level, I will never understand. Teaching is an honor and a privilege, and she did not in any way deserve it.

You may run into these types of professors, and it can really waste your very precious time and, of course, your patience, so do your best to do your due diligence and find out as much as you can about a class and the professor who teaches it before you sign up for the class. But don't hesitate to cut your losses and drop the class quickly during drop/add and pick up a different class if necessary.

U of H LAW

It was also during my sophomore semester in the fall of 1997 that I befriended another student in a couple of classes and study groups. This relationship led to me developing a serious bug to go to law school that I still have today...and that will likely be another great experience and another book. This student, Craig Butler, looked up to me, not only because of my previous restaurant experience, but also because of how I grasped and visualized various food and beverage industry concepts. Craig was a born foodie, an operations guy with plenty on the ball. Also of high interest to me was his adorable girlfriend, Sandy—not a sexual attraction at all, far from it. It was more of a distraction, in that just like Don Corleone he would keep his enemies close, I would keep my rivals for top honors in my class even closer.

I was talking with Kevin, my undergraduate academic counselor, when the subject of the high GPA award came up. On the sly, he inferred that there was a "female someone" who had a perfect 4.0 average going and there was no doubt she would ace all of her major classes. I had heard that she was like clockwork, and I would have to find out exactly when she intended on graduating. I did not want to walk with her, because the best GPA I could come up with in my concentration was a 3.9572, which would never match hers, as the final grades were never rounded up.

I knew this high academic achievement stuff was highly competitive, but I did not know it was so cutthroat and brutal. Kevin also informed me that there probably were a couple of students keeping an eye on me, but because of his professionalism, he just told me to watch and listen. It would be patently obvious that anybody who casually asked me my GPA would be a contender or a rival worth watching with my left eye twitch.

The law bug had bitten, and at the same time, I was seriously looking at doing a dual masters program with a hotel and law degree, both centered on real estate. As I talked with Craig, we confided our aspirations, which often come out at this point in college life. He was a definite foodie and was going where I had been for the past twenty-five years, before I had reached restaurant flameout, that is. In exchange for hearing his burning academic and career desires, I told him about my desire to go to law school. I like to feel that I pointed him in the right direction because he had the drive and burning in his belly to succeed. I could see the determination in his eyes, just like I saw in my own when I now looked in the mirror every morning.

In our deep-rooted conversations, Craig confided to me that his father was a dean at UH Law, but he did not want anyone to know for personal reasons. But he did tell me he would put a good word in with his dad to get me accepted into the school. I eventually interviewed with the dean and showed him my academic resume, accomplishments, and honors. Lo and behold, he opened another magical door for me. He helped me pick out a perfect evening class to prepare; it was titled Real Property. The dean cut through the academic red tape, and I was registered on a fast-track to law school the next day. After checking in with Barbara at the VA, everything was perfect; to my delight and relief, Mr. Perkins approved the tuition funding.

Much to my surprise, the dean himself was teaching the class. He was just like his son, so we got along great for a couple of weeks, until the university dropped the hammer and intervened by reversing my registration because I had not taken the legal entrance exam (the LSAT), or even the GMAT or GRE tests for graduate school. Oh well, what were a couple more rules to break or bother me? I continued to audit Real Property and, later, Contract Law but did not receive a grade. I reasoned that if I decided to go for the dual masters program, I could easily take the same classes over and ace them for the credit. After all, what hardship is one more graduate degree class if two years ago, you were selling stuffed animals in vacant gas stations; five years ago, you had just lost the family farm; and thirty years ago, you were living in a rock cave and shoveling shit?

My grade point average for my first fall semester of nine classes was 3.90, all A's and one B+. While at HCC, except for algebra, I was shooting for C's, but I was getting B's and A's. It seemed that once I had turned on my study habits and new approaches, I could not lessen the process.

CHAPTER FIFTEEN
Finding a Learning Groove and Study Methods

Studying is not just sticking your nose in a book for a few hours after class or when there is nothing else to do. In my mind, I replaced the word "studying" with "learning," as in methodical steps to achieve my lofty goals. Studying for tests came later. After my freshman spring warm-up semester and with two A classes under my belt in English and political science, along with my summer and fall courses at Cornell, Houston Community College, and the Hilton College at the University of Houston, I was getting into a learning groove and was prepared to take on more academic responsibility. I had developed my own system of learning, my own learning cycle, which was now becoming clearly defined and routine in my mind.

DUE DILIGENCE—CONSULTATIONS WITH THE PROFESSORS

As the fall semester progressed, I placed many calls back to Professor Corgel. Just like at UH, most professors were excited about someone who really wanted to learn in their classes. I had also decided it would be good due diligence, and just plain smart, to try to interview all my upcoming professors before I registered or, at the very least, before the first day of class. Because I was already designated as a CHE, my questions were not those of a traditional student. Aside from asking about the type of tests the professors intended to give, I casually quizzed them on the type of interaction and learning methods they were going to present the class with, and went into fairly deep detail about each one. The university professor meetings took longer, as they were not CHEs like their counterparts at the Hilton. The Hilton professors knew exactly how to quickly respond and where I was going with our discussion. This situation is like a catcher talking casually to the umpire between pitched.

There were of course, a number of professors who were averse to my Socratic techniques and would abruptly wiggle out of my interview. I had one professor in particular who suddenly told me that he did not want me to teach him in his class, period. But I soaked up each class like a sponge. During each semester, I was looking ahead to the next semester and tried to interview possible future professors, get their standardized syllabuses, and evaluate them to see if I should take their courses. I also talked to many students and asked them their opinions of the courses and tests, and I checked in advance whether the end-of-course final was the type that I could learn and score highly on. Today, this can be accomplished by going to Cramster, CourseHero, Enotes, Koofers, and other academic websites.

The time between the end of one semester and the beginning of the next gave me a chance to talk with my upcoming professors without the hectic environment that was soon coming. When I would conference with each professor in advance, it was a get-to-know-you session, with strategic questions interjected into the conversation at various times. As I conducted numerous of these conferences at the university and in my major courses, I got quite confident at performing in the academic environment; I felt natural and relaxed without a clipboard and questionnaire.

The first thing I wanted to know, but didn't actually have to ask, was if they spoke English. I needed to make sure I could understand what they were saying and that they could comprehend what I was saying. This sounds crazy, but it was easy and essential. Other students I observed would blindly book classes based on their convenience and location alone, then learn the hard way later that their professor had just come over for two weeks from a foreign country and could barely speak English. Or, even worse, the lecturer barely spoke English and "taught to the board." In other words, students saw the professor's lips move only a couple times during the semester, because his or her back was always to the class. I needed the interaction.

I was not going to be in a situation where I would have to drop the class and replace it at the last minute. If that happened, I would run the risk of being locked out of the schedule that I needed, because certain classes were only given one semester out of three, so missing one would really wreck the entire year or curriculum. So, if I couldn't understand or hear a professor in the first thirty seconds of the interview, I would simply ask them for a syllabus and quickly leave.

If I could understand and hear the professor, the professor could understand me, and he or she gave reasonable answers to my questions, we were off to a good start. I would explain to the professor that I wanted to take his or her class because, based on the course description, it was something that I really want to learn, even if it was economics, physics, or geology—their class was something that I was truly interested in. I really was interested in every class that I took, and there are some classes I still wish I could've taken, such as more statistics, more economics, logic, foods in space, and others.

In the meeting, I would also convey to the professor why I was attending college and briefly explain what my expectations and goals were and how I felt his or her class could help me achieve my goal of graduation. I never had a professor laugh, scoff, or demean me in any way. In fact, except for a couple, everyone was very supportive of my goals and helpful.

Next, I would ask for a sample current or upcoming syllabus. I never left empty-handed. I would then ask, after looking briefly through the syllabus, if there was anything in particular that I needed to know or that I should read between the lines. For example, besides the stated percentages for grading, there was usually a subjective range of percentages that the professor would give more personal weight toward, or sometimes there was something that wasn't written that the professor was considering putting in the upcoming course syllabus, such as class participation.

If the types of tests were not listed, I would ask what type I could expect. If I really got along in the conversation, I would also ask if I could have a copy of an old test. If the professor said no, I knew he or she probably had tenure, lazy and didn't change the questions from semester to semester.

Finally, if it was far enough in advance, I would ask professor if I could monitor one of his or her classes. That way I could get a foresight of what I could expect. Inevitably, in a session like this, the professor was directly teaching to me. No matter how many students were in the room or auditorium and no matter where I was sitting, when the professor was making a point he would always look at me for acceptance, and therefore, I was learning at my speed. If I checked into the actual class, more often than not, the professor would pick up the same thing and would teach the class at my rate of learning.

I would always end these brief meetings with a firm handshake, looking directly into the professor's eyes and thanking him or her for the time with a smile. Even if I didn't take the class, they knew me well enough that when I was walking down the hall or saw them in the library, each professor would acknowledge me. Of course, I would warmly acknowledge them back. They would generally ask how my studies were going and if I was meeting my goals. I did have a few who would always say they wished I would take their class. I'm sure by the time I reached some professors, my interview, as well as my reputation, had preceded me, and some professors actually acknowledged that fact in advance. I could always tell if the professor really wanted me in his or her particular class or not.

After an interview, I would always write down on a 3"x5" card the highlights of the conversation, because at that point I wouldn't know which classes time, location, and schedule would allow, or force, me to take. If I was backed into a jam at registration time over the phone, I would need to make split-second decisions.

Also, if that class didn't fit into my schedule one semester, it might the next. When the thick course schedule came out on that thin, flimsy paper, I could highlight my courses and match them with my cards and syllabi, even if they were a year old.

At home, I would critique the syllabus contents, inside and out. I also inserted a brief critique of the professor on his or her index card and put it in a file. I gave each professor a grade. This was an interactive learning experience, so I felt each professor should also be graded too. As I was certified as a hospitality educator, I had the insight to grade the professor in what I had learned. Upon taking or monitoring a class, I was knowledgeable enough to give the professor a final grade. Why not? It was my money paying them. Well, not exactly...but it was my time.

ATTENDING CLASS

The first day of class in a new semester was always exciting because I felt like I was already ahead of all the other students in the room. Invariably, the professor would acknowledge me because we already had a good start. The professor would not have to look very far, because I would always be in the front row, just to the left of center because of my hearing and bad eyesight, and to tape the class. Every day I would get to class early so I could secure my seat.

Sitting in the front row had many advantages, and I learned everything much more quickly and easily. The only disadvantage was that I could sometimes hear whispering behind me, asking me where my apple was to give as a teacher's pet. I was also known not as a curve breaker, but a curve wrecker, and I was disliked by some students for that reason. That was rare, however, because when I asked the professor after the first lecture if I could start a study group and for interested students to raise their hands, inevitably, numerous hands went up. We would then meet in a social circle at the end of class where names and phone numbers would be exchanged and we would set a time that everyone could meet. As semester after semester quickly went by, the groups were getting too big to handle, so I had to limit them.

SOME TECHNIQUES IN THE CLASSROOM

I would always ask if I could tape the professors' lectures. Taping the lectures greatly increased my chance of success. I am a very visual, graphic, and interactive person. Maybe this was why I was never any good in online classes, but sometimes that could not be avoided.

In a typical class, I generally had one or two book bags or a large legal briefcase from my time in the legal profession. In this case, it was not just a tool bag but an educational arsenal, including different recording devices to tape the lectures and lots of other portable tools and toys.

I accumulated several audio recorders and wished that I had developed this master plan from the beginning. Depending on permission to tape and for concealment purposes, I had two basic sizes: cassette and mini-cassette. I could keep the cassette on the desk in classes I was allowed to tape, or I would turn it or the mini-cassette on in my legal briefcase in classes I didn't have permission to tape. In Texas it is legal to tape a conversation as long as one party grants permission to be taped; in these cases, that party was me.

But as time and semesters went by, it did get a little out of hand. For example, I would start out using only the minis for a certain college or type of class, such as all university or my major classes in HRM, but something would always get me off my plan, like running out of tapes or batteries, or using two sizes of tapes for the same class. Before it was all over, I had a discombobulated mess of tapes, but I managed to get through each semester educationally unscathed and only humanly frustrated with my own organizational skills.

TAKING NOTES

As a freshman, my note-taking ability was inadequate, but as time progressed, I got better, faster, more abbreviated, and straight to the point. I got to a point where I did not have to rely on my tapes to fill in the blanks and would use the tapes only to go back over the lectures in my car, then again and again as necessary. To master note-taking, I used different colored highlighters for information of different levels of importance in the textbooks. I would use a bright green highlighter if the lecturer would say definitively that a subject would be on one of the tests. If one of the graduate or research students was in class and suddenly made some kind of reaction, pointed at the professor, or gave a thumbs-up at a particular point in the lecture, it meant that that topic was going to be on an upcoming test. I used a standard yellow if I just thought it could be or if I had a hunch that it was going to be on a test, and also for general note-taking. If I missed something, I could always refer back to my tapes to listen to the professor's voice, intonation, and inflection.

Additionally, I used acronyms and abbreviations like other students used Coors and Budweiser...to an excess. In the course of being a student, I calculated that I had about fourteen thousand flashcards in my filing cabinet, all including acronyms, abbreviations, math models, and definitions. Today, this exercise can be completed with iPod apps where the electronic cards can be multi-sorted in a click.

DATA SCAVENGER HUNT

When preparing for upcoming projects, I used the computer labs and printed out everything in sight, based on the keywords that I extracted from my research at home and each syllabus. I would then have a mountain of paper for each class, but I got the majority of everything that I needed off the Internet. During the course of the semester, I would eliminate paper unnecessary to the project while highlighting those pages where I saw something useful. I went to the computer labs because the printer ink was from a laser printer and did not bleed when I highlighted the necessary data. Reinforced by what the professor said, this information made the outline easier when it came time to start on my project, and the final product was easiest. For any loose ends, I would stop by one of the numerous libraries available to every student and, in some cases, especially to me.

At the Conrad Hilton College there is a library that held and still holds almost of all of Conrad Hilton's hotel memorabilia. I knew the archivist Kathleen Baird extremely well, and on many occasions she would let me through the door to the inner sanctum of a private collection of hotel antiquities. Again, another door had opened because I had knocked on it. Some of the items I saw there included Mr. Hilton's first hotel ribbon-cutting scissors, a gold key from the opening of the Hilton in Ankara, Turkey, and an engraved Baccarat Mille Nuits Flutissimo sapphire-cut wineglass. From my expression, one would have thought I was looking at the Holy Grail. My mind wandered back to earlier conversations I had had with Mr. Hilton, decades before, when he was alive and I was very young. I think he would have been proud of where I was now, and how I was standing.

I also had access to libraries at the University of Houston's main campus, architecture and culinary libraries at the Hilton, and the Nestlé Library at Cornell, which has one of biggest collections of hotel books on the planet. I had access to some of the most incredible learning environments in the world at my very fingertips, simply because I asked if I could open the doors.

After I assembled my required and suggested reading books, Internet printouts, library materials, and classroom notes, I would prepare a dynamic outline for each class's upcoming project. Even if the professor did not ask for an outline submission, I usually asked if he or she wouldn't mind looking over mine. I would do this right at or just before the semester midterm break. This way the professor was usually not too busy and was delighted that I was ahead of the typical class. When the professor did look over my project, I would have an insight to a perfectly arranged paper and could forge straight ahead to a good paper.

PART III

SUGGESTIONS & RECOMMENDATIONS

CHAPTER SIXTEEN
Types of Tests—How to Study and How to Take Them

TYPES OF TESTS

There are a dozen or so types of tests, including objective, subjective, comprehension, comprehensive, fill-in-the-blank, true/false, multiple-choice, mix-and-match (A,B,C to 1,2,3) short answers, essay, vocabulary, open-book, and mixed examinations. Some of these are more conducive than others to individual study methods and ways of thinking. Though I am by no means an educational expert on test-taking, it did not take me long to figure out that if I memorized both sides of a stack of flash cards, the vocabulary, fill-in-the-blank, mix-and-match, and short-answer tests—or at least parts of them—would be very easy. Conversely, if I knew that a professor was predisposed to intense essay questions or total course-comprehensive brain stretchers, I would see a red flag and rethink taking that course, unless there was no alternative.

The two types of test I always hated the most were the objective ones (as in algebra) and the ambiguous, subjective ones that were best answered with wishy-washy, qualitative BS. I always got a kick out the instructions on the objectives ones, which always began, "Solve..." as if we needed a push.

The true/false and multiple-choice exams were like high school quizzes on steroids. As in junior high, the general rule was that answers containing "usually," "sometimes," or "generally" are typically correct, while those containing "never," "always," or "every" are typically wrong. In college and beyond, students are expected to gradually elevate from purely regurgitating information to synthesizing it, which really pushes the brain. At this stage, the true/ false questions can have a single or double negative twist.

I dislike multiple-choice questions because the questions often throw out a double or triple twist with the "all"-or-"none" feature. For example, one hypothetical question might be, "In the situation where A = B and B = C but C ≠ A, is this not atypical of a typical situation?" In this case, it's simply a process of logic to think about the negatives, such as two negations canceling a positive, or three negations resulting in two canceling out, therefore leaving a positive. But natural language does not work like this, so we are unused to having to think this way, and it's especially hard under the stress of an exam situation. We can usually handle double negations, but beyond that, the brain reaches its cognitive limits. At least mine did.

Whenever I spoke to anyone who had taken an open-book exam, they always said they hadn't done as well as they had expected to. It seems that when the professor told them at the beginning of the semester that the test would be open book, almost every student had taken that as a signal not to bother studying. Wrong! It was really a signal to prepare fragmented answer outlines, somewhat like boiler plates, that could be mixed and matched to make a cohesive paper. This is how I see newscasters and politicians use sound bites and talking points. No matter how they read the teleprompter, whether upwards, downwards, from the left or the right, the individual sound bites always make sense in any order. So why not in an open-book exam, I reasoned.

In addition, I always used a bundle of pull-tabs on the three open sides of the textbook for important pages and highlighted different passages in different colors, so if I got a brain fart or writer's block in the middle of a sentence or paragraph, I could quickly refer to the appropriate page of the book. To make my look-ups even quicker, I would also thoroughly go over the index of the book before the exam, not during it. After all this preparation, I not only knew what to expect, but the answers would practically jump off of the page at me.

ORGANIZE MATERIALS

My organization phase for test studying actually started before the semester began. When starting to study a course, I would first want to get the big picture of what the class was about, from the course description and the syllabus. Next, I would start creating my flashcards; some would list all the important topics, points, concepts, data, and facts of the subject, while others had all the keywords, acronyms, and abbreviations from the syllabus and from each of the chapters and the glossaries of all the course textbooks.

Then I wrote out an abbreviated course description to reinforce the general theme of all the topics in the chapters of the textbook; the full explanation would come from my notes. Writing about each chapter reinforced my retention percentage. Say, for example, the course was sanitation. I would jot out the description, "Sanitation prevents the dining public from harmful food-borne illness"; it would be something very short, and I would list all the chapter headings in order.

Next, I would write all the keywords in each chapter from my flashcards and also from the keywords in the back of each chapter. Knowing the keywords is more than half the battle. There could be as many as fifteen or more per chapter, so I would arrange them all alphabetically and by association, vertically down the side of the page. This is not a new technique, but one that worked very well for me.

HOW TO STUDY

For actual test studying, I would first assemble my flash cards from the glossary, including the acronyms and abbreviations that I had picked up during the course, and maybe some from other related courses. Flash cards are good in the beginning of studying for a test, to warm up for the mental gymnastics. At this point in the semester, it was just a rehearsal. If there were any cards that I had trouble with or tripped over, I would set them aside, or if I was preparing for a midterm exam, I would set aside the cards on things we had not yet covered. Then I would assemble all my mandatory books, recommended readings, pass-out sheets, class notes, Internet printouts, and any pertinent calculator(s) from all the rooms in our home, under the beds, car, trunk, and backpacks.

Most importantly, I would always prepare a master cheat sheet for tests for each course. Not a little wimpy cheat sheet that would fit in your sock, under your wristwatch, behind your tie, or on the palm of your hand; that was junior-high stuff. This was college, so I would prepare a two-or three-page cheat sheet that would compress all the knowledge of the course into as small a space as possible by using acronyms, abbreviations, and portmanteau. Although there have been many volumes and professorial classes written on classroom testing, I came up with a method that worked for me. I called it my C.H.E.A.T. sheet method (Correct Hand-written Exam Answers every Time), but it would never get me in trouble, as it was just an extremely useful shortcut to memorizing the necessary material, with massive recall.

For example, if the test (again) was on sanitation, I would end up with the word CATS written vertically down the side of the paper as one of my keyword acronyms. The C was for “campylobacter”; the A was for “AIDS,” which could be expanded to “Acquired Immune Deficiency Syndrome”; the T was for “trichinosis”; the S was for “staphylococcus aureus”; and so on. I would continue creating acronyms and abbreviations on the sheets for all the keywords and material in the book, until I had all three sheets full of them. Then, all I had to do was memorize all the words, acronyms, and abbreviations on my cheat sheets, and I would be able to remember all the information associated with them!

That was just the beginning. As soon as I’d finished my complete master C.H.E.A.T. sheet, I would write it out again and again, only each time leaving off the parts that I had locked in, so it would eventually fit on just two sheets instead of three. Then, I would repeat the process again, this time reducing it to one single, compact sheet. I would go over and over everything I'd written, sheet after sheet, until I could quickly process any particular cheat sheet by memory. Now I knew the material in detail and the essential facts were reinforced by the cheat sheet. I was always amazed at how many master cheat sheets I could memorize in a row, especially during test week. It didn't matter to me what type of test it was, or if the professor threw a curve by changing the format; after all, it was his test and he was the master of his domain, but I had his material memorized in every conceivable format I could think of.

I used this method successfully when one of my professors asked me to do him a favor and tutor a girl who was flunking his class very badly, averaging just above 30% with only half the semester to go. If she flunked it, she most likely would be turned down for the graduate program she desired and had her heart set on.

For her to catch up, we had to start all the way back at the beginning of the course. First, I had to teach her how to study. I had her make 300 flash cards of her own and memorize them perfectly. Next, we went over the required reading book and I taught her how to read the chapter names to get the big picture first, then zero in on each chapter's first paragraph, then the chapter quizzes.

Finally, we went over how to make her cheat sheets. This was a foolproof method; just like me, there was absolutely no way that she could get caught using my cheat sheet method. She asked me how this could be; "Where do you hide your cheat sheets?" I told her in my brain, or what was left of it. That's what made my method perfect; it was simply a fast-track to being able to retain and recall the information needed for the tests. Much to the professor's, the girl's, and my delight, she pulled a low B, and eventually graduated with a masters degree.

Once I had made a link and association and locked it down through repetition, I could not forget it even if I tried. It's like a song that gets stuck in your head. When I applied my simple processes, I could expand them to colors, days of the week, or anything I chose. After I started applying A, B, and C as algebraic consonants to apples, bananas, and carrots and X, Y, and Z to x-rays, yellow, and zebras, there was no stopping me in any one of the four maths, because I was converting unclear and ambiguous mirages into concrete pictorial graphics my brain could process and remember.

I would also retain knowledge by mentally linking certain words and ideas to the face of a QWERTY keyboard, a pattern on a numerical ten-key calculator, or a phone keypad that would be readily available within eye-shot during a test. In other words, if I was stuck on a problem, I could pre-link the answer to something before the test—just all basic memorization tricks because after the material was locked in and all the dots were connected, how could I not remember any answer?

When preparing to study for tests, I completed the hardest subjects first and did my favorite subjects last, that way I had something to look forward to and I stayed excited. Sometimes I liked them all, so had a hard time prioritizing them, but some were just extra special or I really liked the professor, like Dr. Barth. By tackling the least-enjoyable subjects first, my mind was fresh and I could concentrate at a very high and methodical level. I would get faster as the study session continued because I was looking forward to getting to my favorite topics. I would be tired, but I could take a nap and fall asleep peacefully, knowing that I had made a good start and had only my preferred subjects left to study.

HOW TO TAKE TESTS

The actual process of taking tests was fairly easy for me, as long as my attitude was positive. For this, I again used Tony Robbins' techniques, which, after much practice, I had developed to an extremely high level. I had successfully reversed the effects of many years of negativism. When I arrived at the Disability Testing Center (DTC), I would first check in all my books and bags and then ask to go directly to a cubicle rather than a central table. The central tables reminded me of a public cafeteria, where different people who did not know each other all sat next to and across from one another, which is somewhat like an English picnic table type food service, in which you end up looking across into the eyes of someone who is also dumfounded and groping for answers. That wasn't for me.

Once I was assigned a cubicle, the student proctor would unclasp the envelope, let me verify it was the correct test, and ask me to sign off on it. Invariably, the proctor would look up at the ceiling corners, notifying me that Big Brother was monitoring me in another room through several cameras. Sometimes, just for the annoyance factor, I would pull all my pockets inside out, pull up my shirt sleeves as if I had ten watches to sell on a street corner, show my socks by pulling up my trouser cuffs, stick out my tongue like Houdini, and pull my cheeks apart with my index fingers. This display proved that I was definitely not cheating. They would never catch me cheating, because my so-called cheat sheet program was always foolproof...it was in my head.

Usually, by the time I finally sat down to take a test, I felt totally prepared and had tried to think of every eventuality. I had meticulously organized my study materials to learn the course and reduce every bit of it to memory in a way I could efficiently recall it in my mind. From my past experience, I had tried to calculate every contingency I could think of. I knew the type of test, how I was going to take it, and what I could most likely expect. The extra effort I put into studying, understanding, and completely memorizing the material, plus my extra effort in being prepared, was absolutely key to my success in getting A's on my exams and thus my success in college.

Getting A's is damn hard work. In the end, you can only rise to the level of the grade you have put in the effort to get and that you really deserve. I worked intensely hard because I wanted a 4.0 and top honors and that is what it took to achieve that level. If that is not your goal or concern, I hope these methods will help you study better and test better and achieve the grade you are striving for. In the end, you will always get the grade you worked for. Not everyone has the goal of graduating summa cum laude, but these studying and testing techniques really worked for me.

After completing my sophomore semester, which was in the fall of 1997, I had eased up on taking all my exams in the DTC because my panic attacks during tests were finally diminishing, as I was either too tired or too busy reading and writing to distraction. Sometimes I had to switch back and forth between the DTC and the classroom because of scheduling difficulties. However, by my last senior semester, I was back to taking all my exams in the DTC. This was because of the insanity and pressure the final examinations generated in me. Whenever I got discouraged, I would remind myself what Dr. Barth had once told me: When he took his Bar exam, he had gotten all the way to question 176 before he finally knew he had gotten one dead right.

So, my personal key to success in studying for and taking a test was four-fold. First, my <u>attitude</u> had to be positive and focused on study. If I had a positive attitude, was organized, and knew the material, taking the test was the easiest part of the semester. Second, I <u>organized</u> the material meticulously. Third, my organization allowed me to <u>learn</u> the material and subject matter inside out. Finally, I could <u>efficiently</u> reproduce my master cheat sheet by memory with 100% accuracy, and got faster and faster each time with my A.O.L.E. system.

"Nothing can stop the man with the right mental attitude from achieving his goal; nothing on earth can help the man with the wrong mental attitude."

Thomas Jefferson

CHAPTER SEVENTEEN
Second Spring Semester, 1998—Conquering a Nemesis

NEW EXPERIENCES

Now that I was in my second spring semester in 1998 my positive attitude was contagious, and by this time I seemed invincible, at least to myself. Unfortunately, it was now or never that I would have to face my nemesis, algebra. To my immense relief, Professor Smith, my algebra professor ended up being very cool and would be the pivotal figure in helping me conquer my fear of my nemesis. One of the first things Professor Smith, who was a clone for Colonel Sanders, did was urge all the students who had just bought the brand-new textbooks to return them and get their money back. He did not feel they were worth the ten thousand dollars total that the students in the auditorium had collectively paid, at fifty-plus bucks a pop. He went on to explain that we didn't even need books for his class and he didn't need a course outline or a syllabus, either. For tests, he would put up all the test questions on the board as the class was coming in. In other words, nobody was going to rip off his tests from last semester, because he didn't even know what they were until the class started.

His philosophy was that algebra had not changed in centuries and anyone could pick it up just as well out of a cheap book as a fancy $50 rip-off so if we really wanted an algebra book that would help us, he said, we should simply go to a dollar bookstore and pick up three or four at fifty cents a piece. He instructed us to work some problems out of each book and then, if we don't like how the author(s) presented them, go on to the second book or the third book until things were explained the way we could understand and the methodology was cemented in our long-term memories. I did exactly what he said, immediately took back my book, went to a dollar bookstore, and spent a whopping $4.50 out of my own pocket.

Professor Smith and I had many lunches together over bologna sandwiches and a beverage, but his was usually an adult beverage in his thermos. It wasn't only that I could identify with my algebra professor during our lunch hour, but I felt like I could talk to him. I told him of my lifelong battle with my nemesis, and he helped remove my fear of the subject. He took the time to peel back the layers of the onion and walk me through algebra in baby steps, from pre-algebra on up. With his help I finally saw a clearer picture; I finally learned and understood the difference in basics: ABCs were constants and XYZs were variables...it was actually so simple! Somehow, I had never quite picked that up while Brother Matzinger was flipping my desk and me over on the floor or while Sister Alma was screaming at the top of her lungs at me in high school and beating me with her thickest ruler. They could have been speaking Swahili or Martian for all I knew, but they sure hadn't been teaching and I had not been learning.

It turned out that my fear of algebra was just the fear itself. Professor Smith removed the fear, and my grade, for my tenth attempt after the eight F's and one D, was an unbelievable and solid A. I still had three more maths to take, but the feeling of getting an A in algebra was liberating, exhilarating, indescribable, and thoroughly and utterly unbelievable. I felt I had beaten a thirty-five-year-old cancer and conquered the world at the same time. At first, I thought that Professor Smith just might have given me the grade, but I went over and over the final test in my mind and again on paper and knew it to be accurate.

BACK TO CORNELL

During spring break, Professor Corgel got me caught up on our video course for the first half of the semester in the spring of 1998. He answered the many questions I had and then laid out the second half of the course, which was the harder of the two because of the class project. During my eight days at Cornell, I worked on finance programs and models about twenty hours a day and arrived at the answers to the problems he gave me sometimes at four, five, or six o'clock in the morning. I did not care how little sleep I got; I knew that I was not going back empty-handed or not having completed every challenging assignment he gave me.

I was transfixed by crunching problems and learning everything set out by the professor. There was still snow on the ground, so I ended up having a lot of food delivered to me. I ate a lot of cold pizza and drank a lot of warm, flat beer, unlike my peers who were partying semi-naked on a Mexican beach or running around completely nude at Hippy Hollow Park in Austin, Texas, with hot babes and cold beer.

Although spring break was about halfway through the semester, I still did not have a clue what the undergraduate or graduate group project was about. I was glad I was there in person and one-on-one with its author, who gave me a personal road map to the class project by having me work on problems from several recommended textbooks he just happened to have stacked on his numerous book shelves.

Professor Corgel's classes in the second half of the semester were difficult enough, but the class project ended up consuming almost as much time as the course and all of the other courses I was taking at the University of Houston, the Hilton, HCC, and Cornell combined. It incorporated several financial "black boxes" from highly reputable hotel investment and Wall Street consulting firms such as Green Street Advisors and BT Alex Brown.

The project was real-world stuff, the kind that was highly practical and very expensive if completed by a consulting firm. The guidelines were very stringent: Each group was to arrive at a dollar figure as a solution to the problem, outlined in a maximum of five pages, following specific parameters for font, characters per inch, line spacing, header and footer designations, etc. Because I was based in Houston and all the other students were at Cornell full time, I was alone in a select group of one.

The crux of the class project was that we had to arrive at the price that the LaSalle Hotel Properties (stock ticker LHO) stock's initial public offering would "settle" at thirty days after it went public. I called a broker and received a packet of information; the data included in it could have choked both me and a horse. After spending spring break with the professor, however, I had learned how to extrapolate the golden nuggets of data within it. But this period also marked the beginning and return of numerous panic attacks as I looked at the impossible hurdles before me. At night I would wake up in a cold sweat, feeling the adrenalin of a combat situation mixed with the fear that I would not complete my academic mission. Sometimes I would wake up thirty minutes after I went to bed and was so worried I would get up and start working on one of the enigmas within the global context of the analysis.

Finally, when back in Houston, I turned in the project by sending it FedEx for the tracking, but I also sent in, with permission, electronic copies in Microsoft® Word and Adobe® Acrobat PDF formats. I was sensitive about sending the project as an email attachment because in this delivery method was not specified the syllabus and it's not a good idea to piss off the professor just before he analyzes your project under a beady microscope.

After I sent the hard copy of my project to the professor, he in turn sent me the last VHS tape of the class. Subsequently, I crammed and audio recorded it and sent it back to him. Not long afterwards, he sent the final test directly to our testing center at the University of Houston; now I had nineteen hours worth of exams to take, but studying for the finals would keep me busy while my mind wrecked itself in worrying how I had made out on the project.

A HARD-EARNED BUT VERY SWEET SURPRISE

Much to my surprise, when the student proctor and I signed off on the FedEx package containing my final examinations from Cornell, I opened it to find out that my project was also enclosed, I presumed with a grade. I was shaking like crazy, because I hadn't expected it and I could see heavily pressed red writing on the inside, right through the front cover. I could not turn the page because I knew that at that moment I was holding my entire scholastic future in my hands. If I had bombed the project, there was no use in taking the test or even thinking about transferring to Cornell. The student-proctor interrupted my immediate thoughts by noting the time for my test, then glancing at the Big Brother camera overhead as he left my cubicle, wishing me good luck on the way out.

I carefully pried open the first page of the project, even though I knew I was taking valuable time away from the test, which was just underneath my project. I couldn't slow the rapid pounding in my chest. If I did not look at the project, I could not concentrate on the test; my mind was racing between the project, the exam, and the big decision at hand. If I took the test without knowing the results of the project, I would certainly blow the test, but I could also not afford to lose too much test time. I was in a mess. However, I was powerless to resist the lure of the project. It would only take a minute to look and find out, one way or the other. I could examine it more closely later.

The first thing I noticed was that it had plenty of red ink all over the inside cover and looked covered in bright-red nosebleed splotches in the abstract. My vision started tunneling, and I gasped. I staggered from the cubicle and quickly asked for a timeout. I immediately got on the floor with the project in hand and did some breathing exercises to temporarily stop the clock. My tunnel vision struck the bottom of the page, where a very large letter was encircled. It was an A. I flopped onto the floor, flailing around like a fish just out of water. Above the A was a note, which said,

"This is an excellent report, the best in the class!"

There was also a separate note attached, which stated:

Claude,

Well, this was quite an experience! The projects you did were <u>excellent</u>... I come away from this with a great deal of respect for your work ethic and general abilities to perform. Stay in touch,

Jack

The LaSalle Hotel Corporation's stock came out at $11.00 per share, like most initial public offerings did at that time. But, just like the spinning Wall Street wheel of fortune round and round it goes, where it stops, nobody knows. It is easy enough to just guess a number, but when we calculated each regression run and arithmetical model and cracked each black box (or not), it would spin the calculation off into mathematical cyberspace. After all of the thousands of calculations and iterations I performed, I had projected that a share of LHO stock would settle in at $16.58. I was told later that the other students groups (of two, three, and four) had turned in projects with amounts from a positive $240 to even an impossible negative dollar figure of $80 dollars per share. The numbers could not be bent, because they were finite. It was kind of like a juggler balancing an array of fruit—if the fruits were not precisely in sync, they would all fall down. My projected number (16 7/8) was extremely close, and on exactly the thirtieth day after the initial public offering, LHO's stock opened at $16.62 per share!

I was still on my back on the floor of the testing center, now feigning a panic attack to buy myself time to get over the shock that I was reeling from. This particular attack was really panic's psychological sister, euphoria. I think I was levitating for about a half hour as I dizzily fought to hold on to a chair to get up, wash my face, crack my knuckles, collect myself, and continue with my test. Even then, instead of starting the test immediately, I reread the analysis at least two more times, then reread the notes a couple more times just to make sure I had every word in permanent ROM memory.

After I had completed my last final, I kind of floated from the DTC to my car and sped home to have Gloria read the notes on the project herself. I then immediately called the registrar's office at Cornell to check on the possibility and the timing of my going full-time and graduating from there. I knew that new freshman had already received their acceptance or declination letters a lot earlier and didn't know if I was past the deadline. I found out that I would be classified as a transfer student inserted into a junior year, as I had already taken at least one class "in residence." Because I had already successfully completed two (fantastic) classes, it would be a smooth academic transition.

On the following Monday, I was waiting at Barbara Kinseth's office at the Veterans Administration before she even arrived. The one question I had was whether the Veterans Administration would allow me to transfer to Cornell and also pay for it? A week or so later, Barbara informed me that Mr. Perkins's committee had approved it. After many meetings with Barbara and several with Mr. Perkins, I eventually ascertained that his committee was as fictitious as my Board of Directors.

Everybody I knew who was a success in the industry had either gone to or taught at Cornell. There were Borsenik, Chernish, Ignatiev, Springer, Rappole, and Corgel on the hotel side and several foodies on the restaurant side. While I was at Cornell, I could see myself graduating from there, but I had felt the same way when I had been at the Hilton.

In this whole academic quest I had embarked upon, I had five major decisions to make. The first two had meant huge transitions in my life. First, there had been the decision on whether to go to college, followed by whether to study the restaurant or hotel curriculum. The former was definitely harder than the latter, but the latter was the fork in the road that would shape my final destiny. At my age I could not flip-flop around, losing more time and more money.

Decision number three, which college to graduate from, now consumed my every thought. It was like a toothache I couldn't get rid of, until I made the final decision to go to the dentist. I devised a couple of different scenarios to help me decide.

Option A:
If I went full-time at Cornell, there were several advantages: I would only have to rack up a total of 120 hours; I would not have to take algebra, and the VA would pay all my academic expenses. However, I would have to spend an extra year there, would have to commute from Houston, and the VA would not pay for my room and board. That meant that the three disadvantages canceled out the three advantages.

Option B:
If I graduated from the Hilton, I would have to fulfill 132 hours, take algebra and three other math classes, and face some envious professors who would drop my GPA like a Chevy truck. So I had three negatives for the Hilton, and fewer obvious positives. Now I was getting somewhere. It looked like I would be a runaway to Cornell...I thought.

Before I could pack my bags, however, I took a long guilt trip. If I went to Cornell, I would let down all the Hilton professors who had opened doors for me and helped me, which far outnumber the Cornell ones. I would especially be letting down George Nolan, who had originally gotten me enrolled and started back to school to begin with. I would also not be starting a family tradition like I so desperately wanted to. So now I was back to indecision. I couldn't sleep that night for worrying.

When morning came, I flipped one of my casino chips. I looked at the result, then said to myself I'd flip it three times and take best two out of three. Then it became three out of five...I knew that wasn't going to work either. Damn, damn, damn, damn, damn.

Then I thought of Conrad Hilton. What would he think if I told him I was going to graduate from Cornell, after all his kind mentoring and his financing of the Hilton College? Yes, I had made him a promise, but not a vow. No, actually I had just made a declaration to him. But this was not his life; it was mine.

The biggest consideration for both colleges was that for me they were *FREE.* Can you imagine having a free college education at any age at two prime colleges and even being paid to go, and still not being able to decide? I knew, dollar for dollar, the Hilton was a much better "bang" for the government's buck, but I also knew the professors there had much more operational and industry experience. Their operational experience was tied directly to the theoretical models that would shape our transition into industry. Additionally, every Hilton professor and lecturer is a Certified Hospitality Educator, but no one at Cornell is, to my knowledge. And at the Hilton I was able to secure more field trips and internships, almost in every class if I wanted. I had tried through Cornell to get an internship or an entry-level position on Wall Street, but the only jobs that were hiring persons my age were for janitors sweeping up the floors at the end of the trading day. Like General George S. Patton, I have never been one to fight for the same real estate twice, so I was unwilling to digress thirty years to my Union Carbide midnight janitorial shifts. I further knew that Cornell was a little more spit-shined and formal and there I would always be pushing the wheel uphill, whereas at the Hilton, if I wanted, I could be a BMOC.*

In the end conscience played an integral part but it was the nexus between the operations, which I worked around for years and the research path I would take after graduation, made the difference – for me it was a perfect fit at the Hilton. The dream of going to Cornell, which eventually became a realistic goal, had carried me through many challenges for many decades. In the end, however, I further decided it was only right to finish what I had started and where I had started. I would dance with and take home the girl I had brought to the prom. I was proud of my accomplishments at both colleges, but I would proudly graduate from the Conrad N. Hilton College of Hotel and Restaurant Management at the University of Houston with no reservations or misgivings.

That second spring semester, I had taken five classes, for a total of 13 hours, and gotten two A's, two A–'s and an S, for a 3.83 GPA, plus the three credit hours from Cornell and three more from HCC. I had also finally made my decision on where I was going to graduate, and life in the fast lane was getting better, and for those that can remember the Rolaids commercial, relief is spelled R-E-L-I-E-F!

* BMOC—Big Man on Campus, is a Roaring 1920's term.

CHAPTER EIGHTEEN

Second Summer Semester, 1998—Hitting Overload

MY SECOND SUMMER SESSION BEGINS

My second summer semester began in 1998, and I was slated to start calculus, a short, fast, and dirty summer-school class. It was bad enough that the class was accelerated down to five and a half weeks, but then, the air conditioning in the building went out. The building had been designed with sealed windows that could not open, so the whole building had to be sealed and the class was delayed almost a week and a half getting started. This meant that half the class would drop out because of too much stress and the pressure of a now even shorter period of time to complete the class. I was too stubborn to drop and persisted in taking the course. Again, I hired a tutor, went to the math labs when they were open, promptly sought out my professor for assistance, and was in a couple of study groups.

At home I would often stand in the shower and do calculus on one fogged-up piece of glass and algebra on the other. My calculus professor had advised me that I still had not made a sufficient link between algebra and calculus and I should monitor his algebra class for the remainder of the semester. That would make the eleventh time I had taken algebra and still would not be the last time I would take it, for credit or not.

In general conversation, I had previously told Gloria about regular downturns in the hotel business cycle, which, over the past century, had become highly predictable, and what was probably going to happen in the near future of the industry. These downturn cycles typically lasted from a couple to several monthly quarterly periods, were usually accompanied by a hiring freeze, and were approximately five to seven years apart. Since the last downturn in 1992, seven years had already passed, so we were overdue for another hotel slump. I needed to finish even faster than I was going, graduate, and find a job.

I thought back to another economic downturn, and an encounter that had really opened my eyes, while Gloria and I had been in New Orleans for a long weekend during the regional oil depression in the 1980s. After chatting with a waitress in a nice second-story café for a little while, we had found out that she was working on her PhD at Tulane. She had then told us that, in fact, almost of all the servers in that café were working on either their second masters or their doctorates, as there were no jobs, only student loans to live off and repay. Remembering this, I decided I would quickly see about signing up for even more classes before the next recession.

Envisioning the next recession, I told Gloria I felt I would have to complete more classes in less time. I studied so hard and took so many classes that it had only been a full year between my freshman and senior "years." I had had only one semester as a sophomore, and because I had gone from freshman to senior in twelve months, I had completed my junior term in two semesters, and one of those was a short summer semester. It was Gloria who discovered this fact during my senior year, when she saw an updated transcript, which I needed for the plethora of scholarships that I was applying for.

She noticed it because she was helping me keep track of everything and she was always trying to push me for various reasons. It was mostly because of the fact that she had tutored me since Algebra 1, almost forty years before, so she felt she had "dibs" on me and my education, but also because she was now the one "bringing home the bacon." In high school that had not been the issue, but now, like all wives, she wanted a bigger paycheck, for the home front and our children, and sooner rather than later.

Gloria then went so far as to register me for an online course at Wharton College. After that, a serious argument ensued, and my battle plan, ahem…our battle plan…had serious holes shot in it. I was absorbing information faster than in all my other fifty years combined. I was almost putting more into my brain than I could biologically comprehend. I told Gloria to get her money back from Wharton, and then I told her, "We do this together and by choice, my choice...but I won't be badgered into learning like the sisters and priests back then. My time is fully devoted and maxed out! I've got full professors, associate professors, assistant professors, full professors in Houston, a professor in New York at Cornell University, and several at the University of Houston and others at the Hilton College that I am now beholden to. If they ask me to do a favor, I cannot refuse them because of a lack of time!"

Intellectually, I was absorbing so much information, I literally thought my brain was going to explode. But I did get to cross one goal off my long list of goals to accomplish: conquering time management. It's amazing, but when I had started doing Tony Robbins' activities before school and made out my "bucket list," I only had about seventy or so goals, but when I graduated college, I had almost two hundred. It is like Gloria's laundry list for me...after thirty-plus years of working on it, I've come to the realization that I will never get caught up, as the list keeps growing. I told her that she is going to put me in an early grave and she will outlive me by so many years she will forget whose name was on top of that list.

That second summer semester, I took five classes, for a total of 15 hours, and got three A's, one B, and one B+, for a 3.66 GPA, my lowest scored semester.

CHAPTER NINETEEN
Chains of Command

Here is a breakdown of the college administrative and teaching chain of command and its Marine Corps and Army equivalence to give an idea of how each is set up. I am including this as a primer because it really is a good idea to understand the hierarchy and therefore the politics involved in the university system. This will hopefully help you to understand a little better what really motivates faculty members of any level and how to better approach them and interact with them.

Remember, developing mutually beneficial and pleasant relationships with your professors can be a very important part of having a successful, complete, and rewarding college experience. These people are there to teach you and usually always willing to help someone who really wants to learn. They can be of invaluable assistance to you.

Academic versus Marine & Army Military Equivalence

University Chancellor	General
Vice Chancellor	Lieutenant General
President/Provost	Major General
Dean	Brigadier General
Associate Dean	Colonel
Department Head	Lieutenant Colonel
Professor	Major
Associate Professor	Captain
Assistant Professor	First Lieutenant
Lecturer	Second Lieutenant

At the Hilton College we had only one dean, while at Cornell, we had a dean and a couple of associate deans. The dean has the ultimate administrative responsibilities for approving faculty hiring, setting academic policies, overseeing the budget, raising funds, and carrying out other duties for the college. Such a dean is usually a tenured professor from one of the departments but gives up most teaching and research activities upon assuming the deanship.

The Dean (Brigadier General)
Leaps tall buildings in a single bound.
Is more powerful than a locomotive.
Is faster than a speeding bullet.
Walks on water; Gives policy to God
Anonymous

I knew every one of the four consecutive deans who were in charge of the Hilton College from its inception until I enrolled, but I knew the founding dean, James D. "Jim" Taylor the best, because I knew him before the college was even founded. He was an excellent fund raiser who personally energized the Houston Restaurant Association, the Hotel & Motel Association, and the women's auxiliaries of each to support the new college. During high school I had been president of the junior branch, where we would wash cars and sell cookies that the women's auxiliary would bake for people and groups, to donate to our promised school and its upcoming scholarships. In effect we were just hotel and restaurant brats.

I also knew Dean Taylor as a personal friend when I was president of the Houston Restaurant Association. Jim Taylor and I had a good personal relationship, where I would ask him to come speak to our association meetings and he would ask me in turn to come speak to one of his college classes about life in the food and beverage trenches. The dean was a wine connoisseur par excellence and hosted the Fred Parks Wine Cellar, a highly prized donation to the college.

He would always get very excited when I would come to speak to one of the classes, and at the luncheon afterward, he would always have his chef prepare a memorable meal, from the amuse-bouche to the after-dinner Grand-Fine Champagne Armagnac. All the while, he would have breathing a 1959 bottle of

Department Head (Lieutenant Colonel)
Leaps short buildings with a single bound.
Is more powerful than a switch engine.
Is just as fast as a speeding bullet.
Takes a few steps on water.
Talks with God.
Anonymous

Dean James Taylor, patted by Gloria at the Shamrock Hilton, January 1979.

Château Lascombes Margaux, which was a magnificent vintage year for Bordeaux. But, like all business-like deans, he was always trying to draft me into his school. Looking back, I remember he had always told me that when I did go to college, I would set the school on fire. It would be almost twenty years before his prediction would come true.

At the University of Houston, I had two classes with department heads. One was Professor Sloan, a tenured professor who had been assigned in various positions at five presidential libraries for political science. The other was Professor Jaynes, who could spot or feel anyone cheating through the back of his head—in any higher math course anywhere in the university. I would bother Professor Sloan over numerous vegetarian sandwiches and would sit at his feet and argue like hell about politics. In class, he would pick a fight with me in front of an auditorium full of twenty-year-olds. He put a magical and highly humorous spin on politics, which guaranteed his students could not forget anything he lectured on. His lectures were so riveting, I would play his tapes all the way home just to laugh and learn.

Professor (Major)
Leaps short buildings with a running start
and favorable winds.
Is almost as powerful as a switch engine.
Is faster than a speeding BB.
Walks on water in an indoor swimming pool.
Talks with God if a special request is honored.
Anonymous

Student professors, in order of increasing rank, come in three flavors: associate, assistant, and full professor. At the Hilton College, out of about twenty-eight total professors, there were three full professors, seven associates and about as many assistants, with the rest being lecturers. At Cornell, there were about forty total professors: fourteen full professors, fifteen associates, and seven assistants, with the rest being lecturers, adjunct, visiting, and emeritus faculty. Dr. John B. "Jack" Corgel is a full professor, and now the Baker Chair of Real Estate and Finance. He was, and still is, one of the best teachers at both schools.

Associate Professor (Captain)
Barely clears a Quonset hut.
Loses tug-of-war with a locomotive.
Can fire a speeding bullet.
Swims well.
Is occasionally addressed by God.
Anonymous

I personally knew and had classes with several associate professors, some with and some without tenure. I had two semester classes with Associate Professor Ron Nykiel, also the Conrad N. Hilton Chair, and learned more about marketing in one class from him than in my thirty-five years in the trenches.

As I mentioned before, Dr. Stephen Barth was one of my favorites, and he also asked me to proofread his manuscript, which became a staple textbook across the nation for Hospitality Law. *Hospitality Law: Managing Legal Issues in the Hospitality Industry* is now in its third edition. He gave me a double honor after that, by asking me to critically analyze his extremely successful website, HospitalityLawyer.Com, before it went public.

Assistant Professor (First Lieutenant)
Runs into brick walls.
Can get run over with a go-cart.
Is able to fire a really mean pellet gun.
Swims okay with floaties.
Occasionally hears angelic voices.
Anonymous

There were assistant professors at every turn, feverishly writing and submitting papers to various journals so they could be promoted to associate-level professorships and the eventual academic prize of tenure. This group of professors was always fertile ground for requiring papers and projects to be resubmitted for perfection because, unbeknownst to the student, he or she was doing the prep work for a new paper that the professor was writing.

Lecturer (Second Lieutenant)
Makes high marks on the walls
when trying to leap over tall buildings.
Is run over by locomotives.
Can sometimes handle a gun without
inflicting self-injury.
Can tread in two feet of water.
Anonymous

I had three of the greatest lecturers and senior lecturers the Chapter 31 GI Bill could afford: Rodolfo Casparius, Ron Jordon, and James D. Wortman, casino and gaming teacher extraordinaire. When I took my first class from Jim, I thought I might go into the burgeoning lodging and gaming side of the industry, in case the next recession came too fast and I could not find employment. His course was so good, I took another.

Instructor

Climbs walls continually.
Rides the rails.
Plays Russian roulette.
Walks on thin ice.
Prays a lots

Anonymous

At the Hilton College, our informational technology courses were taught by instructors with masters degrees in their field. These were good guys to know for help with your computer and to copy software and get freeware from.

Graduate Student

Runs into buildings.
Recognizes fire trucks two out of three times.
Is not issued ammunition.
Can stay afloat with a life jacket.
Talks to walls.

Anonymous

At the Hilton College, Lydia Westbrook was anything but clumsy. She was the epitome of a graduate student, as she set the bar extremely high for me and others to follow and would later be awarded for her achievements. She and I would be in a very fierce competition for the high GPA honor—although when I chatted with her after we graduated, I learned I was the only one aware of our competition.

Undergraduate Student
(Claude's First Semester)
Falls over the doorstep when trying
to enter buildings.
Says, "Look at the choo-choo!"
Wets himself with a water pistol.
Plays in mud puddles. Mumbles to himself.
Anonymous

Besides all the aforementioned assistance, with teams of people to help one in any situation, there were the professor's assistants, which included: administrative assistants (full-time employees), technical assistants, graduate assistants, and research assistants. With all this help available, all I had to do was come up with a question, and I always had at least one person to answer it. If I asked a question and didn't get the answer I was looking for, or wanted a deeper insight, as with the fifty-cent algebra books, I would ask someone else until I was satisfied. But like a true follower of Socrates, I still always had one more question.

This type of Socratic questioning is another shtick that I most likely developed mixing over an estimated million-plus drink in my life. As I never really told a good joke, I always asked questions, especially to the inebriates who were there to mumble over some type of problem, of which everybody has at least a few!

CHAPTER TWENTY
Networking and Self-Help Techniques

NETWORKING

While tending bar, I would average mixing almost a thousand drinks a day, with about three hundred at lunch and about seven hundred at dinner. I could naturally work several conversations at one time on a long bar, some of them lasting for days, like a good chess match. Some guys would come back four or five days in a row and wait for my rush hour to subside, just to tell me about how their days had gone, thus actually cheating their wives out of good conversation. That part was kind of weird.

I once had a double post-doctorate petroleum engineer from the Shell Research Laboratory, which was just down the street, come back thirty days in a row before he noticed that I never had a day off (neither did he from drinking). We talked incessantly about the molecular structure of futuristic gas additives and other such topics. Eventually, by golly, together we solved a problem that had been racking his brain since his first doctorate class, all over three great double Stolichnaya vodkas straight up, and a couple bucks' tip every day, to boot.

Networking such as this is important. Ask questions, and really talk to your professors and peers about your subjects and the topics you are interested in; you will be amazed at how rewarding it is. A little schmoozing never hurt anyone, either. You might be surprised how valuable networking can be, how much it can help you, and how many doors it can open for you.

Of all the professors I had, the majority were overwhelmingly helpful, and I just couldn't believe how they would give me every chance available, if I just asked. Most of them were younger than me, some were my age, a couple were older, and one was even over seventy, which made me feel really young. The dedication that I saw in every facet that they taught at the Hilton, whether in hospitality law, controls, management, sanitation, or others, was outstanding. They were all willing to impart their particular knowledge into every student.

Each college had its own area of expertise, but the one lacking at the Hilton College was hotel and restaurant real estate finance. That is one reason why I went to Cornell—in addition to completing my personal goal and gaining the prestige, honor, and self-fulfillment that still fills me today. I pride myself in the knowledge that I could have gone to and graduated from any college that I so chose. Words cannot convey the indebtedness that I feel to both colleges and universities for all the assistance they continually gave me.

In most schools at any university or college, all the professors' offices are clustered together next to one another, in a kind of professor's row. In my freshman year I was hesitant to walk there, or to stop and chat with various professors or draw any attention to myself, mostly because I felt awkward and undereducated compared to them, who were mostly younger and highly educated. But as time went on, the professors accepted me as I accepted myself. It was a different, evolving feeling because I finally felt like I belonged.

In addition to the benefit of the doubt, the professors gave me up-to-date, useful information. No one gave me the answers to tests, and no one gave me a grade I didn't earn, but they gave me an edge and a chance to do extra credit or asked me to tutor other students failing their classes.

As more time went by, I believe, I was seen as someone mature and trustworthy, so some professors would even confide in me their outside-of-academia plans to cash-in on some idea they had or open their own restaurant, start their own online business, or promote a seminar. One even wanted me to go into a restaurant business with him. Along the way, the professors gave me support, as well. A few would openly thank me in front of their classes for my support.

One confidentially asked me how I had managed to pass the CHE's rigid curriculum the first time around when I had been only a freshman and had never taught. It was obvious he had not passed it, so I told him, as best I could without putting him down, that others had chosen really dry subjects, like profit-and-loss accounting statements or cash-flow analyses. I thought, *How boring can you get to nineteen-year-old college students?* I then told the professor that although I was going to the hotel side of the degree program, my class instruction for my CHE had been on flame cooking, more on the restaurant operation end of the industry. What junior college student could resist the flare of flames dancing over a tableside guéridon?

SELF-HELP TECHNIQUES

During my time as an adult student, I had to use every advantage possible. I was very resourceful with little bandages on big hemorrhages and big tourniquets on bigger problems. Some of the tools that I pulled out of my bag of experience were the elements of time management, public speaking, reading, and name and number recognition. I enhanced these with up-to-date and modern innovations to give me an edge over my peers. It was not only a way to keep up with them but to surpass them.

To pick up speed in areas that I was weak in, I came up with my own inexpensive techniques. For example, I knew that I would be taking a hospitality accounting class where I would be adding up hundreds of columns of numbers and would need to keep up with kids thirty years younger. I would need a cutting edge but a bleeding edge. A snail was faster at adding numbers than I was, so I decided to adapt a system I had used years earlier on a ten-key calculator, when they were not connected and driven by electricity. Those were the days when you pulled on a handle for the addition function to work. To practice back then, I had learned a trick from the old-time accountants and started by adding up the numbers in a telephone book. So, as a cheap, burgeoning, and financially struggling freshman, I combined that old-school, free system with updated technology. I used a local phone book and an old electronic "ten-key" calculator to add up the columns of the first three numbers in each phone number down the whole page and write the total on the bottom, then re-add it to see if I had come up with the same total. For example, each phone book in Houston at the time had the same area code, so the numbers would appear like:

523-7840
621-0133

So, I would add up 523, and 621 for a total of 1,144. If I added up that complete column again and again, I would get faster and faster. Then, after mastering the three-digit numbers, I graduated to the four-digit numbers: 7840 plus 0133 totaled 7,973. Then I would learn to add up the combined columns of all seven as fast as I could, always arriving at the same total.

A semester later, I purchased an electronic typing course called Mavis Beacon® Typing Tutor, and it helped me tremendously. I highly recommend investing in it. I did not realize how much my fingers had aged. I had arthritis where I had broken all the joints on both my hands when I was a tank loader. When our tank had been in firefights, ambushed, or in major operations, as a loader, I would swing a three-foot 90-mm round from its secured cradle and slam it into the breech. Everyone would be screaming, and I would be intermittently kicked by the tank commander, who was yelling orders; we were all visibly shaken and were mostly just excited teenagers trying to act tough, and save our own asses. I had to maneuver the round while the tank was braking, jumping around, and suddenly accelerating and while the turret was reversing directions, while the gunner was elevating and de-elevating that big-ass gun in an extremely hot, claustrophobic closet. At the same time, I was half bent over. If I was loading a beehive round with darts, I would have to set the range on an egg beater-type fuse with one hand while covering the shell butt with the other so as not to let the round hit the primer and explode. In the meantime, I would be trying not to bang the other end of the canister into any other piece of metal to thereby detonate the round.

In tank school, we had learned that if the round did go off, there would not be any Purple Hearts awarded or general or special court martials doled out, because there would not be enough of a body to process. As a result of trying to stab that cylinder into the big gun, our knuckles were constantly sacrificed. There were plenty of metal objects to rake a finger knuckle off, one at a time or all at once. On more than one occasion, my skin was peeled back, leaving the bone and cartilage exposed, with no time for a Corpsman's attention. Knuckles were primary casualties while wrists, elbows and shoulders were secondary, and damage usually resulted in only bruises or cuts. Because of my height, however, I took several lumps on my head as well.

To help my hands more in college, after I bought the Typing Tutor electronic course, I bought a couple different types of ergonomic keyboards to help me with the burning pain in my fingers and wrists. Because I lifted weights, my lats under my arms were too wide, which made my arms at an angle, so using traditional QWERTY keyboard was a painful exercise. But just like in a speed-reading course, over time, I would take the intermittent typing tests which proved that I was gaining ground. I would never be Mavis Beacon, but as long as I typed faster than my peers, I would be ahead of the game I knew (but they didn't) we were playing.

When I consistently scored at the equivalent of more than 100 words per minute on the ten-key, I stopped taking tests, because I knew I could pass my peers, as my fingers were actually flying over the ten-key and the calculator keys on the keyboard. Eventually, I would adjust the decimal-place slider on the ten-key to simulate the telephone book and other short mental gymnastic exercises. For example, I would take the last two entries per page, as I turned fifty sequential pages, until I arrived at the same total. These exercises especially helped in the accounting course in the practice of coding invoices in real-world applications.

The typing software was so helpful that I decided to double-down and go for a speed-reading course. I think I read a slower number of words than I typed; it was dismal. I could tell that I was extremely slow compared to other freshman students and that reading was definitely on the top of my long list of much-needed improvements. The first thing I did when our credit card was reinstated for the umpteenth time was order the Evelyn Woods Reading Dynamics speed-reading course. I almost cried when I took the beginning test to see where I would start. But as time went on, I gradually went from fast to faster to fastest and wound up at a pretty respectable 600-plus words a minute. It wasn't long before my peers would see my index finger methodically traverse one textbook page after another, almost at rapid-fire speed, with over 95% retention and recall of material.

With Typing Tutor, I continually tested myself, with Gloria watching to keep me honest. She would post my scores on a white board under three title headings: Ten Key, Typing, and Reading. Over time, I consistently improved each one to its max, and myself along with it.

In my professional career as a restaurateur, I had taken a Dale Carnegie public-speaking course to improve my confidence in the dining room and because I had volunteered for various different civic and industry associations where I needed to speak. That Dale Carnegie course two decades earlier had cost me, I think, about a thousand dollars. Now I was a student and could not even afford a refresher course. Instead, I located a Toastmasters public-speaking course for students on campus for about $35 per semester. In short order, I was being positioned on a fast track to be nominated as the president of the Toastmasters club, as I had been in my Dale Carnegie class. Because of my height, maturity, and my first couple of speeches, I looked like a natural leader and speaker to all of them, while inside I felt less than my stage in life. Most of the speakers were on the eighth and ninth levels of the ten-step program, while my pipes were all rusty. These were the type of student speakers who would go to the adult Toastmasters speaking tournaments and win. What they lacked were the leadership and organizational skills that were two of my three main advantages, the third being my efficiency.

The Toastmasters program was great and, of course, nonaccredited, but it definitely helped with my confidence because of all the encouragement from students less than half my age. This was reciprocal, because when I gave a certain student a standing ovation for a good two-minute speech at a weekly session, he or she gained just as much confidence. In that I was expressing more confident exuberance, I was becoming accepted and known by numerous students in several other university colleges. Now when I walked through the campuses, I would often receive a Tom Cruise *Top Gun* thumbs-up and a military-type salute, a nod, a victory sign, a wink, a double thumbs-up, or a UH Cougar hand sign, all with a smile. No more one-finger salutes.

My mortal enemy was now my perception of time: the time left until I graduated and the compression of time for studying numerous projects within a semester. If I could've taken a time-management course, I would've done so in a New York minute...pun intended. But I couldn't, so I had to develop my own personal course and path. Because classes took up the majority of non-sleep time, I started analyzing there. My college courses were generally scheduled on Monday and Wednesday or Tuesday and Thursday, with class hours doubled up on Fridays, and some intermittent night classes at the community college. On the weekends, most students do what they do best at their age—drink beer and run semi-naked on the beach.

For someone like me, there was no time to waste. When I had Saturday and Sunday off, I studied thirty-three hours and took one hour for church. When there were three days—Friday, Saturday, and Sunday—I would hit the books for fifty-one hours, about seventeen per day. On four-day holiday weekends, I could give it a straight sixty-eight hours, and on longer holidays like Thanksgiving, I could finish up the semester early. There would be no break for me until I finished.

To help with my rusty memory, I balanced the veterans hospital medications and supplemented them with gingko biloba and massive doses of various vitamins and minerals. Beverages included coffee in the morning and 100 ounces of water for the rest of the day. The evening consisted of more power studies and many trips to the restroom.

TUTORS

Tutors basically come in two flavors: paid and free on-campus tutors. Like self-helps, paid tutors are optional and can get expensive, but they are available at odd hours and on weekends, and can make house calls. I used on-campus free tutors in the math and English labs, but the disadvantage with them, besides the limited hours, was that I would never get the same one twice, so in effect, I would be starting all over again each time I went to a lab, because they didn't know me.

A personal paid tutor knows exactly what your strengths and weaknesses are and where to pick up in each session. Mine also asked what I had learned from my class or classes since we had last met. Often, these tutors will also have taken courses from the same professor whose class you are in, which has definite advantages. After using several paid tutors, I also knew their strengths and weaknesses. If I had an important paper to write or if I could not figure something out as in a math problem, I always had someone to contact, including a phone session or a house call at odd hours.

Then there is the second type of paid tutors and labs off campus that I thought was a little seedy but was actually recommended by some professors, as I mentioned before. The University of Houston was geographically in the poor side of town, near downtown; really an oasis in the middle of a ghetto. The paid tutors were located in a strip shopping center along with a tattoo parlor and a chop-shop that sold spree wells and really "hot" wheels, probably selected from the 35,000 cars in the parking lots just across the street at UH.

The band of legal test-taking tutors were a shifty bunch but were always on their knees five times a day on their prayer rugs. These guys actually lived in the shopping center and took showers in the gymnasiums on campus. What I liked about this crew, led by a guy named Shugar, was that they were very resourceful and were born hucksters, like me.

I could tell that Shugar thought I was looking at his outfit through a jaundiced eye, and he abruptly told me, "Mister, you look pretty smart. This is a prep class; some professors like us, some don't. For poly-sci, two of the profs even give us their old exams, and for algebra, some tell us where to focus. If you wanna stay, throw your ten bucks in that *shukr* (hat); if not have a great life, God be willing, and please close the door behind you."

Even if they were as religious as they appeared, I still believe they had a dishonest side that they were not going to disclose to me. I always thought they thought I was some kind of spy from the provost's office on campus, so when I came into their store they were always on their best behavior, dripping with honey, kind of like Eddy Haskell on *Leave It to Beaver*.

One night, when I was going through their file drawers, the investigator mode came out from years before, when I had managed a two-office law firm in Dallas and Houston, where I also had done very private investigative work. I went through drawers that were verboten and I accidentally stumbled on one that had about three or four hundred driver's licenses and student IDs within. Then I knew how they were getting their tests: friends with fake identifications. But over time, I actually did see Shugar talking with different professors in their offices.

In the end, I reasoned these guys were just like the Princeton-type reviews, only cheaper and specialized on the fringe of honesty. In the beginning, whenever I took a class or went over previous tests that they had obtained, I always looked at who was at the door and imagined the university provost coming in and taking names with the university police. The environment just felt clammy. But remembering my Russian tutor and these gypsies, and all the nationalities and diversity I saw tutoring in the on-campus labs, it appeared that the foreign students were far ahead of us here in America.

The first line of offense in crunching information is using anyone who can help you master certain knowledge, whether paid or unpaid, and that means first the professors who are already paid and their assistants. After that, I never forgot about past teachers who were always readily available and would always assist if it was in their domain of knowledge, if you had made a good grade, had good rapport with them, and had stood out in their class.

STUDY GROUPS

After tutors, professors past and present and their assistants, like TAs, RAs and GAs, who are never around when you need them but always show up around the end of the semester, there are the students themselves. Study groups are great and a way that a small group of people can crunch a massive amount of material in a minimum amount of time, especially in situations where you *almost* knew what the professor was trying to get across, but you could not quite grasp the concept(s) or connect the dots. I always had at least one study group per class, sometimes two.

After class on the first day, I would get everybody's attention with my drill-instructor voice and raise my hand for my announcement of starting a study group. As the semesters rolled by, people who knew me would cling next to me so as to sign up first. I never minded trying to help a D student, but I tried my best to weed out all the D students just vying for an easy A.

Study groups are also a good way to keep up if you have to miss a class (say, in case the same grandmother dies twice during one semester) and not only get caught up afterward but get tutored by several classmates. In this way, your classmates become more educated on the subject because now they are reinforcing what they have already learned. I never did mind when I was asked to be a leader, but I always turned the chalk or dry marker and the board over to someone else when there was something I did not know.

HOME OFFICE

"There's a world where I can go and tell my secrets to
In my room…"

The Beach Boys

In the fall 1997 semester, our younger son, Travis, was at Texas Tech in Lubbock, Texas, studying finance and bound for law school, and I had taken over his old bedroom as my study space. Every square inch of his old room had an educational purpose that I devoted to accelerated learning. Over time, my sacrosanct home student office became extremely organized and efficient.

While the academic tools and supplies I accumulated were first class, the furnishings had started off bargain-basement. I think I eventually managed to replace everything, with the exception of the desk, which was a ten-foot-long banquet table left over from one restaurant or another. I loved this huge desk and would sit at it in an old dining room chair.

Whenever I had other students over, whether it was to study, tutor, or be tutored, when they first entered the room, they were always blown away and amazed at my scholastic inventory and all my educational toys.

My study walls were adorned with USMC, UH, Hilton, HCC, and Cornell college pennants decals and bumper stickers. I posted all my test results on two new white boards. Next to the white boards was a wall mirror behind a desktop podium where I could practice my public speaking.

The room was laid out with the desk facing a window; my bookshelves and a bed were on one adjacent wall, with a long closet opposite. Behind me as I saw at the desk were a treadmill and recumbent bike; I was constantly trying to keep my weight in check now, as I had pretty much given up my active lifestyle. On the bookshelves were hundreds of neatly rowed and labeled audio- and videotapes, including a jacket of Tony's tapes, and a VHS combo television to play them. Next to the tapes was a handsome library of recently published educational books. The rusty two-door filing cabinet from a restaurant was finally replaced with two new four-drawer models that I easily and quickly filled up with all kinds of tapes, flashcards, and other magical academic tricks.

On Travis's leftover bed were plenty of stacks of papers for each course, with a syllabus on top of each stack. As each semester progressed, I accumulated other reports and projects in various stages of completion. In due course, the space under the bed was filled with finalized reports, kept safely away so they could not be touched by a dirty hand, stepped on, or creased accidentally. They were always marked with a large, gold-looking brass paper clip and handled with kid gloves.

To prepare for the final push each semester, I placed a mass of books for the current semester in neat stacks on the floor in front of a double-wide clothes closet.

At first, there were only two stacks, then five and finally ten. Behind each was a stack of flashcards.

The scholastic equipment on my desk was the fastest and baddest money could buy. I bought the fastest computer possible and had two monitors and three printers: a black-and-white Epson dot matrix, a Hewlett-Packard color ink jet, and a black-and-white Hewlett-Packard laser workhorse. There was also a Xerox copy machine. I had the latest electronic accessories at my fingertips, with various sizes of tape recorders, computer microphones, headphones, phone chargers, a palmtop, and, finally, a land-line phone.

I had every conceivable item for speed, efficiency, and organization, including a dorm refrigerator, microwave, coffee pot, and warmer. I also had a mounted water dispenser and a custom-made multibook book stand. In the closet I had no less than twenty types of expensive paper in different sizes and weights, matching small and large envelopes, and transparencies with and without cardboard borders.

I kept a stock of dry markers, signs, stickies, a telescopic manual pointer, a couple of laser pointers, magnifying glasses, and an electric pencil sharpener. I replaced the typewriter that I had bought twenty-five years earlier and upgraded it to a used 1990-ish IBM Selectric for labels and odd typing projects. I even had a paper cutter.

I truly had a professional office environment, photo shop, duplication center, and a personal academic production center all in one. While I was a freshman, I went to places like Kinko's for my computer needs and to copy the papers I had written in those all-nighters; by my sophomore semester, I had my own personal Kinko's in our home. The only thing that I didn't have in my office was a metered postage machine. But if I could have gotten a Pitney Bowes model on less than a five-year lease, I would have done so.

I also bought several types of software that the VA would not reimburse. These included Photoshop; Crystal Ball—a Monte Carlo simulation program—Microsoft Office Suite, complete with Publisher; and algebra, calculus, finite, and statistical programs such as SAS. And of course, the Mavis Beacon Typing Tutor and Evelyn Woods Reading Dynamics speed-reading course were all purchased with scholarship money, a scholastic discount, or both.

Finally, I had ready-made and custom-made ink stamps with Draft, Confidential, Faxed, E-mailed, Received, and Resubmitted, very boldly formed, with a line underneath where I could date and initial it, and a supply of red ink pads. When

I turned in a paper it looked very organized and ultra-professional. I resubmitted papers regularly. Whenever I had a paper returned to me with a note on it telling me the shortcomings or where I could make an improvement, regardless of the grade, I would always ask permission to resubmit it. For example, if it was a midterm project, I would always redo the paper, make the improvements, and get it back to the professor. Whenever I would ask a professor if I could redo a paper, I would ask if they would mind taking their valuable time to look it over, but I would never ask for a re-grade.

A couple of professors would ask me if I was trying to improve my grade when I did this. I would generally respond no, that I was trying to improve my knowledge with a perfect paper. I did this even if I made an A or if the semester was over. I always asked them to do it at their own convenience, even in the next semester. In that case, I would always give them a self-addressed stamped envelope to return it to me. I would appreciate their valuable time if they did it between semesters. I'm sure the word got around, because this was something out of the ordinary. But I was just an ordinary person doing extraordinary things that I enjoyed.

ADVANCE READING

I have never been a voracious reader, but I did manage to find another way to chisel my way through the mountains of books that were stacked up for me. After testing out at about six hundred words per minute after the speed reading course, I came up with a second way to pick up speed. I would select a book and slowly read everything at the beginning, including the table of contents, preface, and foreword to get the big picture. I would then go to each chapter in turn, reading the first paragraph in full, followed by the first sentence of every paragraph in that chapter.

Finally, at the end of the chapter, I would concentrate on the last paragraph, chapter quiz, and keywords. If I could not put the puzzle together, I reread the chapter in detail, but that didn't happen often. If I felt my level of concentration was above the ninetieth percentile, I could speed through almost any textbook in an average weekend or an especially good evening.

FINANCE AT THE RECUMBENT

Believe it or not, most all of my reading, as well as some of my communication with my peers, was done on my recumbent bike in my home office. This academic tool was like my car environment; I always had specific accouterment within arm's reach. It also took the enormous pressure of my 250-pound weight off my feet, while still giving me a good workout. One of the major advantages over my car was that I did not have to look where I was going and could use my senses of sight and hearing purely for study. I would read hour after hour, book after book.

Sometimes if the text was problematic, like mathematical equations in finance, I would exclusively use the bike. I also rode for health and ideas. While riding and sweating, I would drink quarts of water, and new thoughts, solutions, and ideas would pour out from me at a phenomenal rate. I was at that time concentrating on Professor DeFranco's finance class but was always interrupted by so many ideas that I spent half my time writing down side notes or recording quips onto a paper pad or a tape recorder so I could play them back in my car.

At the same time I was studying on the bike, I also could cut and file my fingernails, swab my ears, brush and floss my teeth, groom myself with an electric razor, or even eat a snack. Because I incessantly drank quarts of water, I kept about twenty extra gallons in the closet just in case. I will never be without water again after the food and water rationing at Khe Sanh. I also always carried water in all my book bags, in my car, and in the trunk.

Within reach of my bike were two phones, one a land line and the other a cell phone. Straight ahead was a combination television and VHS tape player, where I continually played "borrowed" video tapes from the Hilton and Professor Corgel's tapes from Cornell. As I had lots of audiotape recorders in various rooms, including by the recumbent, I could play two sizes of audios if my eyes were tired, strained, or burning. The tapes probably quadrupled my retention rate. All in all, I made about three hundred cassette and micro mini tapes to study by. It is amazing how much extra I picked up listening to the lectures a second time, not to mention the fill-ins on my notes, plus any corrections I made.

BEDROOM SETUP

In our bedroom, I had yet another academic tool bag that allowed me instant access to anything that was nagging me before I went to sleep or when I first woke up. It comforted me that if I couldn't sleep and was lying awake in the middle of the night with my mind churning with questions, assistance would always be just an arm's length away. Gloria was working a shift where she would have to be at either Houston's Hobby Airport or Intercontinental Airport at four in the morning, so she had to wake up at two or two-thirty with her alarm. During the majority of time I was in school, our household was running twenty-four hours a day. After I heard Gloria's car back out of the driveway, sometimes I couldn't get back to sleep. I always had numerous nagging problems to solve, and then there was always Gloria's growing honey-do list to think about, including, like a typical husband, how I could put everything off or at least on hold.

It's hard to stay in bed sleeping when your significant other has to get out of bed at 2:30 am for work and considers you lazy for lying around until 4:00. I could never fault Gloria for that, because just like she wrote me every day while I was overseas, she would take a phone call from our children in the evening at nine, ten, or even eleven o'clock, knowing she would have to get up for work just a very short time later. I would get furious, not at her but with the children, with their small problems and gossip that they presented her with night after night, disturbing valuable minutes of her precious sleep. But these were the qualities that I had married her for, and I admired her for her work ethic, but even more as a person, a mother, a wife, and a lover. What more could any man or husband have asked for? It was her time to spend as she wished; my responsibility and job were to make her as comfortable as possible.

My night tool bag was set up on my nightstand and consisted of electronic calculators and an English Dictionary Assistant. Additionally, I would have a pad of paper and a flashlight for reading and a couple of the suggested reading textbooks under the bed. I have never believed in the old adage that you have to get a good night's sleep the night before a test; I don't think that was written for Marines.

I think I kept 3M in business by keeping stickies in every conceivable place, including on the headboard and in my clothes closet, as well as posting last-minute thoughts on my bathroom mirror. If I needed to listen to my lectures again, I had both players also close by, with earphones so if Gloria was home, she could sleep through my studying. Sometimes, if I was real lucky, when I extended my arm across the bed in the morning, my beautiful wife would still be lying there next to me.

CHAPTER TWENY-ONE
Types of Courses, Registration, Books, and Materials

TYPES OF COURSES

As in high school, in college, there are specific courses that you have to take to graduate or to pursue your specific degree, but at the college level, there is a much wider variety of courses you can take to accomplish your goals. These will be the same at both the university and college level but will vary depending on what you specialize in. The course structure and the different types of courses are set up almost identically to the course configuration in high school, but with some major differences that you should clearly understand to take better advantage of them.

In the beginning, along with my core classes, I wanted all the easiest and fastest electives courses like Underwater Cake Decorating and Food Fights in Space II. I did take Rocks for Jocks because I figured I had already had the lab in an actual cave, when I had lived in the Rock Quarry in Viet Nam. I wondered if I could get extra credit for that...I didn't. But as the semesters went by and I matured academically, I gravitated to the specialized electives and courses that I really wanted to take, no matter the difficulty, and without regard for my GPA.

Core Courses

As in high school, your core courses are the classes that you are required to take to graduate or obtain your specific degree. There is no getting around any of your core classes, as I knew by facing my nightmare with algebra, only one of the four core maths I needed to obtain my degree. You will be well aware of these courses in advance, so you need to come up with a strategy that works best for you, as I did, on when and in what order to take them. There is really not a lot of wiggle room with these classes; basically, your fate is sealed. I wish you the best of luck. I survived my four maths; you can do it, no matter what class it is, remember millions of students have completed and passed it before you.

Elective Courses

The courses that I took at Cornell were counted as elective courses, which were not the easiest, nor the fastest. In fact, they actually consumed more than their fair share of time. Elective courses are the classes you take that are not required for you to graduate or obtain your degree but still go toward your degree in some way. Or some you can take just for fun if you can work them in. They are, in a sense, the opposite of your core class requirements. These are the classes you choose to fulfill your credit-hour requirements, aside from your core classes.

The importance of electives is that these are the classes that will allow you to specialize within your degree, so any electives you choose should be chosen very carefully and with consultations with your counselors and professors, in order to get the most out of them for what you are trying to accomplish with your degree goals.

Unconventional Elective Courses

Beside traditional courses, I also looked into the unconventional ones including special problems courses, College-Level Examination Program® (CLEP) courses, opportunities to test out new classes, and the latest emerging online courses.

Special-problems courses, which are more like independent research assignments, are metered out in extraordinary circumstances at the request of the student or the suggestion of the professor. Permission is usually only granted by the dean after everything is in order. Usually, a professor-student contract is affirmed and signed off on after a firm course outline has been submitted and approved, as well as a subject outline for any project. It all has to be in the best interests of both student and professor. Certain completion dates are also specified. I thought these courses would be easy and fast. Wrong. I took two of these, and one lasted almost two years, as the professor kept on adding material and changing the rules. I guess I could have gone to the dean, but what the heck. I could have also just said no, but I was learning. Proceed with caution.

CLEP courses give you the opportunity to receive college credit for what you already know by taking any of thirty-four examinations and earning qualifying scores. This existing knowledge could have come from work such as independent study, prior course work, on-the-job training, or internships and was material covered in the first two years of college. I was excited at the possibility of taking CLEP exams, as I would be given the same amount of credit as students who had studied for two years. Unfortunately, however, I did not qualify to take even one of the thirty-four examinations.

I also investigated online courses. There are a lot of advantages in taking an online course or degree, but ultimately, I decided it just wasn't for me. I thrive on the interaction of a classroom setting; I did not want to feel as if I was studying in a void. For time and logistical reasons, however, this may be exactly what you are looking for, so definitely look into online courses.

REGISTERING FOR CLASS

Registering for classes using the phone system is enough to send anyone into stress mode—especially nontraditional students working full- or even part-time, those who are married or single with children, have a business, travel a long distance, use a commuter bus with deadlines, or, like me, sign up for too many classes at more than one university or a couple of colleges.

Our oldest daughter, Christina, warned me about the hurdles of registering by phone, but again it went right over my head. She was correct that several thousand students would be standing by to enter their schedules at the same time so the institutions assigned registration times based on the first letter of your last name. Even so, it was a mad dash at the assigned time. When I first heard this, I panicked, as I was at the end of the alphabet, V for Vargo, but the order was scrambled each semester so it was fair to all. The first semester was very hectic, but from then on, I sped up the process by getting super-organized.

First, I would make a decision tree for every what-if scenario. In other words, I had an instant alternate selection if the class was taken or interfered with another class. A twelve-hour, four-class semester schedule was heads-up easy, but as you added class numbers five, six, seven, eight, nine, and ten, it became first geometrically, then exponentially, difficult. Besides the times of the class, there were other considerations, such as the times of associated laboratory classes, prerequisites, wanted and unwanted professors, and physical distances between classes. Who wants two classes only ten minutes apart with a two-mile trek between them, or a geology class at 7 am and the lab at 8 pm? How about a one-hour-and-twenty-minute class only taught on Fridays, with a thirty-mile trip through Houston rush-hour traffic to get there?

If you were prepared, you could be the first in the phone line and get all the classes you wanted the first time around, every semester. After making all my what-if scenarios in an easy-to-read decision-tree chart, I would use two charged-up phones that blocked any outside call-ins and started dialing the number about seven minutes in advance of the prescribed time and place the number one phone on speaker. It would not ring busy but just keep ringing; no one would ever answer until the university switched the system on. If you stayed on one line continually ringing you would be registering after everyone had – hours later.

I would keep leap-frogging the two phones until I received a prerecorded voice welcoming me to the system. The connection was generally made at between five and three minutes before the prescribed hour, and I was patched in minutes before hundreds and hundreds of other students with a last name beginning with

V who were waiting for the second hand to strike the hour. Rarely did I have to make a correction to my first class selection, but I always had a backup just in case. However, my peers were registering for only one institution and I had chosen to dance around a couple of others, like a nut.

BOOKS AND MATERIALS

After successfully registering in the courses and colleges that I chose, it was time to buy books and materials. To me it was an exciting time because each course was a new adventure. I was fortunate to have been approved in the Chapter 31 program, so my books were free. There were two types of books in each class: required reading and suggested reading. The VA naturally would pay for the required books but refused to reimburse students for the suggested books and materials.

I was lucky, however, because I believe my caseworker Barbara Kinseth really liked me. Because she had an obvious fondness for me, our mandatory meetings were generally longer than anyone else's. On her side, it was both because she was meticulous and wanted to see me do well, and on mine, it was because I wanted her to approve the suggested reading books and materials. The banter between us always ended with her holding the receipts. I used to almost feel guilty that it could be construed that I always took advantage of her fondness, but in the end, she was happily surprised that someone she had oversight for had graduated with as many honors as I had. I really did deserve the glowing reports that she gave her supervisor about me, so I believe that the playing field was level and we each achieved our mutual goals.

I didn't wait for Barbara to approve my book purchases, I just went ahead and took all my eight, nine, or ten new syllabi and bought all the books that were required and suggested. I would worry about the details and receipts later with Barbara, who always said that she was going to approve them only this time, and that I shouldn't count on it next time. I so appreciate her kindness and her faith in me.

Buying books at the campus bookstore was great. I was like a kid in a candy store, with all the sugar candy being free. How could a fifty-year-old kid with a sweet tooth ask for anything more? I would methodically go through each syllabus and go row by row until I had a stack that would almost overflow the basket to take to the cashier. With so many syllabi, I naturally had several stacks of books, or a couple baskets and usually, when the cashier started to ring the books up he or she would give me the professor's price first. After a couple semesters, I learned to tell them in advance that I was just student, generally with a jaundiced look.

Finally, I would always ask for assistance to help load up my books, which I thought would be as exciting as asking for assistance at a grocery store or Home Depot. But at school, a student would always be happy to help. I usually said, "Please bring those outside while I bring my car up." The student would bring a stack of books on a two-wheeled dolly to my car and would inevitably say, "Professor, I'll go back and get the rest." As the young man quickly left, I wouldn't have the heart to tell him that I was a student just like him, and only a sophomore or junior at that. He wouldn't have believed my story anyway, because frankly, I still didn't either. When he returned, I would usually give him a five dollar gratuity and wish him well in his studies. So, whenever I walked through a university, several students would always acknowledge me as a middle-aged professor.

After buying the books and whatever else I needed, which might include a chef's uniform, I would go home and start methodically stacking books for each class. Each course had a primary and secondary stack of books for the required and suggested readings. It's one thing for a student to ask a question about something in a required book, but quite another when it's in the suggested one. That meant I was probably one in a hundred, a cut above my peers. This was where Evelyn Wood's speed-reading course really paid off. Today, I would also recommend that you look into RocketReader®.

CHAPTER TWENTY-TWO
Different Types of Class Projects

You will be able to become involved in various types of class projects that can and will impact your grade. These are mostly all optional, but as I will explain, there are many reasons I highly recommend becoming involved in any and all class projects that suit you.

EXTRA-CREDIT PROJECTS

I loved extra-credit projects, particularly on subjects I really wanted to learn about, or something the professor was working on, especially if the professor was working toward tenure. I always asked about extra-credit projects if I was overly anxious about the course itself. Teachers know that students who ask about extra-credit projects at the beginning of the semester really want to learn, as opposed to the failing students, who ask at the end of the semester simply because they are worried about their grades.

For example, I would ask for extra credit in every class that was essential for me to take but in which I thought I might not really excel. This could be because of a scheduling conflict, where the only available teacher was the professor from hell, or when the class was only taught once a year.

The two classes where I definitely had to go to the professor and ask for an extra-credit project up front were, of course, algebra and macroeconomics. Other students told me I was crazy asking an algebra teacher if I could do an extra-credit project or paper for the class, but I asked anyway. The professor said yes very enthusiastically, the project title rolling off his tongue as if he was very familiar with it. He said, "I would like you to write a ten-page, powerful paper on time in algebra or algebra in the dimension of time." He said it so confidently and quickly that I asked him why that title. He related that when he had been a freshman algebra student some fifty years before, he had written the same paper. He explained that with the Internet being new, he wanted me to research that topic to see the difference a half century of knowledge could make, and that no one in all that time had asked him to write an extra-credit paper. We never discussed what merit I would get for a producing a good paper. I just learned more.

I also did an extra-credit report for macroeconomics because I saw all the graphs and algebra I was faced with between the pages of discussion. There sure were a lot of x^2 graphs in that textbook, so I did a five-page critical essay on the economic theory of the department store Filene's Basement in Boston, where they kept marking down the price daily until someone bought the merchandise. It paid off big time.

INDIVIDUAL PROJECTS

At the beginning of each semester I would take all my syllabi and my pre-made flashcards to the computer labs at both the university and the college. In each syllabus, I would highlight the keywords I felt were a gimme to the course, especially in the section outlining the project. I would take these keywords and certain combinations of words from my flashcards and insert them in the major search engines of the time, Bigfoot and WebCrawler.

I would simultaneously use multiple computers to download information on every keyword in each syllabus. Generally, I used four computers at a time, two on each row, turning all the monitors and keyboards to face me for speed with a slow academic Internet. If I could not log in to more than one computer, I would throw a couple bucks to the IT guy so he would flip the right dip-switch or click the right button to make my shortcut happen.

A few times, I pulled several all-nighters in the computer lab at the beginning of a semester, downloading and printing pertinent pages for each class. I'd get it done then, because in the first few weeks of the semester, the computer labs would be virtually empty; conversely, at the end of the semester, when all the term papers were due, a waiting line faced the flocks of students desperate to get just one computer. Having your own laptop was still an expensive luxury at the time. In 1997 not all students even had a computer at home, and computers at places like Kinko's and Copy King, which were off campus but close to the university, were also full. At the beginning of the semester, I would have computer labs and their technicians all to myself, for an abundance of personal assistance.

Once I had completed my exhaustive Internet search, I would divide the printouts into common stacks. After I had arranged everything, I would come up with three ideas for my paper, which I would take to the professor to see which one he thought was the best or if he had a favorite topic he could suggest.

After that, I would complete a first-draft outline and submit it again to my professor. I always wrote this as three-tiered for easy reading—for their ease of reading. Usually, sometime after the midterm test, I would focus on the project fully, and ask permission to submit it early. Most of the time I could request an early grade if they had the time; otherwise, I would receive it at the same time as the rest of the class, no biggie.

GROUP AND TEAM PROJECTS

Unfortunately, the dreaded group and team projects usually lived up to their reputations. Up until this time, grades were derived from individual efforts, but in group projects it's somewhat like group therapy...an emotionally filled and frustrating roller coaster.

The group work was good, as long as I was not the leader. However, I usually was in charge or stepped up to the plate when a leader was fired by the group and somebody had to step in. If the group was voluntarily picked between the class members, the damn D-graders and some international exchange students always made sure they sat next to their A-grade peers for an easy semester ride. I really resented them, especially because we were only allowed to fire the leader, and then we had to drag them around for the rest of the semester.

This was another reason to check out the professor before the semester started, not only his character but also if there was a group project and how the groups would be picked. There is nothing worse than doing the work for three extra deadbeats all semester long. On the other hand, just like the volunteer study group, three or four people working well in unison can crunch an enormous amount of data, edit, and create a terrific project.

Whenever I did a search on the web for "college group projects" all that appeared in the browser window were the negative headlines like, "How to Survive Group Projects," "Surviving Group Projects in College," and "How I Survived the Groupies." The main theme here was stress and survival. Today, this has been somewhat abated by project-management software programs that help take the student interaction and anxiety out of the equation, much like working with a virtual team in industry today.

For the most part, the groups were okay, but I did sometimes have to pick up the slack or raise my voice a little. I think everybody understood that if I was going to lead, they were going to have to tow their loads. I think I was pretty well known as the flash-card king, because I always showed them a stack and expected them to have pre-read all the material that was scheduled—or else.

I wasn't in college to spoon-feed a bunch of babies, and I let them know that upfront. At the same time, however, the kids could be a breath of fresh air. In one of my groups, I was standing at the board and showed the group a stack of cards, then turned my back on them to write something on the board. When I turned back to look at them again, several of them were holding up a huge stack of much larger cards, in comedic defiance. Little did I know then, my toughest group project was yet to come.

PART IV

MY ACADEMIC GOAL LINE

CHAPTER TWENTY-THREE
Second Fall Semester, 1998

LEARNING TO LET GO; MY MORAL REDEMPTION BEGINS

In my last two semesters of undergraduate work, in the fall of 1998 and spring of 1999, I had to complete forty-two semester hours to have the 132 hours total I needed to graduate. That meant I could pop out twenty-one hours for each of the remaining two semesters to finish. That was if the classes were available and I could schedule them to work out—therein lay the rub. There were a lot of hurdles; for example, some professors only taught their specialized courses in one semester or the other, so there was no room for error, no drop and add, and no other college I could attend. But I was able to work out exactly what courses I needed in advance and which semesters I had to take them in, so I was totally prepared when it was time to register, then used my phone technique to get the classes I needed.

Now I dug into my second fall semester full-speed ahead, ready to kick ass and take names if that's what it took to get my GPA where I wanted it. As it would turn out, that is exactly what I would have to do. I suddenly found myself with one annoyingly big problem on my hands...my old friend Nyugen from Viet Nam. I had never really thought about him at all since having the class with him earlier at HCC. I had no idea he was also a UH student, until he popped up in one of my lodging classes at the Hilton College and was assigned to our team project. There were four other team members, and I was again voted the leader. The team also voted for the project to lean towards the food and beverage side of lodging because I had extensive experience in the restaurant business. I gave them the benefit of the doubt; no favoritism and no undue overwork. I tried to balance the workload evenly, but I took on the meat of the project while they took on the buns, so I knew that the project would be an A from the beginning. No one complained.

As work on the project moved on, things played out pretty much just as I had suspected they would. When we received permission from a particular hotel to interview the food and beverage manager and chef, two of the team members did not show up. One was Nyugen. He told us via cell phone that he was dreadfully sick, but we found out later that he had gone on another group project outing. We also found out through the grapevine that he was just going to let us do all the work and ride our coattails to an easy A. The rest of the semester was pretty much the same. It was excuse after excuse, until he told us that he would do a certain part on his own and turn it in as proof that he was still working on the project. As I had four children and had seen most, if not all, of this kind of childish chicanery before, I smelled a rat.

The semester rolled by with not a word from Nyugen, until two days before the final report was to be turned in. He and I met in one of the computer labs, and he handed me a packet of papers and a diskette that he informed me he wanted inserted into the report. I in turn informed him that I had already turned the report in that morning and that would be the end of any discussion. He then asked me for a copy, which I gave him. In his opinion, there was something grossly wrong. His name was not on the cover page. It took him about a terasecond to realize that he had just flunked the course, so he demanded that I insert his part and his name into the completed report. I could see that he was about to explode with rage at being academically out-snookered, so I somewhat acquiesced to his demand by at least looking through his bundle of papers. "Not good," I told him sternly, then continued, "This is just a copy, paste, and print job of trash that probably took you about forty-five minutes to complete, if that."

This was one of the few times in my life that my cooler head prevailed, as he went berserk on me. I don't know who he thought he was fooling with. I was twice his size and still had (have) a highly explosive temper, which I have only been able to control with the help of heavy medication. Even medicated, I can still become highly agitated and inflict severe pain and damage on someone who's asking for it. I did well this time and kept my cool without completely destroying him and the computer lab; I just left him physically exhausted and fuming and cussing at me in Viet-French.

I wish that had been the end of it, but unfortunately, it wasn't. He had obtained my home phone number from our initial exchange of information for the project at the beginning of the semester. He started calling our house, hanging up on anyone who picked up the receiver, except me. He threatened that if I did not put his name on the report, he was going to kill me. He said it not once but several times, so I taped him. Then it went further. He also started yelling belligerently at my family when they picked up, telling them what he was going to do with me if I did not put his name on the project analysis.

After checking with Dr. Barth and taking his advice, I took a copy of the tape to the provost's office. I told the provost's representative that I just wanted them to be aware of the situation for the safety of my family, but I did not press any charges that could hurt Nyugen's career, and I never heard from him again. This was one of the first times that I did not blow it. Maybe finally, this late in the game, I was learning to forgive my enemy, because this time, I was actually able to just let it go, instead of throwing him on the back of my tank, dead. My personal moral redemption, just maybe, was now overriding my temper.

On a lighter note, in a successful group project that semester, a great friend and classmate of mine, Kyle Bowman, and I assembled a group of students who belonged to the Club Managers Association of America (CMAA), and we collectively wrote a 100-page feasibility study on a potential country club within the Harris County limits. This report would be looked over by a professional consulting firm as a representative project that showed what the students at the college were capable of producing. This meant that in the future, this international hotel consulting firm would hire students on an ongoing basis for internships and eventually permanent employment. This also meant the Hilton College would be taking market share away from other prestigious colleges and universities, including Cornell. It paid off for Kyle because a couple of years after graduation he went to work for that exact consulting firm.

CHAPTER TWENTY-FOUR
Third Spring Semester, 1999

MY LAST UNDERGRADUATE SEMESTER

In my last semester, I had to take nine courses, for twenty-three hours, so it wasn't just because of the stress that I requested to take my examinations at the DTC or for the extra time I was allowed there. It was for just the opposite reason; it was all about how the exams were scheduled at the DTC. I could space five exams out over one day and four the next, in the sequence of my choice. Each professor would submit their exams to the testing center and specify the range of times I could take them. The only condition was that I stayed at the center for the duration of the exam. Of course, I could not be allowed to leave and get the answers from other students or tell the others what would be on the exam. As a serious and convicted curve-buster who was very conscious of the students' Academic Honesty Policy, however, I would never have jeopardized my degree for anything or anyone.

When I received my test papers, I immediately set them aside while I filled out my blank sheets with a perfect copy of my cheat sheet outline of the course material. If I forgot something, I just went on; it would usually always come back to me. After I finished the outline, I surveyed the test to see how many pages and questions there were, looking for any surprises. If there were any bonus questions, I would read those first so I could be thinking about them in the back of my mind. Sometimes one of the earlier test questions would trigger something in my mind that could be useful for a bonus question.

The rest of the test process was pretty much like in high school, except that by the end, I knew I had all the answers. If I did not know the answer to a question, I would pass and come back to it. If I felt that the answer I had selected could be wrong, I would look at my cheat sheet outline and figure it out, especially for those multiple-choice questions that also had the twists of "all of the above" or "none of the above." If I still did not know the answer, I would go to the next question. At the end of the test, I would make a mental note of anything that I was really unsure of. Outside the test hall, I would write these points down to remind myself of them when I got home after the test.

After each test, I would immediately look up anything that I had written down during the exam and determine the correct answer from the textbook or my notes. This was a small quirk, but it saved me a lot of sleeplessness before the grades came in. At least that way I definitely knew whether I had got the answers right or wrong and could predict my final grade with some degree of accuracy.

So, in my last two regular semesters, fall and spring, I had pumped out twenty and twenty-three hours, respectively. The twenty-hour fall semester would have been easy, because after all, I was now in one central location, had it not been for finite math in a university class, which took up a lot of extra tutoring labs again. But in the fall, I ended up completing eight classes with six A's, one A–, and an S, for a 3.94 GPA. Then, in my final semester, I took nine courses, plus I was finishing up a facilities course from three semesters earlier; I aced all eight grade courses and got two S's, for a 4.0 GPA in my final semester. Those nine months are pretty much a blur, and I don't remember too much, as I had become a study-robot to all but fall over the finish line.

CHECKING MY GRADES

After all my hard work, I couldn't wait to check my grades. I always felt a mixture of hope with deep angst and desperation beforehand. It was like asking Gloria out on our first date or, conversely, looking at the WIA, MIA, and KIA list in the "Stars and Stripes" newspaper. Whether I checked my grades by picking up the phone or going to a board, it was usually a tremendous rush, sometimes a complete downer, but always terrifying.

When I asked Gloria out on our first date, it's not what she said that I remember the most, but how her mother and father reacted. Back then, I knew her parents well enough and had their respect. Gloria's brother and I were Boy Scouts, and their father was our troop leader. Gloria's mom was always courteous and friendly to me while her son and I were friends. But when I placed that phone call to ask Gloria to ask her to go out in my '32 Ford Model B Roadster (with 650 horsepower) for an ice cream cone, you would have thought I was an ax-murderer drooling after their daughter. It was bad enough that before the call, my heart had been pounding out of my chest. I did not know what high blood pressure was then, but I remember my heart was throbbing so hard, I'm sure I had it. I should have been awarded a medal for my bravery in asking that thirteen-year-old eighth-grade girl on a real mini-date. Little did I know, it wouldn't be the last time that I would have to pluck up courage to pick up a phone to receive or give either good or bad news.

ONE TRANSCRIPT & MULTIPLE GPA'S

It was during my junior semesters that I really got serious about tracking and projecting all four of my GPAs. By using a software program called Crystal Ball, a Monte Carlo simulation program, I was able to analyze one transcript and forecast multiple GPAs based on different what-if scenarios. I started with my standard, standing GPA, which was just from my work at the Hilton College and the University of Houston. Next, I tracked my major or concentration GPA, and then my graduating GPA. This was calculated as the standard GPA, minus the last senior semester. Unfortunately, I did not know this until it was too late, so I miscalculated it.

Finally, I calculated my lifetime GPA, which is considered for graduate school and is the aggregate average of all my college and university classes. I was advised that if I was looking to go to graduate school, I would have to submit all my transcripts from all the institutions I had ever attended, without conveniently losing or forgetting any courses or transcripts, especially those that were not flattering. If I did, I would get dropped for dishonesty. That is why they have academic standards and rules.

My major or concentration GPA was obviously the highest, and the lifetime GPA was the lowest, because it considered every course I'd ever taken, including all the D's, F's, I's, and W's from the junior college. However, I still had fun seeing how high I could move the needle. I then started to write semi-complex algorithms in Microsoft Excel and my own extensions in Crystal Ball, which was, of course, the half-price student version, paid for by the scholarship monies that I was receiving regularly. The statistical Excel add-on for Crystal Ball could configure a half million iterations of what-if scenarios in a couple of minutes; that would give me a probability of what GPA I would wind up with if I made a certain, and realistic, grade in each class.

Naturally, in my Excel spreadsheets for various GPAs, I would start with five classes—fifteen semester hours—in which I made a B+ in every class, then an A–, and finally an A. I would then increase my odds by increasing the number of classes until I was taking up to ten courses, to see the effect that would have. A total of ten classes with all A's will really jump-start a sagging GPA. It was all maybe a bit anal, but it was still fun, gave me a better picture of where I was at, and was good mental exercise.

A CLOSE CALL THAT WAKES EVERYBODY UP

"Life is not about waiting for the storm to pass…
it's about learning to dance in the rain!"

Vivian Greene

It was late one afternoon during this time, as I was leaving the Architecture & Art Library at UH after working on a hotel room design research project, that it started to rain. Of course it was Texas-style rain, which meant it went from dry as a bone to flash flooding within minutes. These floods and raging gully washers could actually sweep a car off the road, instantly and totally unexpectedly. A manager at one of my restaurants had once left the University of Houston in his brand new Pontiac Trans Am. As he had driven under the I-45 underpass, his car had been caught in a flash flood and turned over. He had had to swim for his life, and his two-week-old car had been totaled and lost forever.

So in the rain that day, I broke out a dinky, fold-up emergency umbrellas and proceeded to jump and avoid the puddles as best I could. Everything below my knees was soaked, as I tried as best I could to cover both of my backpacks. As I peered out from under my umbrella, I could see all the studly young men were getting soaked down to their undies because they thought it looked too geeky to walk with an umbrella and they'd never even think of wearing a raincoat or galoshes. They would rather run into a nice, freezing, air-conditioned schoolroom and get a super-summer cold because looking cool was the most important thing. I was glad my days of vanity had passed. Now, as lightning lit up the sky around me, I cursed myself for not checking the daily weather and not packing an emergency raincoat. It reminded me of when I would golf with my father-in-law in a lightning storm. After the first bolt would crack past us, he would yell, "Hurry up, now we can cut right through and pass the two foursomes ahead of us!"

My weight was against me as I pushed forward into the oncoming wind, trying to keep on the asphalt sidewalk, when a group of kids bumped into me from behind while trying to get past me and knocked me off the sidewalk. I attempted to push my fogged-over glasses up to see, but to no avail. I stumbled helplessly into the road, which was now covered in ankle-deep water, and I began struggling to cross over to the less flooded side of the street. As I fought the wind and rain and strained to see how far it was to the other side, I saw a tree get hit with a bolt of lightning. It was an amazing site as the tree twisted itself in utter anguish, finally submitting with a loud crack and collapsing fairly close to me. It hit close enough to spray me with an extra shower of water and a terrific double gust of wind, which I guess came from the bolt itself and from the leaves.

In Khe Sanh, I had seen and become almost immune to explosions, and as a TC, close lightning strikes when we were out in the bush had been commonplace. Whenever we were on ops chasing Charlie, we often had nothing around us for miles but the companion tanks, which were ten feet high and weighed in at fifty-two tons of pure fighting metal each. We had been sitting duck magnets for up-close and personal strikes from lightning, so the storm and the lightning strike on the tree didn't rattle me at all, but what I saw next really shook me.

When I finally made it to the other side of the street, which was now also quickly filling with rising water, I was horrified to see a wheelchair, stuck in water where the curb should have been. Slumped over like a drowned rat in the chair, feebly trying to protect herself from the pounding rain, wind, and lightning all around, was a petite young lady. *Holy shit!* I thought; not only was it a metal wheel chair in a lightening storm, it was a battery-powered electric chair that had stalled out. Having such an explosive temper, I was of course immediately furious that the punks who had just blown by me must have either tried to help her and given up or, even worse, just hurried straight by.

Because I needed both hands for my new mission, I let my umbrella turn against the wind and blow inside out, then let it go. I tried to push the wheelchair forward with all my might, but it would not budge—either because of the underwater curb or the stalled electric gear mechanism, I didn't know which—so I spun the chair around and pulled it backwards with all my might. At first it lunged away from me, but then I had the measure of the weight and knew I could make it. The nearest building was not too far away, but it was utterly exhausting to pull the weight of the chair, the thirty-or-so–pound battery, and the girl and her book bag while carrying my own book bags. When we finally arrived at the building, the only thing I really wanted to do was flop down exhausted in the mud under the trees.

But instead of collapsing, as there was no handicap ramp into the building, I put on my best drill-instructor voice (that's the one that I could make my children wet their pants with) and yelled at a couple of kids with earrings and dry hair to give me a hand to get the poor girl out of the storm. The voice didn't let me down, and thank God the restrooms were close to the entrance. The kids helped us, and we pulled the chair into the women's room to get the poor girl some kind of dry. Although the few shocked occupants of the ladies' room initially gasped at my invasion of their privacy, they quickly realized the gravity of the situation. The girls quickly pointed two electric hair-dryer nozzles at the woman's wet, trembling limbs and started to gently remove her sodden clothes.

As I turned to exit the restroom, the girl appeared to summon all her strength, turned, and blurted out, "Thank you...what's your name?"

I called back, "Claude Vargo...what's yours?"

"Ashley, Ashley Pate," she replied with a weak but grateful smile.

As I hurried out of the freezing building before I caught pneumonia, I thought a lot about what had just happened. The whole situation was a wake-up call to me. First, there was no curb ramp in the road. Second, there was no ramp into the building, and third, the restroom was so narrow, it was impossible to maneuver a wheelchair without assistance. I had never been one to be an activist, but this needed my attention before I ended up in a chair myself. Like any other family, my kids would rag on me from time to time. Christina especially would always chant, "Hey, Pops, in a couple of years when you are even older than you are now, we are going to push your wheelchair down the driveway and take your Social Security check!" Following the day's events and with Gloria's prodding, the idea of forming a disabled students fraternity was born.

THE DISABLED STUDENTS ASSOCIATION—DELTA SIGMA ALPHA—DSA

I didn't see Ashley Pate again until several weeks after the incident in the thunderstorm, when she came into the DTC. I didn't really know it was her at first, but then I recognized the bumper sticker on the back of her wheelchair. I tried to reintroduce myself to her as she sat at a table in the middle of the room, but she was in the middle of an exam and let it be known that I was hassling her, so I just left.

A few days later, I saw Ashley again, as we were both checking in our book bags at the testing center front desk. As soon as she recognized my name on my Cornell book bag, she blurted out my name. She told me that she had never really seen my face during the storm and apologized for not having had a chance to formally thank me.

After we both completed our tests, we chatted in generalities, then I broke a silent moment between us with the idea I had come up with after Gloria and I had talked about the incident, to formalize a fraternity for the disabled students on campus.

We began holding meetings at the testing center and sometimes at a pub across the street from the campus. Within a month or so of beginning these meetings, the Disabled Students Association (DSA), or Delta Sigma Alpha fraternity, at the UH was formed. It was also during these meetings and our numerous conversations that it struck me she had a beautiful complexion and an indescribable inner beauty. I could only imagine if she wasn't in that chair, she would be a sure thing for being voted in as a college cheerleader. She would make a great vice president and a better president after I graduated, and I wanted her resume to look outstanding.

During my senior year, as president of the fraternity, I organized numerous colleges and students in a multi-semester project that would inventory and make recommendations for disability provision at all student facilities at the UH central campus. Not only was this desperately needed, it was also legally necessary and politically mandated because of the implementation of the Americans with Disabilities Act a few years before. As a publicly funded entity with huge grants and federal funds at stake, UH was under the gun to catalog all the points of interest that applied to the law. We didn't make any corrections or construct anything, but we did inform the administration what needed to be fixed, as well as what was being corrected.

This project comprised multiple teams of students and colleges, primarily engineering students, who represented more than 50% of the total volunteer force. It took more than a year to inventory all the parking spaces, water fountains, doorway widths, staircases, sidewalks and ramps, restroom facilities, elevators, and anything else that had to be brought up to legislative standards. The engineers now had many problems to solve, and with the energy of numerous disabled students with purpose, this group met weekly and did a magnificent job of inventorying the entire central campus of over 550 acres, a couple hundred buildings, and countless parking spaces and miles of streets.

When I assembled, printed, and presented the 450-page compendium to the Vice Chancellor of the University, one of the first things he asked me was, "What grant are you operating under?"

When I told him we were working on our own recognizance, he told us we should have applied for a grant and could have had thousands of dollars to work with. This would have come in handy, as I had big ideas for the association, including having national speakers come to speak to us as a group, where we would have an open invitation to the entire university and the community to kick off the National Disability Employment Awareness Month of October.

I looked for and contacted several noted speaker bureaus and decided that the best person to come to our rally meeting to drive membership was John Hockenberry, who had most recently written the *New York Times* Notable Book of the Year. John was also a correspondent and program host for ABC News and NBC News. His book was aptly titled *Moving Violations* because John had achieved all this from his wheelchair. The New York Times Book Review, among numerous other noted citations, called his book "Full-throated, driving, and highly affecting….Moving Violations could be described as an Invisible Man for the disabled."

After reading that review, I bought his book, which had been published less than a year earlier, and I knew this was our guy. There was only one hitch: When I checked with his agent, she told me his fee was $10,000; that did not include hotel, airfare, and miscellaneous expenses. I would really need to pull off something big to pay for this one.

I decided to use my resourcefulness and started a door-to-door campaign begging for money, starting with the director of the disability center and working my way up the chain of command as my conscience in protocol dictated. My requests became an obsession, and although a couple of doors were shut in my face, word spread rapidly. Surprisingly, the person who could make the decision and write the check called me instead, saying that if I could cause that much commotion and ruffle that many feathers, I could definitely market the project, get a large crowd in attendance, and bring much-needed awareness to our cause. It was the vice chancellor who cut the check, and we gave John Hockenberry the golden keys to UH.

John gave a tremendous speech to a very crowded auditorium and a very anxious group of students, faculty, staff, family, and friends, which kicked off our planned awareness week that October. The moral of this vignette is that we not only got the big bucks but also ended up shaking an even bigger tree.

I found out about a year later that our fraternity's compendium was to become a model for all other Texas public colleges and universities and was encouraged and supported by the Texas state legislature. The DSA was also instrumental and the impetus in pushing the need for a new disabled student building through the Center for Students with Disabilities (CSD), which was completed after I left.

When the disability group met every other week, it reminded me of some of the wards at the veterans hospital, but I held back and hid those innermost thoughts. Outwardly, some there questioned and may have even resented my position, because in reality, I had all my limbs and most of my five senses. Inwardly, I had been put back together with Band-Aids so often that only more operations and therapy would be able to keep me physically fit and sane. I also knew that when I graduated and the study groups ceased, the panic attacks would return in spades and I would be back on my medications with necessary and compulsory group therapy.

I strongly feel that when all the Marines and soldiers returned from Viet Nam, we should have received at least some kind of debriefing or mental evaluation. Some Viet Nam vets went straight from a firefight in the jungle to the streets of

America in a matter of hours, which is staggering to think of. I had Gloria, but most had no one, and none of us had a disability group then. I think these are a lot of the guys we see underneath our nation's bridges.

CHAPTER TWENTY-FIVE
Two Pet Classes and a Second Epiphany

ART HISTORY

I had two classes in particular, totally unrelated to HRM, that I thought were both challenging and very interesting. They were probably also my favorites. One was art history, in my first fall semester, and it was amazing. The art history textbook, *Gardener's Art through the Ages, 10th Edition: Renaissance and Modern Art* has 1200 pages, with hundreds of replications and photographs of stunning color paintings, frescoes, reliefs, sculptures, and buildings with magnificent columns. Before the first class, I had my routine chat with my professor to make sure I could communicate with her and to learn about the class. I asked her if I could have an early copy of her syllabus or, failing that, an old one. She gave me a copy of the previous semester's syllabus and penciled in some changes. She also gave me an insight to the midterm and final exams. She said they would consist of somewhere between 25 to 50 works of art that we would have to know seven facts each about, including the artist, name of the piece, year (within a decade), medium, size, country of origin, and pertinent description. In addition, there would be a glossary definition section.

The first thing I did was make 600-plus flash cards on the definitions in the glossary. As the semester progressed, the professor would explain, compare, and contrast, maybe fifteen to twenty works of art during each hour-and-a-half class. After about thirty classes, she had covered approximately 500 pieces of art. Right away, I decided that after each class I would color copy each artwork from my book and scale it to approximately the size of a 3"x5" flash card. On the back I would put the seven critical pieces of data and keywords that we were required to know for test purposes. For example, on the back of one card, I wrote

Object:	Princess de Broglie
Artist:	Ingres (Jean-August-Dominique Ingres)
Year:	1853
Medium:	O/C (oil on canvas)
Size:	4' x 3'
Country:	France
Description:	Romantic, realistic aristocratic; ice-blue gown (like taffeta).

In the two tests of the semester, I would remember the description and then expand and embellish it into a full, yet short and powerful paragraph.

After the first couple of classes, I started flashing the pictorial cards every morning while sitting on the commode. The session was perfectly timed and did not get longer, because after so many minutes, I turned on the hot water in the shower next to me and waited for it to kick in. By the end of the semester, I had a stack of 500 picture flash cards upstairs and 600 more glossary text cards downstairs. As the semester progressed, I raced through the stacks and rarely missed a data point.

After I aced the midterm exam, I began a proactive method of Xeroxing the possible upcoming artworks. Starting where the professor had left off in the previous class, I'd copy all fifty to seventy-five of the upcoming artworks that she might display and discuss in the next classes. Then, during class, I would comb through and pick out the objects as she described and discussed them. I could then write down the exact keywords that she mentioned in her description of a particular piece, and use the exact same verbiage and nuances on the test. For insurance, I always taped her lectures, which I found extremely interesting. If necessary, I could replay any class in the course because I never missed a lecture.

As the semester progressed, when other students saw my flashcards and caught on to what I was doing, a couple tried copying me. I didn't care, because the course was on the leeward side, and besides, they couldn't catch up anyway. I had already ruined the curve at midterm, and by the final, the curve was a total wreck. It was a great feeling to be on the highest end of the statistical bell curve instead of the lowest downside, three standard deviations away from the top. This would be just one course where I would blow the curve for the entire class. On the final exam, I made a 108%, a perfect score, because I got all four of the extra-credit questions worth two points each. The bonus questions were where we had to write a narrative and describe new pieces of art that we had never discussed in class, but I had studied in the book.

I also did two course projects that were related to architecture. One was on the old Harris County courthouse downtown, with its magnificent pillars, dentils, and giant portico that had been built almost one hundred years before. When I was doing the report, I passed the building many times, took pictures, and one day stopped to go inside. I asked to see the building superintendent for permission to inspect the building from the inside. The superintendent gratefully acknowledged my passion and love for the subject and personally gave me a tour of the facility and the magnificent dome inside. Just before we went up to the dome, he said firstly that he hadn't been up there for maybe ten or more years, since the roof had last been redone and secondly that he didn't know if he could remember where he had put the key to the antique mortise lock, but he found it and we went inside. I felt because of my education he was opening another door that I never would have walked through and could never even have imagined earlier. It was well worth the price of admission.

PHYSICS

My two junior semesters, spring and summer, included twenty-eight hours at the University of Houston and the Hilton College, plus six hours at Cornell and Houston Community College, for a total of thirty-four hours, which put me into senior standing. It was during my second spring semester that I had my second favorite university class, a great physics course in a large auditorium at UH, given by a noted and distinguished full professor who fittingly bore the nickname The Mad Russian. Professor Alex Ignatiev was not only one of the university's premier professors but had done his doctorate at Cornell University in astrophysics, as a graduate student and assistant, under none other than Carl Sagan. To top it off, he was the Director of NASA's Space Epitaxy Center. Of course I knew of Carl Sagan's illustrious work and basic views of the universe, and I equated this professor to Alexander Graham Bell's assistant, Mr. Thomas A. Watson, in the phone call heard around the world.

I was early for the first class so I could sit center of left in the front row as usual, and as there were plenty of empty seats, I put a bulging and heavy book bag in the empty seat next to me. The book bag was an extra one that I had bought at Cornell, purchased out of pride and as a badge of honor, like any college student flying their proud colors. Anything you bought at Cornell, including toilet paper, had their imprimatur on it. As I generally either carried two bags or switched off to another pre-sorted bag from my car between classes at different locations, I didn't just carry the Cornell bag at Cornell.

When I carried it outside Cornell, sometimes I would get a smirk from a fellow student or professor, who thought that I was pushing a rival university in their face. I did not see the necessity in lowering myself to figure out which classes had people who did not like the book bag that I carried—such triviality. As I walked through any of the faculty parking lots, I saw many different university and college decals; everyone loved to proclaim to all their peers where they went to school. I just loved the academic politics, as long as I didn't bear the brunt.

As I sat in that first physics class, an attractive lady in her late thirties or early forties came in and sat diagonally behind me. Within the next three minutes, I had her life's story. She quickly blurted out everything about her recent divorce, the statistical 2.5 kids, the car that needed repair, how Mr. No-Good was going to have to help support her return to finish up college; all without taking a breath. I did not know her husband, but I remember thinking we would most likely have gotten along pretty well together. I got everything but her name during her true confession. It wasn't long afterwards that she gave me one of her bank deposit slips, with the account number torn off, so I would know her name and address and so we could study together. I did not know how to respond. I again calmly twisted my worn wedding band.

In the few seconds when she wasn't catching her breath, she was gushing about everything. This included the professor, the size of the auditorium, the hundreds of students filling it up, the massive floor-to-ceiling blackboards with chain winches being moved around by graduate students, and the choreography of the A/V department technicians who were setting up equipment in the booth in back of the class. It was all totally exciting, but she somehow made it less so as she prattled on about all the pretty colored pictures in the 622-page textbook *Abell's Exploration of the Universe* by Morrison, Wolff, and Franknoi. What I saw in that book were models, exponential and mathematical calculations, postulates, hypotheses, theories, and the 680 or more flashcards I would have to make and memorize.

The mad Russian finally entered the room, full of confidence and with a hint of justifiable arrogance. He proceeded to give us his short biographical spiel and shtick to impress the kiddies. All I heard, however, was the lady's mouth, which was now in high gear. When I turned around to ask her to please be quiet, the mad Russian chucked an eraser at my feet. He proceeded to write on one of the nine blackboards "Sheet List" and, underneath, "#1," then asked me my name. He knew it from previous conversations, but he wanted to make sure everybody else did too. Daring anyone else to be "#2," he put his fists on each side of his hips. Shortly after, when the professor turned around to write something else on the board, I heard the exit doors in the rear of the auditorium open and close; I imagined that several students had bolted from the class to "drop and add."

Then the Russian went off on all nine boards at once, writing mathematical formulas, starting with and inadvertently placing the equation of the luminosity of the sun on the board as:

$$L = 4.0 \times 10^{27} \text{ watts}$$

He ended over an hour later at the coup de grâce of physics:

$$E = mc^2$$

Every time the professor turned around to us to say something like "Do you see what I am saying?" he would look around the room to gaze at all the little lost sheep like me with dazed looks on their faces. By then when he would turn back to the board, both the rear and front doors were a free flow of students quickly exiting the auditorium. As I closely watched the professor, when he heard another door slam, I caught a split-second smirk on his face. This was the same smirk I had seen on several other faces: priests, brothers, nuns, drill instructors. That just then confirmed for me that he was playing off all the kids who were not taking this class seriously. He was preparing to teach a very erudite course and was eliminating the students who were not serious.

Astrophysics made simple

When we had about ten minutes left, the professor turned around toward the class for the last time. He was just now starting to feel his Wheaties, while everybody else was approaching exhaustion. As he had my name on the board, I raised my hand, and he asked me if I was asking to be excused. I told him I would like to ask a question. He turned his palms up and shrugged his shoulders as if to say, "Why not?"

With a little difficulty, I started to speak. He asked me to speak up so everybody in the large hall could hear me. I don't know why, but I proceeded to ask him if all the equations were interrelated, so as to balance at the end. He turned his palms up again and nodded affirmatively; he was by this time a little hoarse from talking nonstop loudly enough for everybody to hear him. I pointed to the first equation on the board, the luminosity exponent, and asked him if it was off by one digit and would it not spin all the following equations and his whole hypothesis off just a little.

He zeroed in on the equation when I asked him if the exponent should have been 26 instead of 27. Well, that did it. He knew I was going to be trouble from then on, as he grabbed a book from one of his GAs, threw it at the board, and strode off out of class, exactly as his reputation as the mad Russian had suggested. As I turned to lift my book bag, I noticed that it had gotten very quiet behind me; the divorcée's seat was vacant.

For this course, I formed two study groups. I was not going to let this opening debacle produce a failing grade, which looked like a real possibility now and could cost me a dive in my near-perfect GPA. On the midterm exam I made an A– and was so furious, I couldn't sleep a wink. Without shaving or showering, I went to the professor's office and staked him out. I didn't care if he had office hours then or not. He had asked two questions that were so twisted, in my opinion, as to not be valid or, at the very least, appropriate. I did not go there without ammunition.

During the semester, I had befriended a fellow student who was in one of my study groups and had learned that he was also a pilot for Delta. Everybody called him Roy, but his real name was Elroy, which sounds a little, no a lot, like a geek, but This guy was single and the girls in class would fawn all over him, whispering about how "really cute" he was. After studying with him in the student cafeteria at lunch, I found out that he also had a bachelors and masters degree in physics. I knew this guy was too sharp to be in an undergraduate physics class, because he always came up with the correct path to arrive at all the answers.

At one of our sessions over lunch, he told me that he was returning for his doctorate but because it had been so many years since he had graduated, he had to catch up with many prerequisites before he could start his program. He also told me I was correct in my hypotheses of the ambiguous questions on the midterm exam and that the professor was teaching way above where he was supposed to be. That quickly ended my leadership in that study group. At the next group, I quietly but quickly passed Roy the chalk baton.

In addition to the groups Roy made two requests in return for personally tutoring me. First, he asked that I would not tell anyone that he had advanced degrees or that he was a commercial airline pilot. He didn't want the professor to single him out in class as a potential PhD. He also asked that I introduce him to a certain young and attractive associate professor at the Hilton College whom I knew personally and had a class with earlier. I had been unwilling to do this for my earlier Russian algebra tutor, but Elroy was closer to my age and wasn't a pathological gold digger trying to marry an American. He was just trying to get a date with her. In my day, we would have said he "had the hots for her." He further told me that he had tried to ask her out twice, but that she had spurned his advances. I asked him what was really up and why all the nineteenth-century formality. He told me he had given it his best shot and had really felt put down, but now it was a challenge. We both knew she was single but didn't know if she was seeing anyone else. Elroy didn't understand why his charm had not worked and wondered if he was he losing his touch. I didn't get anywhere with getting her interested in him, either, so I told Elroy a big white lie that she was gay, just to ease his battered ego.

The semester was hard, and I went to see the professor several times, until I would say we had a situation of détente. The final exam was a complete shock for the students who were still enrolled, however, because he gave the exact same test for the final exam as for the midterm, which had smacked down the class.

I assume his contention was to test everyone's level of retention rather than last-minute cram rate. If I concentrate, I can still hear the students moaning and groaning when they realized that all their studying for that test had been for naught. Those who had made good to great grades at midterm were trying to remember the material, to make sure that whatever they'd gotten correct on the midterm was still answered correctly on the final and that they could correct whatever they'd gotten wrong on the midterm.

In effect, it was a double-whammy, because the students could have gotten an answer correct on the midterm but wrong on the final, as they couldn't remember the right answer or the material to work it out again, or just wrong on the midterm and still wrong on the final. From the gnashing of teeth, loud crinkling of paper, and pounding on the desks, I assumed no one had studied the first-half semester's material again; that is, except for me. I had made sure to mentally re-study my midterm cheat sheet in the days leading up to the test.

As I had aced the midterm and could quickly rebuild the midterm cheat sheet in my head, I did the test in one of my fastest times ever. I did not have to work any problems on a scientific calculator or a blank sheet of paper; I just had to write down the same answers as before, which were all correct. So whatever challenge was thrown at me, with a positive attitude I would come out on top and decimate another curve. I looked at the grades when they were posted, and I made an A- for the course, but I decided not to stalk the professor or contest the grade up to an A. I had got what I deserved.

Whenever I talked to other students about which physics class to take, I would always recommended the Mad Russian because he really taught his subject. He was extremely dedicated and serious, and I was forced to learn. I am proud to say that every time a scientific breakthrough is in the news, I not only understand it but still have my textbook to study its background and where it fits in with the world around me. Additionally, the Mad Russian turned out to be a truly patriotic American professor.

MY SECOND EPIPHANY

In a hotel finance course I was taking in the last semester before graduation, we were assigned to cover in detail just the first half of a textbook we were reading, as the latter half was for a subsequent master's course. I believe the book was about thirty chapters, so it was about fifteen chapters per semester. But something magical happened as I was reading chapter fourteen...I had another epiphany. Everything I was reading came into perfect harmony, and I'm not just talking about the numbers, equations, or course; I mean the whole freaking world and my being. It seemed like the entire universe from the beginning, thirteen billion Big Bang years earlier to the present, all came into focus, how everything was divided and where I stood in the middle of it all. I mean everything about everything, lined up perfectly. My education was the key that had opened the most miraculous and thrilling door in my existence. My life took on a new and wonderful meaning. I just felt different in the way I looked at my environment and the world around me.

It was about two in the morning when I finished the entire book. When Gloria came in to go work at 3:30, she interrupted my semiconscious, transfixed daze. I could not stop thinking about this wonderful change of direction in my life. I didn't really know what it was, where it came from or how it had come to me, but I knew then that I wanted it to last.

CHAPTER TWENTY-SIX
Scholarships and Internships

SCHOLARSHIPS

When the other students heard I had applied for certain scholarships, some actually called me out for even applying. They felt that more worthy students deserved them—they being the more worthy, of course. They were, I assume, the guys and girls who had been turned down because their grades were not high enough. They had either submitted mediocre applications and their lackadaisical attitudes had shown in their work, or they were the ones who liked to party more than study.

By the time I had completed that year's spring, summer and fall semesters of 1997, my GPAs were registered as 3.83, 4.0, and 3.9 respectively. This was good enough for thirty semester hours at UH and HCC to qualify for the scholarship season, which started around February. This was a new and exciting way to complement my education, and my back pocket. You may not realize this, but there are so many types of scholarships, so many avenues to getting them, and so much money available, it is actually mind-boggling. You'd think that with the hundreds of thousands of college students out there, everybody would be applying for free money. It's actually just the opposite, though. I certainly didn't realize before starting school and looking into the scholarship system how many scholarships were available and how few people were applying, and neither did most other students. I quickly became very knowledgeable!

I had a great friend, Eric Morse, who, like me, was a returning student, around 30 years old, and needed cash and lots of it. Between the two of us, we applied for nearly every scholarship available to an HRM major, and then some. Eric had the initial idea, and I quickly followed because he discovered there were holes in the scholarship process. We capitalized on those holes, and the rewards were quite handsome. Because I was a switch-hitter between hotels and restaurants, I made scholarship home runs in both parks.

Eric Morse between Eric Hilton and me at Barron Hilton's induction ceremony into the Hospitality Hall of Honor.

The first key in scholarship applications is having the grades. Anything over a 3.25 average and claiming the minimum of honors is acceptable. The second key is to have extracurricular activities, including association memberships. Officerships are preferred, and being a president or chairman is a Rolls-Royce opening. Awards from associations and further scholastic achievements are the whipped cream and cherry on top, so volunteer for organizations and have some fun. The next task is to prepare is boilerplate paragraphs of short-term, intermediate, and long-term goals. The linchpin of these is to have a great answer to the question, "Why do you think you deserve this particular scholarship?"

Once all this is done, the last task is to assemble as many applications as possible and file all the appropriate papers and applications, which means more writing. The majority of students don't apply because they think they won't qualify because of their grades or because they were not president or an officer of an association, or simply because they lack time in the struggle to study and work.

When I went through UH, there was very minimal housing for on-campus students. The university's central campus had 33,000 students but could house only about 4,000. The campus is located adjacent to downtown and was surrounded by inner-city ghetto pockets, so most students drove many miles to attend and often worked in a third location equally far away. Conversely, Cornell is a destination institution, and the majority of students live on or very near campus.

With the vast majority of students at Houston working, it was easier to rely on the certainty of a paycheck than take a chance on the apparently slim hope of a scholarship. Eric worked as a waiter at one of Houston's notable full-service restaurants for extra cash, but we soon discovered that with scholarships, we could concentrate on the books full-time, thereby generating more money in scholarships from our better grades. It was a self-fulfilling and self-perpetuating cycle.

Our initial idea came when we went to see our counselors, who gave us a couple of different applications to fill out for scholarships available directly within the college. The bulk of the application deadlines ran through the spring semester; however, the more we searched for and applied for scholarships, the more the twelve-month calendar filled up.

It was in our initial applications that we found an immediate difficulty. We discovered a common problem in the scholarship application forms. The forms that we received were generally copies of copies of copies, so the lines on the paper were so wavy and crooked that they were hard, if not impossible, to fill out, especially on antiquated typewriters. When I tried, I ended up with toner dots and smears on third-, fourth-, or fifth-generation copies. Eric and I overcame this by redesigning each and every application from scratch, with various computer programs, until the final product was flawless and camera ready. Because there were two of us working on different applications and then combining our efforts, we already had the process in second gear and were ready to put it into high.

After converting each application, we would electronically exchange them, competing with one another to see how many we could each produce. We not only had simple applications but had complete portfolios that wowed each scholarship committee and produced very favorable results in return. Each portfolio had an application; a short autobiography; a statement of short-, mid-, and long-term goals; an up-to-date certified transcript; a pre-typed custom letter of recommendation from an advantageous professor; a color photograph transposed to the matching bonded paper; a list of academic positions, offices held and group memberships; a list of association memberships with a short sentence describing duties, highlights, and awards; a dynamic industry resume; color copies of any pertinent award(s); and, finally, an electronic sample diskette with one or two scanned papers from the courses that were most relevant to the scholarship in question. The scanned copies would also show our professors' personal notes, which were always the good ones.

As the final scholastic coup de grâce, we would prepare a diskette containing an electronic version of the new and reengineered application form. We'd enclose this with a cover letter addressed personally to the chairman of each scholarship committee, explaining what we had done and how they could distribute the form to future applicants, making their committee work easier. Sometimes I would include that I recommended inserting a tidbit piece of information that most other forms had but that a previous committee had left out. We also encouraged each group to post the new form on their new and upcoming websites for maximum student distribution and ease of use.

My packages were assembled in an expensive leather portfolio cover, embossed in gold with my name. Within the portfolio was distinctive and expensive paper, some running at two dollars per sheet, purchased as seconds at a paper manufacturer and wholesaled at student prices. For extra measure, I had student business cards made out of heavy card stock; they were embossed with rose-gold ink and very classy. I would then attach two cards, one externally and one inside, for a professional look with a gold-looking brass paperclip. To top it off, the original was sent to the committee chairperson, and if needed, I sent a half a dozen or so copies for the committee. While we saw other students prepare their toner-dotted, wavy applications and send them in the regular mail "To whom it may concern," I over-nighted mine to the chairperson, with American Airlines dependent or student-discount pricing, of course.

Each package was tailored to the respective entity's business. For example, if we applied to Exxon Petroleum, we placed the emphasis on their food service division and wrote our goal paragraphs highlighting our intentions in that direction; if we were applying to the Knights of Columbus, we would give them glowing reports of how we would like to follow in our great-grandfathers' footsteps. By the time they received our peers' typewritten applications, there was no contest. Our counterparts were begging for money, while Eric and I were extending them our burgeoning careers. In my case, I naturally left out the first half of my resume so no one could figure out that I should have graduated high school thirty years earlier, thereby nixing my chances of a scholarship.

In that first year, our efforts were cumbersome, but by the second cycle, we were a motivated team machine. My total gross in almost three full seasons was more than $100,000 in awards. But in scholarship terminology, there was a difference between "applied to," "gross award," and "net cash" scholarships. This was because, in some scholarships, they would directly pay the school the remaining balance in the scholarship recipient's account, while others would pay the student directly. In other words, although the scholarship awarded might be $1,000, this really meant the scholarship entity would fund the balance of your student account up to the $1,000 limit, so if you had a $625 balance owed to the college or university, that's all the committee would pay. It was a one-time deal; they did not wait around until you accumulated more debt for them to pay off. Because my balance was always zero as a result of my Chapter 31 award from the VA, I would not be funded any money from some scholarships. Luckily for me, the majority of scholarships just sent the recipient a check and paid cash on the barrelhead. These were the ones that Gloria and I liked most.

I did have one scholarship that was most rewarding. I was selected for it by one of my finance professors, Professor Agnes DeFranco. She told me at the outset that there was no money involved in this scholarship from the International Society of Hospitality Consultants (ISHC). I applied anyway, and received the honor, because I was targeting a certain international hospitality research and consulting firm, of which they had several consultants as members. Each year they offered and granted two scholarships to HRM majors and provided airfare and hotel expenses for the trip to receive them. I was honored to accept one of the two slots that year, and I proudly went to Nashville to receive the award on their association's tenth anniversary.

Dr. DeFranco witnessed my academic maturation because she had been one of my two CHE class instructors when I was a freshman. She would later also recommend me for another very honorable international scholarship. Later, in graduate school, I was very pleased that she was in charge of my thesis; I am extremely indebted to her as one of the principle educators who challenged and shaped my mind.

The other young recipient of the ISHC scholarship that year was from the University of Michigan, which meant the Cornelians had been usurped by two competing HRM program students. The hotelies from Cornell had had a lock on both positions for the previous nine years. It was a shock to many of the mandatory attendees that any other school would even be offered the privilege. I found this out when several attendee consultants and Cornell alumni bought me drinks in the bar at the Nashville Gaylord Hotel. While I sipped an adult beverage, the Michigan recipient had to be satisfied with a cola because of his age. I thought back to the time when I had come home after two years in a war zone and still could not buy a beer legally. There was something satisfying in this picture, so I ordered another.

I would later classify all the scholarships as internal, university, or general industry. The internal scholarships were directly from the Hilton Foundation and different hotels, restaurants, and suppliers to the industry, such as Bass Hotels (now Intercontinental Hotels), T.G.I. Friday Restaurants, and Sysco Foods. The university scholarships usually came from the Fortune Fifty industries in the Houston metropolitan statistical area that supported the college and recruited new graduates, for example, Exxon Petroleum, Kirby Lumber Company, and Hughes Tools. The general industry scholarships were those we applied for on our own, outside of the college, university, geographic area, or HRM industry but might have a link to outside of education through a family member, especially parents and grandparents. These general scholarship providers were organizations such as the Knights of Columbus, Daughters of the American Revolution, or private endowments.

In the second scholarship cycle year, I was getting prepared during the short Thanksgiving break because I knew that during the upcoming Christmas holiday season I would be taking classes elsewhere. In updating my personal scholarship portfolio, I added and revised my boilerplate paragraphs for every imaginable potential scholarship I could target. My electronic calendar and the interchangeable boilerplates were finely tuned, and if I had had any doubts the first year about applying for any and all scholarships, I didn't in the second cycle, not even remotely. I even applied for and received scholarships that came in handy from a Cattle Women's Association, an aspirin firm, and a few manufacturing endowments.

Part of my preparation for the scholarship cycle included preparing numerous thank-you letters that could easily have the relevant company or association's details inserted and would be printed when the checks arrived. Gloria especially liked licking the stamps for those envelopes after she made out the deposit slips.

TEACHING SCHOLARSHIPS

By the time the second scholarship cycle rolled around, the other students had become aware that Eric and I were cashing in and decided we were ahead of the curve. Whispers from different professors blew our cover, and people began asking questions. We had thought that by the time everybody else caught on, we would already have graduated, but I decided that with my CHE qualification, I would teach an extracurricular scholarship class. Why not; I was certified, right? I taught three classes and then stopped, because "enrollment" grew exponentially and got completely out of hand, to the point where students were constantly stalking me for all kinds of advice, even to write their boilerplates. As my time was extremely limited, I needed to give them a polite "no."

For my class, I decided to use a technique similar to one another professor had used in a class I had taken a decade before that had been an extremely effective learning system. Dr. Glenn Cordua y Cruz had taught a week-long extracurricular class at the University of Houston School of Continuing Education on database management, which involved the use of roughly forty computer stations with the old external floppy disk computers. At the beginning of the class, he had distributed a complete set of that season's baseball cards amongst the stations, so each station ended up with about forty cards. Then, he had divided the class, with the females in baseball's National League and the males in the American League. The exercise was to build a database of baseball statistics, and this technique made the class easy to understand and very interesting. The girls could type faster, but the guys had the advantage of knowing more about baseball.

During the first week, we entered each player's statistical information from the back of each card, including hits, runs, earned run average, bases stolen, etc., until we had a complete statistical database of baseball. During the second week, as I recall, we learned how to create databases and parse the information that we had typed in and the hard data we had entered. Then, by exchanging floppy disks, we compiled all the data and uploaded it onto Professor Cordua's computer. Now, I know the good professor would never use this data for his personal ill-gotten gains or to enrich himself through the use of multiregression analysis to place wagers on the upcoming World Series, as the professor and I developed a friendship that lasts to this day, but the thought did cross my mind.

After the course was over, Dr. Cordua and I formed a partnership in the restaurant real estate business. He would manage the computerized site-location research, and I would use my Texas broker's license and my contacts within the industry to buy, sell, and broker numerous restaurants in Texas. Eventually, Glenn became so enamored with the restaurant industry that he and his brother Michael would open a South American steakhouse called Churrasco's imitate after the El Novillo Restaurant in Miami. After a decade in the restaurant business in several ventures, both Glenn and I would gravitate back to the University of Houston at the Hilton College, he as a professor and I as a freshman student.

In my undergraduate junior semester, I took a hospitality controls class from Dr. Cordua, with an arm's-length symbiotic relationship; we got through it together. It was a great class, and I was amazed at how much I still learned from him. He was one of the many professors who cheered me on, and for that, and also for the A– I received, I am indebted to him.

It was Dr. Cordua's example in reverse that I used in my scholarships class. I had all the information on one disc and disseminated the data in bits, until everyone had the same application as an example template. Not everybody told me how much they actually received in scholarship money, so I could not get a final total for my class members' scholarship achievements, but in my senior year, I was extremely well-liked by numerous students and faculty members alike.

Larger scholarships were now within the reach for Eric and me. Once in graduate school, the scholarships, endowments, and grants are like the second half of the television show *Jeopardy*, where they go into Double Jeopardy, and the $500, $1,000, and $2,000 minimums were elevated to $3,000, $5,000, and on up to $20,000. With the amount of money on the table and the number of students in my classes, we should have easily and collectively reached several hundred thousand dollars or more.

INTERNSHIPS & TRAVEL

Some of the best college times I had outside of the traditional classroom were on internships, projects, and awards out of town. I went wherever I could learn something and forge any link between a class and practical knowledge and experience. Of course I flew to most cities thanks to my wife's personal benefits on American Airlines, but I drove to others if time permitted, as I really disliked flying standby because of my experiences with military hops. As a dependent student (D-2 airline classification), I flew to Boulder, Colorado; Lake Charles, Louisiana; Santa Fe and Albuquerque, New Mexico; Atlanta, Georgia (several trips); Austin, Lubbock, and Houston, Texas; New York City; Nashville, Tennessee; Somerset, New Jersey; and St Louis, Missouri. If I add in the multiple trips to Ithaca, New York, and Atlanta, it would total a dozen cities I went to learn. As a result, I kept a pretty full schedule to not miss any classes, which was one of the agreements I had made with myself, no matter what.

My first internship was in Boulder, Colorado, with HVS (Hotel Valuation Services) International, where I would apply my financial and real estate knowledge to this firm specializing in hotel appraisal, feasibility, and consulting. Because this was my first internship, I did not think to get course credit, but I learned a lot in the weeks during the Christmas break that I was there. One good thing was that Gloria and Amanda came up to see me and got to go snow skiing and enjoy a snowy, holiday vacation season while I worked. Then the three of us flew home like vagabonds to be with the rest of the family. If only one of us made each flight, we could wind up at Houston's two major airports while the last one to go could wind up in St. Louis or Chicago before coming home. After a warm family Christmas in Houston with the family, I returned to an icy Boulder to finish my internship.

I was just as impressed with HVS as I guess they were impressed with me and my work, because they asked me back for spring break. I also helped appraise the Astrodome Hotel, about two miles from my home, during that semester. An additional hotel that I assisted in appraising was the Four Seasons Hotel in Austin, Texas. I drove from Houston after classes on Thursday and worked over Friday and Saturday and studied intermittently in the evenings and at night. Of course on Sunday I had to double up to catch up. Although I believe that I had a standing job offer from the managing director at HVS after I graduated, I've always wondered what would have happened if I had actually gone to work for them.

During the spring semester, I volunteered to go to Lake Charles, Louisiana, where they had recently opened casinos with Class III gaming: slot machines, blackjack, roulette, etc. I was doing a paper for a gaming management class, so I got to interview several of the in-house security, pit bosses, dealers and managers. Because of my maturity and knowledge of tending bar and dealing blackjack, I was offered a position as a shill and a mystery guest for theft prevention. As I said before, earlier in my restaurant career, I had mixed more than a million drinks as a bartender and club manager at the Black Angus, the Red Lion, and Steak and Ale, and I had dealt blackjack in Seabrook, Texas, at Odds' R. Right then, however, I just did not have the time, but I did sincerely thank them for their offer.

During the summer, I headed to Santa Fe, New Mexico, for another internship with a company called Six Hats. The name was derived from the book *Six Thinking Hats* by Edward de Bono and was used with his permission. This was a hotel baptism of fire and probably my most interesting internship, because the Six Hats company had legally taken over the property in a hostile environment. Three of us, from different parts of the country, met in Santa Fe and literally physically took over the hotel...court order and checkbook in hand.

The night before we took over the hotel by force with the local sheriff, we had met with the asset manager (owner's representative) of the hotel, who informed us that the hotel's occupancy had disintegrated from 70% to 30% and that in a short period of time, the hotel managers had cheated the brand-holders out of royalties and the owner's bank out of hundreds of thousands of dollars worth of loans. During an extensive renovation, the managers had skimmed the money for repairs and not put it into the intended construction.

The night before we fired everybody, I had a drink at the huge nightclub that was attached to the hotel. I could tell in about ten seconds that the managers and employees were stealing and double-dealing from both sides of the bar.

Prostitutes were working the single johns, and dope was flowing out of the restrooms. I'm sure that I had been given this simply wonderful opportunity and once-in-a-lifetime experience because of my credibility and maturity but more likely because of my size and my Marine Corps training.

We also figured out pretty quickly that the managers were cooking the books, so the first couple of days were spent balancing records and running off the dope dealers, prostitutes, scammers, and thieves. It was amazing that for the following weeks I was there, johns would call on the phone and come in person looking for hookers, only to find out that we were not running a house of ill repute any longer. Some guys, out of desperation, would ask me where their "friends" had gone. After the first few, I just gave them an address: 2515 Camino Entrada, which, of course, was the City of Santa Fe Police Station.

The owners of this 100-plus–room property had borrowed a couple of million dollars to renovate the building and the property; however, the operating management firm had put 90% of the money into their pockets and 10% into the hotel, which was enough to put a fair curb appeal and a good face on an illicit product, or put lipstick on a pig. The three of us took over and fired every last employee on-site, then replaced them with a new crew, which in turn wasn't really much better. Eventually, we realized that the hotel and restaurant labor pool in the area was finite, so we stopped firing them and just told them to go home, as we knew in a couple of seasons we would have to hire them back again. Tempers flared, people pushed, shoved and demanded excessive paychecks and past nonexistent tips, while the bill collectors were stacked up three deep at the front desk. The brand-holder was also in the process of stripping the brand, the reservation system, and anything with their logo on it, under another court order. At that point, we still did not even have a new name for the hotel.

This was a situation in which the three of us worked around the clock and slept with one eye open, literally. Between midnight and 3 am, I would stand guard duty and study in the general manager's office. On Fridays and Saturdays, we kept a 66% watch (two of us) for strength, until the "trash" finally began abating and business began growing again. After about three to four weeks on the site, when I felt it was safe for them to come, Gloria took one of her vacation weeks, and Amanda, who was on summer break, both came to visit. The girls had another ball, in a desert setting this time, and while I worked, they used my car for their activities and I continued to work and study hard.

When I left that hotel, it had been turned back into a respectable, working property, but only through our hard work, several subcontractors, and a lot of heated discussions. In short order, the grounds were manicured, the rooms were quickly and modestly renovated, the swimming pool was again working, and the hotel was re-permitted by the city of Santa Fe to accept guests. The three of us had reversed the low occupancy and raised it back up to over 75% in a short time. But the damage done to the property through the community at large would most likely take years to repair.

After all was said and done, the Six Hats takeover firm established itself; the bank got its money; and I did a report for college credit, received another good grade, and got some tumultuous on-the-job training. All in all, it was a good trade-off. In retrospect, the course's name was an ironic understatement, because it is listed on my transcript as "Special Problems."

During the last three weeks of my time in Santa Fe, the other two managers of the hotel had encouraged me to study for my GRE so I could attend graduate school. I later took a Princeton Review prep test class for it in Albuquerque, New Mexico. It was during this period that I made about an additional 2800 vocabulary flashcards to score the highest GRE grade I could possibly get.

PULLING A RABBIT OUT OF THE HAT

During the following fall semester, one of my other cousins mailed me an invitation to his wedding, and because he had waited so long to get married and I hadn't seen him in years, Gloria and I felt both obliged and privileged to go. The only problem was that the wedding was in Somerset, New Jersey, in the middle of a semester. This was a three-leg trip with flight changeovers in Dallas and La Guardia and a rental-car drive to Somerset. Another conflict arose because I was now head of a project group of four students for my lodging class that had procrastinated in the early part of the semester in reporting and research. But my time had also gotten away from me, and I felt the group was in danger of turning in a substandard report. I was usually better off working by myself, but the professor had said no, and the group insisted we could pull it off.

As each week flew by and quickly slipped through my fingers, I did not connect the dates of the wedding with the group's completion dates, so I double-booked that crucial weekend to be in two places at one time. I tried to remedy the situation by going to the professor. I knew better than trying to ask for an extension, so instead I asked if we could alter our project. I submitted a proposal that the project would compare and contrast like-branded union hotels against non-union properties from derived income summary statements and labor statistics. I knew that union properties were prevalent in New Jersey and New York but almost nonexistent in Houston. After receiving permission to proceed, I informed the three other group members that they needed to interview Courtyard and Sheraton hotel managers because one was a full-service and the other was a limited (select) service property. Conversely, I got on the phone and made reservations at two union hotels, also a Courtyard and a Sheraton. When the family and I flew up to my cousin's wedding, they again had a ball while I interviewed hotel managers in the New York City and Somerset, New Jersey properties.

I had made appointments in advance with the general managers of the properties that we booked our reservations in and told them of my project. Everyone had seemed okay until I arrived. After I arrived, however, they were very hesitant to give me any information about their properties, especially discussing their profit-and-loss statements. Even after I showed them my student ID, they were still doubtful, so I even showed them the course syllabus. One of the managers actually called my professor to make sure that I was on the up and up.

In the end, when the group assembled the project and turned it in, it was not only flawless, but because the properties were from out of state, it showed distinctiveness, compared to the rest of the groups' only local hotels. The professor was so impressed with the report that he did not want to give the original back. The group didn't care, however, and I had the only "final" electronic copy. It would be up to a year later before everyone in the group eventually wanted a copy back from me to show a prospective employer some work they had completed in college to put their best feet forward.

MORE INTERNSHIPS AND TRAVEL

I also had a couple of internships with PKF Consulting in Atlanta, Georgia—one over the Christmas break and the other over spring break. Later, I would return to Atlanta after being invited by a professor I had known earlier in my career to be a guest lecturer at Georgia Tech. He figured that I was getting all "manned up" with education and could give my insight into an earlier Racketeering Influenced Corruption Organization (RICO) lawsuit in which I had been the lead plaintiff, as the title of my presentation was "Ethics in Business."

Soon afterwards, I attended the wedding of a son of one of my other cousins in St. Louis. By this time, I was getting extremely proficient at interviewing hotel managers. On this junket I got to look at aspects of riverboat casinos on the Mississippi. During a casino management class we were told about how several independent casino boats on the river would moor on either the Missouri or the Illinois side to pick up gamers. It seems that the respective governors of each state had a standing college football bet from year to year and were extremely competitive. When riverboat gaming was licensed in one state, to safeguard the population from the vice, they instituted a $10 limit per bet. Naturally, it wasn't too long before the other state allowed gaming and, to get the boats to its docks, raised the limit per bet to $25. As the story goes, the opposite state then instituted a $50 maximum bet and all the boats returned to the other side. The bet limit was then made unlimited, whereupon the two governors supposedly got into a fistfight. I took advantage by interviewing the juxtaposed parties, the Missouri and Illinois riverboat casino managers.

When I add up all my trips, it seems like I spent more time standing-by in airports rather than in classrooms. Nevertheless, when I was standing-by, I had my nose in a book, was flashing my cards, or had my headphones on, listening to a tape. I was also always lugging around a full book bag or two over my shoulders. But everywhere I went, people were kind and courteous to me. More often than not, people always thought I was some type of professor, and as we politely exchanged our itineraries, they would always cheer me on with encouragement. Even students I sat next to going back and forth from whatever college would notice that I was studying the curse of college algebra and would interrupt me when I paused for a long time and discuss the problem that I was having difficulty with.

The one thing I did not like about flying standby was that if I missed the last flight of the night, I would be scratched and my name would be rolled over to the first flight in the morning, so whenever the gate attendant would turn on the lights at four o'clock in the morning, I would have my elbows on the counter and be the first in line to check in. That way, when I made the first flight out, I could be back in Houston and in class by nine or ten o'clock, unshaven but ready to go.

I always had a tremendous advantage in travel because of my wonderful wife. She was always either at work or at home, which meant she was in front of the computer, and with her inside knowledge of the airlines, she could look at the space available or any diversions of flights on most major carriers. As an insider, she would often reroute me from New York to Chicago or St. Louis, or Dallas to Houston. Because Dallas was American's major hub and corporate headquarters, I would usually go through there but was often rerouted through Miami, Philadelphia, Nashville, and various other places. During inclement weather, like gulf coast Texas hurricanes or wind shears in Dallas, Gloria sometimes rerouted me to San Antonio, where I would rent a car and drive to make a class in Houston by ten.

When Gloria, the kids, and I would all be going somewhere, we would sometimes arrive in three different airports on two different airlines, but Gloria was truly gifted in getting us where we needed to be at all times. In any airport, she could use multiple pay phones, cell phones, and computers to simultaneously call girlfriends behind the desks and counters of other airlines. When she performed her magic, it was rare for one of the family members to get stranded. Before I had registered as a freshman at the Hilton College and the University of Houston, it had never crossed my mind that American Airlines would be of such benefit to me and would prove to be so invaluable.

I did make one other flight to Lubbock, Texas, to see our son Travis, who was still at Texas Tech at the time. The secondary reason I went there was to investigate a Research in Hospitality and Management PhD program. Because I was looking to take the PhD and skip over the masters program, I sought advice from two professors I knew: Professors Frank Borsenik from UNLV and Clinton Rappole, who had earlier been a dean at the Hilton College and was then the Eric Hilton Distinguished Chair; they both advised me to do the masters program first.

After much discussion with both professors, they pointed out that if I bombed any of my courses or if my dissertation did not include enough research to be awarded the PhD, by skipping the masters, I would be left with only a Bachelor of Science degree. This is when I again did a lot of soul-searching about what I really wanted from life and how was I going to get there. When I talked with Barbara Kinseth at the VA again, she cleared the way for me to either do a masters at the Hilton or Cornell, or a PhD at Texas Tech or Cornell.

I turned down numerous speaking engagements at other colleges from professors I had met at the CHE program and knew from the industry, including the University of Nevada, Las Vegas; Harrah's College (UNLV); Florida International University (FIU); and Michigan State University School of Hospitality Business. I turned them down because they invited me thinking I was a PhD professor taking the course. I had forgotten to mention to them that I was only a freshman; no one had asked, so I had never taken off my mask.

ONE OF MY LIFE'S BIGGEST REGRETS

One of the biggest regrets of my life is that I missed the most important event in my son Dennis's military career because of my study schedule. Dennis was in the 23rd Marines Reserve Regiment in the last year of his six-year hitch and was based in Houston. His platoon achieved the Top Gun award for infantry, which is called Super Squad. This award is for the best of the best of the Marine Corps, and Dennis's squad had achieved record-breaking performances. For this, they were each awarded Navy Commendations, which were personally presented to them by the Commandant of the Marine Corps with a full-blown parade with honors at Eighth and I Streets in Washington, DC.

I will always feel as guilty as hell about not going to that event for my son because of some relatively insignificant college crap of mine. I feel as guilty about that as about being a Khe Sanh survivor. These are two scars in my life, among others, that will never heal. If I were to ever have it to do all over again, I would trade all the honors I received in both the military and in college to see my son Dennis presented with that award that day.

The only thing that has somewhat made up for it is that he and his wife, Melissa, have presented Gloria and me with five adorable grandchildren, four girls and a boy, who will be a third-generation Marine and the next Commandant of the Marine Corps. I do plan on hanging around for that one, which is goal number 196 yet to do on my bucket list, and moving up.

Through all the challenges and the perceived times of hardship, though I have turned everything around into one of the most exhilarating, thought-provoking, educational times of my life, and the best was yet to come!

CHAPTER TWENTY-SEVEN
Accolades

In the beginning, I thought if I got the grades I was shooting for, I would just graduate with honors (cum laude), with high honors (magna cum laude), or with highest honors (summa cum laude) and that would be it. Although many universities use the thresholds of 3.25, 3.50, and 3.75, some deviate slightly, with some even as high as 3.8 for summa cum laude. During the eight consecutive semesters that I attended, my last five were on the dean's list, and two of those five were at a 4.0 GPA. My lowest GPA was a 3.66 in a summer session.

When all was totaled, I received a 3.88 GPA with a 3.95 concentration GPA. But, after achieving the academic level that I wanted and applying for numerous scholarships, I started receiving a number of awards and honors that were bestowed upon me, one right after another...none of which I had ever thought of or imagined receiving.

During my senior year, in the spring of 1999, I was asked to apply for, or was nominated for, numerous awards by various professors, deans, and vice chancellors who put my name in the hat. Because UH is not a Phi Beta Kappa institution, some of these were impossible to achieve. I did, however, qualify for the equivalent designation of a Phi Kappa Phi ~ National Honor Society recipient. I was also listed for two consecutive years on the National Dean's List, as well as on the Golden Key National Honor Society (GKN), Phi Beta Delta ~ Honor Society for International Scholars—Delta Iota Chapter, Eta Sigma Delta and the International Hospitality Honor Society, and in *Who's Who Among Students in American Universities & Colleges*.

The highest of ten academic Greek-type fraternities I was inducted into was Omicron Delta Kappa, a National Leadership Society. This award is only given if the academic institution has formed a "Circle" university and is nationwide. Applicants are recommended by the university's hierarchy. Many student recipients are nationally and internationally known. Five basic areas are covered, and the applicant must excel in: scholarship, athletics, campus or community service, social and religious activities and campus government, journalism, speech and mass media or creative and performing arts.

At each participating university or college, only a few awards were given because of the stringency within the institution. If no one qualified in a particular year, then no one was inducted. Past inductees, we were told, were internationally known household names including statesmen, financiers, and laureates. Several nominations from UH included student body presidents, student ambassadors to different continents such as Europe, and gold-medal Olympians such as Carl Lewis, Clyde Drexler, and Akeem Olajuwon.

When I received my notification that I was to be inducted into ODK, I dropped the phone in shock. At the induction ceremony, I received my pledge from a billionaire businessman who had been a recipient years earlier. The two other inductees and I were informed that the individual bar for us was extremely high and we were expected to clear it and make way for others behind us. I hope that through this writing, I can achieve this and cross another goal off my bucket list.

As a student, I held several association positions, including membership in the Texas Restaurant Association (TRA) Cougar Chapter, concurrent with membership in the Houston Restaurant Association (HRA) Student Chapter, Founding Advisor for the International Food Service Executives Association (IFSEA), Founding President of the Disabled Students Association (DSA), and Chapter Secretary for Toastmasters International (TI).

I received miscellaneous awards such as a Writing Excellence Award at Houston Community College (HCC) with a paper titled "Flambé," as in tableside cooking. Another distinction included "Best in Class" Hotel Financial Analysis at Cornell University from a graduate/undergraduate senior course.

OUR FIRST CHC CLASS RING

One other accomplishment that I am especially proud of is that I conceived, designed, and implemented the first Conrad N. Hilton College (CHC) senior class ring. As I look back, it was no easy feat and actually took me about two years to complete because of all the approvals, academic hurdles, and red tape that I had to go through. I designed it with a traditional hospitality lamplight in the center, with the name of the college around the outside border, reading "Conrad N. Hilton College" and including the University of Houston acronym, UH, in the center bottom of the ring. After some research, I included engraved eucalyptus leaves on the left and live oak on the right, which were all symbolic of the university, the college, and the great state of Texas.

As the project progressed and more people and entities got involved, the more the project slowed. Letters had to be written, and, just like in the military, rank has its privileges. Feathers were ruffled in different echelons of academic power. I would take the design to one person or entity and it would be okay, then some person above wanted another change or the project would sit on someone's desk.

Some of the entities involved were the Hilton Foundation; the ring manufacturer, ArtCarved Class Rings; the chancellor, a couple of vice chancellors, several deans; a student committee, plus Eric Hilton and probably several wives.

The first Hilton College senior class ring.

It seemed like I had opened Pandora's Box. Some colleges at UH, such as engineering, pharmacy, and law, had rings, but ten others did not. When one college was granted permission, other colleges wanted the same, so I kept on writing letters, changing artwork, and waiting. After much correspondence and patience, my persistence prevailed, several parties signed off on the project, and a couple weeks before I graduated, my gold ring was delivered, to my personal satisfaction.

To market the ring, I got the student chapter of the Hotel Sales and Marketing Association International (HSMAI) to boost sales and start a tradition. But as always, there was a faction of students who spread the rumor that I received a personal percentage of the sales. This was basically the same group who did not like me getting scholarships or awards, as again they felt I was taking things away from them, whatever.

STUDENT OF THE YEAR

The highest award that I received was the University of Houston's Dean of Student Affairs Award, which unofficially, I guess, is like student of the year. I am not quite sure who put me up for the award, but I was nominated for it, even though I did not even know it existed until I was contacted to fill out the forms. Naturally, I revised the application form and provided the committee with a diskette for their future distribution use instead of completing the copied forms. This was an award for which there were a series of cuts to gradually sift through the vast number of students who were nominated. There were also self-nominations from hundreds of other students. I suspected that students who had been nominated by professors of various degrees, deans, and chancellors would garner the most attention. I would imagine the higher the prestige and title of the nominator, the more weight was afforded the nominee.

I would further imagine that the outlying UH campuses of UH–Clear Lake, UH–Downtown, UH–Victoria and UH–Cinco Ranch had the least amount of pull, while central colleges that had been around since the founding in 1927 had the greatest. The Hilton College was, from what I was told, lower in significance because it was so new, having only been established in 1970. While waiting for my interview, I was also told by the personal secretary of the dean in charge that no one from the Hilton had ever made the cut thus far.

After representatives from each of the fourteen colleges made all the cuts from several hundred nominations, about a dozen or so nominees were scheduled for grueling interviews from the college representatives, including deans, assistant deans, and full tenured professors. Each college's representative was politicking for his or her own college's students.

For openers, I thought about sending a box of chocolates or a bouquet of flowers to the dean's administrative assistant but decided that would be a little over the top and an obvious suck-up. For the interview, I prepared by going to the library and researched each college to find out their founding year, their benefactors and their impact on the community at large and the world, such as Professor Paul Chu's incredible 1987 breakthrough in superconductivity. After finding out who was on the committee, I outlined each member's most recent international awards so I could flatter and pay homage to each representative and his or her college during my interview. I also discovered in my research the number one "want" of the university, the golden nugget that almost all Texas colleges were drooling over: to become the next Tier I facility in the state. I found out what made them passionate: the idea that with "our" university, "we" could conquer and turn that dream into a realistic goal.

Naturally, I was the oldest student being interviewed. When the interview first started, I think my age came into question, although my qualifications were also under close scrutiny. However, the points I made hit hard and were well received, as I looked each representative in the eye with the firm determination that if I could obtain my goals, they could too. Just the tingling thought of turning a junior college into a Tier I multi-college and major university institution in a short time was mind boggling. But when I put the image on the table, the group looked intently between my open palms and saw the vision. I challenged them. Anthony Robbins and Frank Abagnale would both have been proud.

At the university presentation ceremony, hosted by the campus hierarchy and the Dean of Student Affairs, Dr. William F. Munson led the drumroll of awards. First, the honorable mentions were given, then the third, second, and first runner-ups were announced, with all their exceptional credentials: president of this, chairman of that, ambassador to this, that gold Olympiad, etc. After hearing all those back-to-back awards, I clearly remember saying to myself that I did not have a snowball's chance in hell of having my name read. But much to my amazement, out of about 40,000 students, my name was announced. I was given a plaque, and I immediately fast-walked back over to the Hilton College to show the dean what I had brought home for the team.

I felt like I was Mr. America, had just won the U.S. Open, and had just scratched off a multimillion-dollar lottery ticket all at once. It was a once-in-a-lifetime experience, and I still get goose bumps thinking of the exhilaration. Now I feel it is my duty and responsibility to live out my life as a real example to other students and within my family as a dedicated recipient.

CHAPTER TWENTY-EIGHT
Redemption Week

AMNESIA

"If I did not have any flashbacks and panic attacks
I would not have any memory at all!"

Claude Regis Vargo

In an ironic twist, after all my hard work and pushing myself to the breaking point for two years, it was my final exams at the very end that wound up almost killing me...literally. The first day of my finals, I had scheduled the first test at 8:00, finishing at 9:30. From 9:30 until 11:00, I could study for the next test, which was from 11:00 to 12:30. Then I could take lunch and study until test number three, at 2:00. This ran until 3:30, and I would take the fourth test of the day from 3:30 to 5:00.

The first day of finals went really well, and I went home to study for the next and final round of five tests the next day. My schedule for the tests was approximately the same on the second day, except I had one more test to study for, from 5:00 to 6:30. I would take that extra fifth test from 6:30 until 8:00, when the DTC closed.

The first four tests of the next day went just fine, but by the end of the afternoon, I had developed a severe headache and for some reason I was feeling an extremely high level of anxiety and stress. My chest hurt so bad, I actually thought I might be having a real heart attack, and I had to lie on the ground several times to catch my breath. I knew I had no choice but to finish the test, I had made it too far to crash now. The Marine in me and my survival instincts both kicked in, and neither would let me quit or have a stroke and die now. I had come way too far, and I had to finish.

I slowed down my breathing, totally focused, and forced myself to calm down and concentrate. I was finally able to gain some feeling of control over myself, and I held on to it for dear life, just long enough to finish my last test. But during the whole test and afterwards, I felt very strange, like I was in a dream, looking in. By the time I was finally done with my exam, it was very late and I was one of the last ones to leave the building. On the way out I went to the student proctor to get my ID and found out the drawer that my student ID and driver's license had been put in had already been locked up for the night, and I would have to get them the following day.

As I left the DTC and started walking to my car, things continued to get progressively worse, and I was in such a daze I started feeling detached from everything around me. I was walking down the path, but now I was suddenly unable to remember anything about myself, where I was going, or what I was supposed to be doing. It was a very frightening and very strange feeling of being totally disoriented and not knowing where I was going. It was getting dark, and the only thought I could rationalize and cling to was that because I was walking, I must be walking to my car. I grappled with my feelings of confusion and rising panic as I looked around the parking lot and realized I had no idea which car was mine.

A security guard stopped me under an overhead light and asked me for identification. When I could not produce any, he took a step back and, with a radio, called for backup, the security desk or the testing center. As I set my two heavily filled book bags down, I gave him the only fact that I was sure of: my driver's license and student identification were locked up in the DTC. I was verified, thankfully, I guess by the student proctor, and the guard told me I could go.

Still wandering around, looking for my car, I eventually bumped into someone who obviously knew me, although I did not have the foggiest idea who he was. After a short chitchat, desperately searching in his words for a clue as to his identity—or mine, for that matter, I simply told him that I had lost my car. I suppose I didn't otherwise seem disoriented, and for some reason, I didn't want anyone to know, so I just hid it really well. He smiled and responded by telling me it was probably in the basement garage of the hotel in one of the handicapped spaces by the elevator, and pointed in the general direction where I always parked it.

Making my way to the hotel basement, I meandered through the garage until I saw a car in a handicapped space. I did not recognize it all, but it matched with the keys in my pocket. It was an eerie feeling, leaving the university, knowing how to drive but not knowing where I was going. It was sometime later, as I drove around in search of anything that looked familiar, that a cop pulled me over. He told me that I looked dazed or drunk, and he called in my Purple Heart license plate number. It came back clean, and I passed a breathalyzer test.

I don't remember exactly, but he either gave me a warning ticket or wrote my address down on a piece of paper and asked me to confirm my address. When he said 6-5-0-8, I instinctively told him West Chase, which in fact was my address, but I had no clue what the words meant. Because he worked in the small township that we lived in, he gave me VIP service to my front door, after he had me lock up my car on the spot and made me give him my keys. We drove up to our house, and he gave me back the keys, but I did not need to use them, because the cop (who I am actually *very* grateful to) had made sure that he had turned every single light on his patrol car so the whole neighborhood was lit up and knew I had gotten home. When I walked up to the house, a strange, very mad-looking lady opened the front door. I felt a great amount of guilt and remorse, but I didn't know why. I didn't know what to say to her. The lady angrily said something like, "At least you're still alive!" and she showed me where to crash for the night.

The next thing I can clearly remember was Gloria taking me to the veterans hospital to see what was wrong with me. After consultation with a couple of doctors, they diagnosed me with transient global amnesia (TGA). Gloria commented to the doctor that I looked like I had gotten hit by Mike Tyson or Mohammad Ali. I felt the blood in my face instantly drain to my chest when I heard the diagnosis of yet another psychological problem, not knowing why.

Gloria asked the doctor if electroshock treatment would be of any value, and she told him that I had undergone that type of therapy twenty-five years earlier. After several daily visits, undergoing a more civilized type of therapy session, my memory began to return to a somewhat more normal state. Gloria still teases me that I'm almost 50% better. Just like Peter Pan's uncle in the movie *Hook*, she tells me (and everyone else) that we both are still looking for our marbles.

The next week was very slow, but fortunately, all my school work had been completed, except for one more exit test from the university. Over the next several days, Gloria babied me and waited for me to catch up to the world while she administered various medications and massive amounts of love and affection, which I naturally played along with.

I had always thought of education as a purely mental function and had never thought of it as a physical exercise. Most one-off single tests that I had taken earlier in class or in a cubicle were pretty much routine, but this last-semester volley had really taken it out of me. For the first time, I felt my age. My fingers were understandably always a little swollen from the broken bones and arthritis, but now all my muscle groups felt like they were pulling my tendons off my bones. I ached. I had lifted a lot of weights in my time, but this was a combined mental stress and physical release that I had not ever encountered previously—or since. If I had to sum it up, my body felt like it was ready to suffer a total, volcano-like collapse, complete with tremors and aftershocks. My head was ready to explode.

EXIT TEST

"When the goal is in sight, all your physical pain disappears, and your mental determination shall carry you the rest of the way."

Trey Patty

The state of Texas legislature, in all their academic wisdom, had, years earlier, instituted a program whereby, after each potential graduate completed his or her curriculum, he or she should be able to correctly write a term paper, graded by independent proctors, before being given his or her sheepskin. I'd never really heard about it until my last semester, or the news about taking it may have just gone over my head, as I never really had a freshman orientation class. At any rate, the closer graduation came, the more I realized this was not going to be another gimme, as the university was giving prep tests for the "exit" exam.

By this time, I had taken more than forty courses for credit, together with several noncredit exercises, and had written countless papers, so I thought I had nothing to worry about. But then I started thinking that whereas all the papers I had written had been edited by paid and unpaid tutors, this test was in ink and had to be flawless to achieve a pass to graduate. I suppose that's one of the reasons some football players complete all their courses and do not graduate—there is no one to help them through that writing test.

I found out through the DTC that the exam was given once a semester at each state-supported college in Texas. I also found out that there were students who had to come back to the university from all over to retake the test after they had flunked it the first time. In fact, I was told there were students who ended up returning every semester as they flunked it repeatedly for two, three, or more semesters in a row. I had no intention of having gone through all this only to be stopped by one last small and very stupid test at the end. With great haste and renewed determination, I immediately sought out the prep class.

The prep class was uneventful, but all I heard on student break was how hard the test was. These comments, however, were from students who were majors in subjects that did not require narrative writing, such as math and pharmacology. They were worried; I was not. The only thing that made me nervous was that because of the scoring of the test and it being a narrative, it would take a while to grade the papers individually. The test was taken so close to the graduation ceremony that no one would know for sure if they had passed until just before the actual graduation.

I thought about the invitations I had made and sent to practically everybody in Houston. I had done everything except invite the *Houston Chronicle* and broadcast it from the Transco Tower in the Galleria. Now I pondered if that had been a wise decision. What if this was a repeat of high school and I flunked again, right at the very end? I knew if I flunked the exam, it wasn't going to be given again until the following December. There would go graduate school. How would I find a permanent job without a degree, after not graduating again? It was a torturous thought.

I took the exit test back at the DTC, to remove as much anxiety as possible and reduce the chance of any unwanted panic attacks. Like everyone else, I took the test with only a pen and blue book paper so the examiners could see every stroke of ink, the misspellings, punctuation errors, and cross-outs for sentences that did not flow. The subject and the topic were preselected and were generic enough that the subject matter should be easy enough to write about, but, the essay's internal structure had to be perfect, with perfect sentences obeying all the grammatical rules. We were, however, given the choice of printing or writing incursive.

I was now pondering the memory of Sister Marcella again back in the fifth grade, beating me with a triple-thick ruler for not staying on the dotted lines to write incursive. After each of "our" corporal punishment sessions that "I made her do," she would always grab her four-foot rosary with those gigantic black beads dangling from her side and hold them up to heaven. At first I was sure she was going to choke me with them, but in the end she would break out into tears and ask forgiveness, though of course not from me.

"LIVE MAN WALKING"

I physically survived taking this test okay, but I had a couple of days afterwards when the result, and its repercussions, really chewed on me. Psychologically, I was going downhill and starting to work my way up into a fury. I remembered the story floating around from the previous year about Miguel Sanchez. The story started with Miguel standing in line to walk in his graduation ceremony.

Miguel was a brilliant young man from Spain who was expected to be awarded the high GPA for his college, and maybe even his college's Dean's Award. He was in line with a couple hundred other graduates when he was tapped on the shoulder and told to go see the dean. It seems he had not passed the university exit exam and was also a one-hour lab short of completing his degree. The course lab he needed would not be given again until the following spring semester, thereby throwing his graduation off a year. Poor Miguel was not permitted to walk, nor even to sit amongst the graduate nominees. He was physically removed and de-robed in nervous lines of students.

Everyone knew that Miguel's family was in the auditorium, including his new fiancée, who was sure to keep him with her in America for love alone. His family had come all the way from Europe and beyond to celebrate their very special family occasion. What was worse, he had a job at Hewlett-Packard, which was in the middle of a hiring frenzy. His fantastic salary package and agreement was, of course, contingent upon his completed degree. Worse yet, when his fiancée found out the news of his dilemma, she split, and his student visa was soon expiring. Miguel had deservedly thought this day would be special. But it would not be special at all.

I could only imagine his feelings as he was "escorted" out of the waiting area. It must have been just like a man going to the electric chair in shackles, hearing a deputy shout, "Dead man walking!" There had been so many previous exceptions made so students could walk without completing their full curricula that the deans of the colleges and the university had decided there would be no more exceptions, no matter what excuse anyone could come up with, so while all the new grads were waiting in line, there was still some wailing and gnashing. I would not know until the day of graduation that 4.0 Sandy would not walk or that I would not get the high-GPA award. But I just knew that I passed that last damn test and I would walk.

I was so excited about attending my own graduation, to soak up all the pomp and circumstance, that I went to both the university and college ceremonies. At the university graduation, Chancellor Arthur K. Smith was an outstanding master of ceremonies. There were about 3,300 graduates represented, and about 20,000 family and friends—just about the same as the odds as Khe Sanh, although being in the center floor at my college graduation was much more to my liking. Because I was taller than almost everyone and could see over their heads and mortar boards, my eyeballs fixated on the exits and entrances to see who was going where. I had to make sure no one was possibly coming my way with an unwanted shoulder tap and bad news.

As I stood there in the stadium, our financial situation suddenly hit me in a flash. Money was getting pretty tight again, as Gloria still worked, but the expenses for the house, cars, and the children were continually increasing, I was still spending money like a drunken Private First Class in the Marine Corps. But we were at least debt-free, whereas three years earlier, we had constantly had one foot in and out of bankruptcy. I thought back to an incident one day back then, as I had been trying to fill up with gas on a bumbed-out credit card. The pump had abruptly stopped under a dollar, and when it had flashed and read, "Please see attendant!" I had known the jig was up. There was just enough gas to get me home, and I had immediately called the IRS in Austin. They had told me that our house was going to be posted for foreclosure and we had been passed from auditing to the enforcement department. I had quickly borrowed some money at a Mafia interest rate and promptly driven to Austin with a cashier's check and a Release of Lien from an attorney to personally give the IRS.

The only thing that snapped me back into the present just then was that I knew that all the hard work was behind me and only exhilaration was before me. Finally, everyone was seated and the ceremony got under way. No one could stop me now, I figured, because I must have passed the exit test, and based on my GPA, I would achieve the highest honors. I breathed a huge sigh of relief; I just knew I had definitely done it. I had not failed this time. I would shortly graduate and could at last savor the moment.

I thought everybody knew I would graduate at the top, but apparently not, because when my name was called, there was quite a gasping and mumbling. This brought me right back to my high school ceremony. In high school, most students are in their own little cliques and do not look around beyond their own friends to the world outside. When they start seeing the high-fliers being accepted at the most prestigious colleges out of state and discussing the fraternities and sororities they'll rush, they wake up. They all wish they were going, too, and that's when a lot of them start fibbing about where they are going and have been accepted to. The other, non-clique, but also not high-flying group of students are headed to hometown community colleges because of insufficient grades and money. Of course, a lot of the students who went off to the prestigious colleges and fraternities, with all the fanfare that went with it, did not cut it the first semester and were soon back at the hometown community college. Others could only achieve an associates degree or get through college by going to a trade school.

When I left high school, I didn't have to worry about college, grades, or money. My dad had conditioned me to believe from an early age that there was no money for me and I was not college material anyway, so he had told me not to even think about it. Instead, he was always pushing for me to join the Army and go to Germany, then if I wanted to go to school later, I could have the government pay for it. Alternatively, I could wash dishes for him and wait to get drafted. It seemed like he had predestined me to work like hell in the family business under him.

So now there I was, surrounded by about 3,300 students standing in the stadium to graduate. When I looked around at the honor students, however, I knew the group was smaller. The students who graduated cum laude, with honors, numbered about 660, with GPAs over 3.25. Then there were the magna cum laude graduates, with high honors, who had to have GPAs equal to or higher than 3.5; this group comprised about 200 students. This was the group of students who received the most job offers, as their brief but impressive resumes would look after them for life. They would make sure that everybody from their high school group knew it, too, and made the other students jealous and envious with their talk of their future company-paid cars, new professional wardrobes, and vacation homes by the lake.

Finally, there was another group of students who could already name their first employers and already had their new cars and wardrobes picked out because they were graduating on top with highest honors, summa cum laude. These were the students who had the privilege of the chancellor personally reading their names aloud. They were the elite, and most had been valedictorians or salutatorians in their respective high schools. They were now standing up, one by one, to be recognized by tens of thousands of people. These were the students who were expected to be not only grad students but lawyers, doctors, professors, astronauts, and more. These were the students who were expected to bring back accolades to their respective institutions, along with the big bucks as alumni.

Things are emotionally harder and more difficult in high school than college, but unlike high school, in college, the consequences of your efforts are for keeps, they are for life. In high school you can still make up for your past mistakes by waking up and turning things around in college. In college, however, if you do not apply yourself, it's all over; you can't get into graduate school to try to turn things around, nor can you start all over again. You are definitely not going back to pick up any extracurricular officerships or join any fraternal organizations. For most students, it's reality time. The reality is that the top 10% of the class gets its pick of 90% of the good jobs.

As each name was called out by the chancellor, the ooh's and ah's were generous, despite some under-the-breath mumbling. Chancellor Smith proceeded to read the names of the forty-six students who had graduated at the top of their class, summa cum laude. Because my name is in the V's, I was either the last or second to last to have 30,000 people cheer my accomplishment. When my name was finally called, chills ran down my spine, and I think my heart actually stopped.

I stood up, and I think there was now more astonishment than anything else. The murmurs that I heard were, "I didn't know!" and "How did he...?" I just assumed they'd had known I was going for all the marbles. The hair on the back of my neck stood up, and I felt they were all personally cheering just for me. Indeed, I had just won the lottery.

I wish I could remember more of either my actual university or college graduation ceremony stage walk, but it all went by so quickly. I wish it would've lasted longer or that I could remember more to savor the moments. All that work, pain, and effort would be summed up in a thirty-second walk and a handshake, but it was more than worth it.

Claude Vargo's graduation day, May 14, 1999.

Out of the approximately 33,000 students who had struggled through classes that year, I was glad to be one of the 3,300 graduating students standing there at the finish line. I do remember closing my eyes, reveling in the feeling of a unique moment of complete fulfillment in my life, as I grasped that single, leather-bound piece of parchment—one moment that, in retrospect, symbolized the hard work of a lifetime and my total redemption. Every disparaging word, gesture, and crushing comment that had ever been uttered to me had now been made ludicrous.

At that moment, I had finally become smart enough to realize and see how dumb I had always been to doubt myself. If there is not one other thing you take from reading my story, please realize that one single fact: ***You should never doubt yourself, or try to live up (or down) to others' expectations of you. You will never accomplish anything in life that you truly want until you first believe in the deepest recesses of your heart and soul that you really can do it, and then you give it everything you have to achieve it. Never, ever, listen to anyone who even remotely thinks about telling you that you can't accomplish something you truly want to achieve.*** You must go out on a search-and-destroy mission and take no prisoners when you decide to accomplish your goal, no matter what. Ignore anyone who doesn't support you and doesn't believe you can achieve your goal, including friends and family members, but most importantly...yourself!

Personally, I can tell you it took a massive effort and a lot of determination, but with a heck of a lot of help from my wife, family, friends, students, teachers, Tony's tapes, and, most important of all, myself, I "unleashed my power within" and did what had seemed impossible for me.

The first person I saw as I left the hall, when my eyes had finally adjusted to the blinding Texas sun, was George Nolan. I had not seen him for a long time. He had a big unlit cigar that he was slowly savoring under his nose. He looked at me and smiled, then handed me a La Aurora Cristal out of an elegant glass tube. We both lit up with a lapis lazuli- and gold-trimmed Dunhill lighter that I handed him as I had promised. Neither of us said a word; neither of us had to. We silently nodded and toasted each other as we enjoyed the sweet smell of success.

Gloria and I were walking to our car afterwards and discussed the possibility of me attending the graduate program at Cornell, keeping the momentum going. She asked, "What do you think?"

I answered, "Cornell would look good on my resume and great in my obituary, but I can still always say that I went to charm school!"

She interrupted me with, "What?"

I said, "C-H-A-R-M, Cornell Hotel And Restaurant Management school...get it?" She told me I was still too damn goofy.

In the end, I believe that everyone has his or her own unique set of advantages and skills over others, and if we just look into ourselves, we can find them and accomplish anything we set our sights to. Luckily for me, mine had been in front of me the whole time; I just hadn't seen them because a few negative people at critical times in my maturation years had mentally beaten me down. All I ever had to do was trust my instincts and my skills and, most importantly, first and foremost, trust and believe in myself. So can you!

With Bill Marriott when he was inducted into the Hospitality Hall of Honor. I was a featured speaker.

To see my test results, papers, and other academic records from fifth grade high school and college, please go to:

www.GetYourDamnDegree.com

EPILOGUE ~ "GOD KNOWS CLAUDE VARGO"*
*Front Page ~ Houston Chronicle, April 15, 2000

It has now been almost ten years since I graduated, and I cannot believe the time has gone by so fast. Until I started writing, I had not looked back long enough to realize all the things I had actually accomplished. I just thought I had gone through it all rather fast, but I had never really looked back, because I was always afraid that something might trip me up and I might not graduate...like an early death.

As I write this to close, I still get excited thinking about my accomplishments and how much fun I had doing it all, but I am also somewhat sad about how much I missed out on earlier in life. I never considered that I could pass algebra, much less make an A. I still can't fathom that. Although I set many possible and impossible goals, I never in a million years thought I would achieve all of them...and more. I am so thankful for having a second chance and so grateful to all the people who helped me along the way. There will never be enough time or ink to thank everyone.

I think the key for me was always perceiving myself, throughout my college experience, as already being a college graduate and conducting myself as such. This technique came from Napoleon Hill's *Think and Grow Rich*. He was not talking only about money. He did, in fact, teach me about more riches than I could ever have imagined possible, and because of him and a plethora of others, I am a much better person. In my professional thesis, I thanked a multitude of people, but now that I look back, I could have doubled the count.

Besides the total of fifty-two credited courses I took, I still can't forget about the nine nonaccredited courses: the Certified Hospitality Educator program; Evelyn Woods Speed Reading; Mavis Beacon's Typing Tutor; Toastmasters; the freebie HVS internships and Princeton Review course for grad school; plus the D+ at HCC and the two law classes. They rounded out my character...I am told.

Before I made the decision to go back to college, I came up with 100 negative reasons why I could not do it and only five positive reasons why I could. This book is the story of how I made those five positives overpower the hundred negatives and how I did not let my past, and the burdens I carry from it, stop me or get in my way. It was written to inspire others to go for their dreams and to share with the reader the techniques I used to accomplish this for myself.

I ended up having some advantages over a lot of people, but in the beginning, I could not and did not see any of them. My GI Bill had expired decades earlier, and with my dismal junior high and high school record, I had never dreamt of getting any kind of scholarships or money to study. I was totally committed to college, and I paid for the first semesters at all three colleges on my own while I was broke and facing bankruptcy. That is another key, and maybe one of the most important points of this entire book: It was not until I was totally committed, and totally convinced mentally that I could take on the self-challenge and succeed, that doors began to open. But once they did, they kept on opening, one right after the other.

A TIME TO HEAL

Sometime during April 2000, while I was studying like a madman to finish up my masters degree, I was contacted by Allan Turner, a reporter from the *Houston Chronicle*. He was writing a feature article on the twenty-fifth anniversary of the fall of South Viet Nam and told me over the phone that my name had kept coming up over and over again from people he had been interviewing. It seemed like all roads led back to me, and several of these people had told him he should interview me.

Although I was pushed for time and did not feel comfortable revisiting my memories, because of the people he named who had urged him to contact me, I felt obligated to contribute what I could to the story. They were all just a few people on a very long list of people who are very dear and very important to me in my life, so I had to say yes to the interview, out of honor to each one of them. They all know who they are.

The entire interview was a gut-wrenching ordeal of remembering what had happened overseas, with every past emotion instantly returning, along with the personal shame and guilt I feel. But it was also about what happened afterward. Twenty-five years earlier, after the fall of Saigon, the panic attacks that I still live with to this day had begun. This same feeling was now flooding my entire body, and my brain was screaming at me to run or fire, to do something.

Allan sensed the mental state I was going into and asked me a final question that he did not print. He asked me what the failure of the war had really meant to me then. The only analogy I could think of was, if you had worked at something, like a college education, for years and almost died trying to complete the task, only to have it taken away and declared null and void, how would you feel? But, in retrospect, that analogy doesn't come close.

LIFE'S TWISTED JOKES...AND MAGNIFICENT GIFTS

Finally, I want to share with you some of the developments and some ironies that have come to pass over time and since I left school.

- The financially savvy Sisters of the Incarnate Word sold off the thirty-four acres of Marian High School and the convent for several million dollars after the community had bailed them out for years. A developer bought it, turned it around, and sold it to the Episcopal Diocese of Texas for a tidy profit.

- The 1960s-era Viet Nam draft-dodgers who went to Canada were later given amnesty. Now many of the dodgers feel guilt and remorse because they did not go. Ironically, I feel just as bad, not because I went, but because I came back.

- When I came back from two tours of war, I was still too young to legally buy a beer. The very next year when I turned twenty-one, the nation rolled the legal drinking age back to eighteen.

- In 1968 I yearned to vote in the presidential election. When I turned twenty-one, the voting age, too, was rolled back to eighteen.

- After I passed the writing comprehension exit exam the first time around, the State of Texas eliminated the test the very next semester.

- After I had walked at two Hilton graduations, with the strict no-exceptions rule, that too, was relaxed by many of the fourteen colleges of UH.

- After I completed my 132-hour degree, the very next semester, it was reduced to just 123 hours.

- Dr. Jack Corgel, my professor at Cornell, and I are now business partners.

- On November 7, 2008, the University of Houston celebrated the investiture of Dr. Renu Khator as its eighth chancellor and thirteenth president to lead UH. At the time of this writing, the Tier I initiative is in motion and appears to be coming close to fruition with her guidance.

- If the newest status symbol is longevity in marriage, then Gloria and I have fought our way to the top. It has been a harrowing forty years now, and counting faster. We have made it big financially several times, only to lose it again by hitting another brick wall. But we are blessed to have seven granddaughters and two grandsons—and they are all healthy, precious, and beautiful.

- Today, I work as a vice president of operations for the international hotel consulting and research firm that I targeted in graduate school, where we vault all of the highly confidential Hilton financial statements for hundreds of their company-owned and -managed hotels. I think my dear friend and mentor Mr. Conrad Hilton would be proud of my position.

Me, hard at work, overlooking the JW Marriott Hotel Buckhead, Atlanta, GA.

- My beloved Shamrock Hilton Hotel was donated by the Hiltons to the Texas Medical Center. It was torn down; the wrecking ball left only the gigantic pool and a parking garage. Sometimes when I go back to Houston, I drive by, and if I stop and listen, I can still hear the nightlife and the gaiety that will never leave that site. If I close my eyes, I can go back to another time and place, which I am trying desperately not to ever lose. I can taste the Napoleon shortcake and the freshly baked, mouth-watering chocolate-dipped éclairs I used to pinch from the pastry department while walking by...much faster than anyone could ever catch me. In those moments, I am fifteen again.

LOOKING FORWARD

Gloria and I funded the Claude Regis Vargo Family Endowed Scholarship at the University of Houston through the Conrad N. Hilton College of Hotel and

Restaurant Management a few years ago. A portion of the profits of anything I do with this book will go toward furthering that cause, as a way to recycle all of the scholarship monies I received to the next generation and, hopefully, in perpetuity. I also plan to donate monies from the sales to fund a couple of the worthwhile military associations to which I belong.

I still plan on teaching at some point, even if just one class, because it is so rewarding. Then I can cross that off my bucket list, too, and maybe pass on some things I have learned on my odyssey.

Just like I could never pass algebra, I had also convinced myself that I could never write a book, but here I am putting the finishing touches on this manuscript, which I wrote for many reasons. It has been a form of self-induced and directed PTSD therapy, if only temporary. What transpired when I started writing were more panic attacks, doubt, and depression, but now I feel wholeness, a wellness and calm. Maybe I can even catch a slight glimpse of inner peace.

With my semi-Socratic education completed and while my bucket and laundry lists both still grow, I am now more aware of my existence than ever. I am also still working on that law-school itch and maybe dabble in politics.

But the back story in this whole adventure was always my personal moral redemption, because even if the panic attacks and the PTSD are never going to go away or even get worse, I may be able to find some kind of inner peace if I can learn to forgive my enemy and my enemy's children and confront my innermost demons. One of the ways to do this is to go back to the Rock Quarry at Khe Sanh to see if my cave is still there.

Between writing this book and going back there, one way or the other, I will, hopefully, finally dispatch my demons to the back of my tank, where they have always belonged. Then I can finally leave them and that place forever and come home to Gloria...again.

Life is short. Go for *your* dreams.

"Employ your time in improving yourself by other men's writings, so that you shall gain easily what others have labored hard for."
Socrates

APPENDICES
APPENDIX A

The President of the United States
takes pleasure in presenting the

PRESIDENTIAL UNIT CITATION

to

TWENTY-SIXTH MARINES (REINFORCED),
THIRD MARINE DIVISION (REINFORCED)

for service as set forth in the following CITATION:

For extraordinary heroism in action against North Vietnamese Army forces during the battle for Khe Sanh in the Republic of Vietnam from 20 January to 1 April 1968. Throughout this period, the 26th Marines (Reinforced) was assigned the mission of holding the vital Khe Sanh Combat Base and positions on Hills 881, 861-A, 558, and 950, which dominated the strategic enemy approach routes into Northern I Corps. The 26th Marines was opposed by numerically superior forces—two North Vietnamese Army divisions, strongly reinforced with artillery, tank, anti-aircraft artillery, and rocket units. The enemy, deployed to take advantage of short lines of communications, rugged mountainous terrain, jungle, and adverse weather conditions, was determined to destroy the Khe Sanh Combat Base in conjunction with large scale offensive operations in the two northern provinces of the Republic of Vietnam. The 26th Marines, occupying a small but critical area, was daily subjected to hundreds of rounds of intensive artillery, mortar, and rocket fire. In addition, fierce ground attacks were conducted by the enemy in an effort to penetrate the friendly positions. Despite overwhelming odds, the 26th Marines remained resolute and determined, maintaining the integrity of its positions and inflicting heavy losses on the enemy. When monsoon weather greatly reduced air support and compounded the problems of air resupply, the men of the 26th Marines stood defiantly firm, sustained by their own professional esprit and high sense of duty. Through their indomitable will, staunch endurance, and resolute courage, the 26th Marines and supporting units held the Khe Sanh Combat Base. The actions of the 26th Marines contributed substantially to the failure of the Viet Cong and North Vietnamese Army winter/spring offensive. The enemy forces were denied the military and psychological victory they so desperately sought. By their gallant fighting spirit and their countless individual acts of heroism, the men of the 26th Marines (Reinforced) established a record of illustrious courage and determination in keeping with the highest traditions of the Marine Corps and the United States Naval Service.

Lyndon B. Johnson

APPENDIX B

PARTIAL LIST OF CLAUDE'S UNDERGRADUATE SCHOLARSHIPS & MILITARY MEMBERSHIPS

UNDERGRADUATE SCHOLARSHIPS

- Texas Restaurant Association (T.R.A.)
- Houston Restaurant Association (H.R.A.)
- American Hotel Foundation (A.H.F.)
- Ecolab (ECL)
- Appraisal Institute Education Trust Scholarship [A.I.E.T.]
- Sysco Foods Services [S.F.S.]

MILITARY LIFE MEMBERSHIPS

- The Military Order of the Purple Heart
- Disabled Veterans Association ~ Chapter #6, Marietta GA
- United States Marine Corps Vietnam Tankers Association
- First Battalion Ninth Marines Network, Inc. ~ The Walking Dead
- Marine Corps League

APPENDIX C

ACADEMIC ACCOLADES

- Summa Cum Laude ~ 3.9 Concentration - 3.8 Cumulative
- Phi Kappa Phi ~ National Honor Society
- Eta Sigma Delta International Hospitality Honor Society
- National Dean's List ~ two consecutive years
- Phi Beta Delta ~ Honor Society for International Scholars
- Golden Key National Honor Society
- Certified Hospitality Educator ~ American Hotel & Lodging Association
- Founding President ~ Disabled Students Association
- Founding Advisor ~ International Food Service Executives Association
- Who's Who Among Students in American Universities & Colleges
- Omicron Delta Kappa ~ National Leadership Society
- Member ~ Texas Restaurant Association ~ Cougar Chapter
- Student Scholar ~ International Society of Hospitality Consultants
- Student Chapter Secretary ~ Toastmaster's International
- Member ~ Greater Houston Restaurant Association
- Hilton College Dean's List ~ five consecutive semesters
- "Best In Class" Hotel Financial Analysis ~ Cornell University
- Writing Excellence Award ~ Houston Community College
- Conceived and implemented 1st senior class ring ~ C. N. Hilton College
- Invited Guest Speaker ~ Georgia Tech —"Ethics in Business"
- University of Houston's "Dean of Student Affairs Award"

Beyond My Horizon

ORDER FORM

Yes, Claude! Ship me more books.

Name ____

Address ____

City, State & Zip _____________________________________

Phone (   ) _____________________________________

Email ____

Payment   VISA   MasterCard   AMEX   Check (Payable to CV Pubs)

Card # ____

Expiration Date ____________ Signature ____________________

Billing Address if different than above ______________________

____

Total Books __________ @ Total amount ___________________

SEND ORDER TO:

CV Pubs, PO Box 18855, Atlanta GA 31126

Discount *prices available on website at:*

GetYourDamnDegree.Com

Or Call Toll Free ~ 1 - (888) NOW – XLR8

(888) 669 - 9578

If you have an intersting story that you would like to share with me, other non-traditional students and our planet, please go to my website for more details at:

www.GetYourDamnDegree.com

Semper Fidelis, Claude

LaVergne, TN USA
29 September 2010
199009LV00001B/6/P